PROBLEMS
IN EDUCATION
A Comparative Approach

INTERNATIONAL LIBRARY OF SOCIOLOGY

AND SOCIAL RECONSTRUCTION

Founded by Karl Mannheim

Editor W. J. H. Sprott

A catalogue of books available in the INTERNATIONAL LIBRARY OF
SOCIOLOGY AND SOCIAL RECONSTRUCTION and new books in
preparation for the Library will be found at the end of this volume

PROBLEMS
IN EDUCATION

A Comparative Approach

by

BRIAN HOLMES

LONDON

ROUTLEDGE & KEGAN PAUL

NEW YORK: THE HUMANITIES PRESS

First published 1965
by Routledge and Kegan Paul Ltd
Broadway House, 68–74 Carter Lane
London, E.C.4

Second impression 1967
Third impression 1970

Printed in Great Britain by
Redwood Press Limited
Trowbridge & London

ISBN 0 7100 3447 4

CONTENTS

v

Contents

Contents

PART THREE: NATIONAL CASE STUDIES

Contents

PREFACE

THIS book is chiefly concerned with my absorbing interest—methodology. It reflects the outcome of my thinking, over a period of some twenty years, about the theoretical problems associated with the study of comparative education. Fortunately during the past ten years I have been able to clarify these questions to a considerable extent through my day-to-day work with research students, as assistant editor of the *Year Book of Education*, and as a lecturer in comparative education. Above all I am indebted to my colleagues at home and abroad with whom, thanks to their patience, I have had endless discussions. It is perhaps appropriate to acknowledge the contribution of several persons, among many, to the growth of my fascination for methodology in comparative education and thank them for it.

It was Dr Hans who, in 1945, introduced me to the study of comparative education and fired my interest in it. Since then I have met him constantly. To the pleasure derived from our many discussions has been added the privilege of being accepted by this pioneer as a fellow-worker in the field.

Across the Atlantic three experiences should be recorded. During the summers of 1955 and 1956 I was greatly influenced by the rigorous study of theories of social change in a doctoral seminar at the University of Illinois, which was conducted by Professor B. O. Smith and Professor W. O. Stanley, and in which I participated. In Urbana I also met the late Professor H. Gordon Hullfish of Ohio State University, who, in long discussions, encouraged me to feel that I understood a little about American education, and in particular about the philosophy of John Dewey and Boyd H. Bode. Later, during the course of my appointment at the University of Chicago, I had the opportunity of putting many of the theories expressed in this book to the probing analysis of Dean F. C. Chase, Professor C. Arnold Anderson and their colleagues and students at the Comparative Education Center.

Preface

Since preparing the first draft I have worked closely with Dr S. B. Robinsohn in the preparation of an expert meeting held at the Hamburg UNESCO Institute for Education in 1963. Our collaboration sharpened my awareness of the issues—and one outcome was *Relevant Data in Comparative Education*.

It will be apparent, however, that two writers have been most influential in the development of my point of view. In 1945, almost simultaneously, I was introduced to the works of John Dewey and to Professor Popper's recently published *The Open Society*. The conceptual framework presented in this book is based largely on the writings of these two philosophers. But it has evolved during a period of collaboration with the person to whom I owe the greatest debt of gratitude. The influence of Professor J. A. Lauwerys on my thinking has been profound, though I cannot blame him for weaknesses in my presentation. I wish to thank him for the opportunities he has given me and for the pleasure and intellectual stimulus gained working with him at the London Institute and on the *Year Book of Education*. The contribution to this book of these substantial comparative studies (and of a joint editor, Dr Robert King Hall) should, incidentally, be apparent.

Finally I wish to thank several colleagues and students for reading the manuscript at various stages of its preparation and for their helpful suggestions.

B. H.

Institute of Education,
  London,
    December, 1964

PART ONE

METHODOLOGY:
The Problem Approach
in
Comparative Education

INTRODUCTION

DEBATES about methodology have been one feature of the post-war upsurge of interest in comparative education. They have turned upon the possibilities of enabling the comparative argument to be used with more rigour and precision in the reform and planned development of education. Statesmen and administrators have increasingly sought the advice of comparative educationists in international organisation and in the universities. The challenge has been accepted, and attempts have been made to refine the methods of studying comparative education with the intention of improving the contribution it can make to a deeper understanding of the processes of education and to the planning of education.

Disagreements about methodology have no doubt frequently arisen because the basic assumptions of the protagonists have not been made clear. For example, the historical and scientific approaches have been regarded not as complementary but as antithetical. Similarly descriptive and explanatory studies have been contrasted and the relationships between them not fully examined.

One purpose in writing this book was to state the assumptions on which the author's approach is based. His commitment to the 'problem approach' rests on the beliefs (a) that it is scientific and (b) that it can be used as an instrument of educational reform. Both these aims were accepted by some of the nineteenth-century pioneers of comparative education, and Chapter I is intended to place present-day debates in historical perspective. In Chapter II the main assumptions of the problem approach as given by Dewey in *How We Think* are examined and their correspondence with the generally agreed features of post-relativity views on scientific method made clear. In Chapter III, against K. R. Popper's analysis of critical dualism in *The Open Society*, the limitations of planning and the scientific study of education are, by implication, considered. Scientific studies should be concerned with Popper's 'sociological laws', or J. B. Conant's 'predictive generalisations'. It is suggested that 'normative laws' or the 'wide premises of a culture' can be studied philosophically. Both types of investigation are integral parts of well-founded comparative studies. Critical dualism also suggests the possibilities of establishing a useful conceptual framework which can be used (*a*) to identify and classify relevant data; (*b*) to facilitate descriptive studies; (*c*) to identify and intellectualise the source of problems, and (*d*) to suggest the range of consequences likely to flow from educational innovations. These aspects of the problem approach are examined in Chapter IV.

In this section, too, suggestions are made regarding the most general sources of post-war problems. These are identified as (*a*) the explosion of aspirations, (*b*) the explosion of population, and (*c*) the explosion of knowledge. They are regarded as useful starting points in comparative studies, and are re-stated in different contexts in Part II and Part III.

The conceptual framework presented is intended to be flexible, not restrictive. It should facilitate a variety of different types of investigation in comparative education, and, if not acceptable to all workers in the field, should provide a basis for further methodological discussion. Progress depends upon the vigorous promotion of both.

Chapter I

COMPARATIVE EDUCATION AND CULTURAL BORROWING

DURING the eighteenth century many schemes to promote universal education were proposed, but it was in the nineteenth that systems based upon them were slowly and painfully evolved. Many features of the process were common to some countries of Europe and to North America which were passing through somewhat similar phases of development. Old political orders were in process of being rejected for more democratic institutions. New forms of nationalism were emerging. Incipient industrialisation was introducing processes of change on both sides of the Atlantic. The social problems associated with urbanisation and the growth of city slums were becoming increasingly obvious to many people.

These developments were accompanied by a ferment of new, or revived, ideas which helped to instil in men visions of a new and better world. Central to many of them was the crucial role education could and should play in its creation. Education was a panacea. To the 'new' theories of Comenius, Milton, Locke, Descartes, Franklin and others were added the practical proposals of such men as La Chalotais, Condorcet, Thomas Jefferson, and Robert Owen. All of them hoped to democratise education and expand it. Some stressed its political purposes. In his report to the Convention in 1792 Condorcet advocated universal education so that all individuals should know and exercise their rights and understand and perform their duties. Jefferson's statement of the purposes of education in his *Report of the commissioners for the University of Virginia* in 1818 included almost identical phrases.

For Robert Owen education was the supreme socialising agent. The misery of mankind could, he maintained, 'be traced

5

to the ignorance of those who have ruled, and of those who have been governed'. Idleness, poverty, crime and its consequent punishment were 'all the necessary consequences of ignorance'. Later he was to argue that 'No arrangements have ever been formed in any part of the world to well-educate humanity; no such arrangements nor any approaching them exist in this or in any other country.'[1] In his own school in Lanarkshire Owen attempted to make productive work in the factory the very core of education. Nevertheless it was probably not until much later in the century that the possibilities of using education to promote economic growth were seriously debated.

Comprehensive plans for universal education, were however, formulated. Again those of Condorcet and Jefferson were similar and representative of an era of reforming zeal. Elementary schools for everyone were to be followed by selective secondary schools and still more selective institutions of higher learning. The pattern of education was designed to ensure that from the aristocracy of talent thus detected and fostered the State would be able to recruit its leaders. Already, of course, in Europe there existed well-established secondary schools for the few potential leaders of society. Many were, or had been, church or private schools. In America the colonial schools and colleges had served a similar function by training leaders to serve theocratic communities. Some attention had also been paid to commercial and technical studies which had been promoted in Europe either privately or by enlightened princes. On both sides of the Atlantic the dissenting academies had provided curricula more practical in emphasis than was customary in the traditional Latin schools. Among the tasks facing the nineteenth-century educational reformers were the reshaping of this tradition and the expansion of secondary education. In many respects, however, except perhaps in the U.S.A., radical reform was delayed until the twentieth century.

On the other hand, schools for the masses were set up. Even before the end of the eighteenth century many national or state governments had passed legislation providing a basis for universal primary instruction. The practical realisation of these intentions required many decades of effort. By 1880 or thereabouts elementary education for the masses had been established in most Western countries in the face of many difficulties.

6

Certain features of the struggle were present everywhere, but in each country specific factors led to somewhat different results.

The principle of compulsory attendance, for example, though advocated, was controversial. It was not a new idea. Legislation designed to enforce attendance at school had been enacted by the Duke of Weimar as early as the first part of the seventeenth century. Frederick William and his son Frederick the Great had introduced similar laws in Prussia during the eighteenth century. Many parents, however, were reluctant to send their children to school regularly, and the opinion of politicians was often divided. In France, in contrast to the Jacobins, Mirabeau opposed obligatory attendance and Condorcet did not think it necessary. Even in the middle of the nineteenth century Matthew Arnold was to question the value of compulsory legislation in England by describing how easily French parents avoided sending their children to school. Classical liberalism suggests, of course, that public authorities should interfere as little as possible with the rights of individual parents. The advantages of going to school were not always as obvious to parents and children as they were to the pioneers of mass education.

In the event, governments in most European countries participated in the nineteenth-century movements to extend and improve education and make it compulsory. Their authority to do so was challenged by the churches, for which control of education was a traditional prerogative. The nature and intensity of the clash varied. The French revolutionaries were determined to abolish clerical control and the Convention passed measures designed to achieve this end. Later Napoleon, it has been said, 'brought to a conclusion the difficult operation of securing for the remodelled State the sanction and support of the church'. His State *lycées* and the monopolistic system of administration established for some secondary schools and higher education a form of lay control which was not achieved in primary or elementary education (in spite of the radicalism of many teachers) until the Jules Ferry reforms of the eighties.

The position in the United States during the early part of the nineteenth century was very different. In the amendments to the Constitution the formal separation of Church and State was recognised. But the absence of an established national church—or of an all-powerful one—and the existence of many religious groups from different European backgrounds no doubt helped to accelerate the process of secularisation which had progressed rather far even by the end of the colonial period. Many secondary schools, however, were subject to some religious supervision by ecclesiastics as members of visiting committees. But the acrimonious clash between Horace Mann and church leaders in Massachusetts was symptomatic of the fight to make the American schools non-sectarian.

The denominational struggle dominated the educational history of nineteenth-century England. The established Church clung tenaciously to its hold over education, and even to the allocation of public funds. Not until the last quarter of the century were lay authorities made responsible for a system of elementary schools. And not until the early years of the twentieth century did the local authorities decisively enter the field of secondary education. Private enterprise, to Matthew Arnold's regret, was allowed to discharge the role (undertaken by several national governments on the continent of Europe) of creating secondary schools for the enlarged middle classes.

While secondary schools were thus often regarded as a State responsibility, elementary education was invariably left in the hands of the local communities. Frequently these were either unable or unwilling to finance their schools properly, and increasingly public moneys from the central government were provided to support the elementary schools whether or not control remained in the hands of the local authorities. The notable exception to this general rule is the United States, where until recently most of the money needed for the schools was raised locally. Inevitably, whatever the details of financial support the elementary schools assumed national characteristics.

Several methods of achieving some uniformity were devised. Government committees and commissions were set up to look into the state of education and advise on future policy. In some countries a Ministry of Education was created. Even in the United States, where the attachment to local government was most pronounced, a system of state boards of education with an appointed secretary was initiated in Massachusetts in 1838 and subsequently adopted in other states. Hence, in most western countries at least, the practice grew of appointing officials whose special concern was with education. National circumstances determined what inspectors and directors of education could do; but in a very real sense the nineteenth century witnessed the growth of a corps of educational administrators. Among them may be counted many of the pioneers of comparative education.

Several of them were scholars in their own field, and it is hardly surprising that their interest in educational reform was both intellectual and practical. Victor Cousin, for example, was a professor of philosophy at the Sorbonne before becoming in 1840 Minister of Education of France. Matthew Arnold is as well known as an author as for his activities as an Inspector of English schools; William Torrey Harris for his leadership of the American Hegelian school of philosophers as for his work as superintendent of the St Louis schools and as United States Commissioner of Education. Each of the pioneers of comparative education wished in a practical way to understand better his own system and its defects. At the theoretical level each attempted to discover the actual processes of education (rather than formulate ideal systems), to relate theory to practice, and to use his investigations to reform his own schools. Furthermore, some of them hoped through their efforts to assist in the general improvement of mankind. Collectively, their efforts may be regarded as having made a substantial contribution to the development of a science of education.

Selective Cultural Borrowing

Certainly they were not the first men in history to study foreign institutions with the intention of improving their own. Cultural borrowing is an ancient art. Blueprints abound for the reform of one society based upon the study of another. Not least, Plato's *Republic* was inspired by the institutions of Sparta. In more recent centuries governments had occasionally invited foreign 'experts' to advise on the reform of their own institutions. For example, Comenius was asked by Parliament to make suggestions for the establishment of a national system of education in England and came to London in 1641. When some decades later Peter the Great sent officials to study the Royal Mathematical School at Christ's Hospital in England, he intended to

Methodology

set up similar institutions in Russia for the training of naval
personnel and engineers. Henry Barnard's assessment of Peter's
aim was that he 'desired to transplant Western culture to
Russia, and for this purpose sent Russians to foreign countries
and called foreigners to Russia'.[2] Equally significant in these
earlier movements was the procedure adopted by Maria
Theresia. In order to draw up a comprehensive plan of reform
her Imperial Chancellor Prince Kaunitz was given the task of
collecting useful information on foreign improvements in education. In 1774 Kaunitz sent a circular to the Austrian embassies
abroad asking for information about various aspects of existing
educational systems which might be useful in school reorganisation at home. Although with one exception the replies were un-
enthusiastic, this approach to cultural borrowing is of interest.
Some time later in 1801 the Prussian government sent a school
inspector to study the work of Pestalozzi at Burgdorf, and young
men of promise were also encouraged to study there so that they
might return to Prussia better equipped as teachers and
administrators.

During the nineteenth century more and more attempts were
made to learn from other countries. Few of the pioneers of comparative education, however, were uncritical borrowers. Indeed
the principle itself was questioned, for obvious reasons. At that
time each nation was building up its own institutions and
national consciousness. The schools were either deliberately or
implicitly fostering among people an awareness of nationality
and a unique 'national character'. Sir Michael Sadler made
very explicit his view that the greatness of an educational
system was in its 'living spirit', and that 'all good and true
education is an expression of life and character'.[3] William
Torrey Harris in America shared these views. He appreciated
that each nation 'stamps upon its system its own ethnical character and, consciously or unconsciously, perpetuates its own
institutions by its schools'.[4] Ambivalence to cultural borrowing
was consequently inevitable. On the one hand political rivalry
and economic competition among nations encouraged imitation. National sentiment and awareness of special national
virtues discouraged it. Matthew Arnold recognised, for example,
that one obstacle in the way of using foreign experience in
England was 'our high opinion of our own energy and wealth'.[5]

He also pointed out some of the dangers associated with cultural borrowing by reminding his readers 'what different conditions and the different character of the two nations must necessarily impose on the operation of any principle. That which operates noxiously in one, may operate wholesomely in the other.'[6] The prospect that the reverse might occur worried most of the reformers.

One solution—selective cultural borrowing—commended itself to many of them. Although not prepared to accept for imitation a foreign system *in toto* they were willing to select parts of it. Impressed as Henry Barnard was with the Prussian school system his reservations were clearly expressed in his *Common School Journal*. 'Admirable as it is as a system,' he wrote, '—wisely framed in all its details for the schools of that kingdom —thorough as is the instruction in most particulars which it secures for the great mass of the community—universal as are its benefits—still we do not present it as a model for our imitation.'[7] Barnard and some other comparative educationists hoped that certain transplanted features of a foreign system could be made to serve different ends. Cousin spoke as an enemy of artificial imitations, yet, he maintained, 'With the promptitude and justness of the French understanding, and the indestructible unity of our national character, we may assimilate all that is good from other countries without fear of ceasing to be ourselves.'[8] Horace Mann likewise argued that 'if Prussia can pervert the benign influences of education to the support of arbitrary power, we can surely employ them for the support and perpetuation of republican institutions'.[9] In fine, the principle of desirable selective cultural borrowing to which many of these men subscribed was well stated by Cousin. 'The experience of Germany', he wrote, 'ought not to be lost upon us. National rivalries and antipathies would be completely out of place. The true greatness of a people does not consist in borrowing nothing from others, but in borrowing from whatever is good, and in perfecting whatever is appropriate.'[10]

Against this view Sadler argued that such judicious selection and subsequent modification were impossible. He certainly admired the German system and felt that a great deal could be learned from it, but, he maintained, 'No other nation, by imitating a little bit of German organisation, can thus hope to achieve a true reproduction of the spirit of German institutions. The fabric of its organisation practically forms one whole. That is its merit and its danger. It must be taken all in all, or left unimitated.'[11] For his own part while recognising the value of comparative studies he felt that 'National institutions must grow out of the needs and character (and not least out of the weaknesses) of the nation which possess them.'[12]

Another kind of solution was proposed by several comparative educationists, who thought that comparative studies could result in the establishment of general theories which would have universal application and be useful in the reform of all educational systems. Jullien, for example, had pursued this line of thought, and M. F. Buisson, referring to his distinguished predecessor, stated quite clearly that in his view research in comparative education would help to perfect a positive science of education. He had the support of such men as John Eaton, Jr., and William Torrey Harris, both at one time Commissioners of Education in the United States. Harris, like Sadler, felt that there were certain general principles about the operation of education which could be discovered through a study of other systems and applied everywhere. He advocated the separation of 'what is peculiar and incidental to local needs from what is of universal application and useful to all educational systems', and concluded that 'this sort of knowledge it is that gives directive power'.[13] Harris thus touched upon an element—reliable prediction—which tends to be regarded among modern philosophers as extremely important and distinctive in scientific work.

Descriptive and Statistical Studies

With these objectives in mind several methods of comparative study were adopted. Two contributions made by some of the nineteenth-century administrators suggest that, in spite of the many precedents, they should be regarded as among the important pioneers of comparative education. The first was the systematic way in which they collected, classified, and disseminated information about foreign educational systems; the second, the attempt to interpret data and develop general theories of education. Thus the accumulation of historical data, legislative details, and statistics provided a basis for comparative descriptions. As for interpretative studies at least two somewhat different approaches can be distinguished in the historical and the social-scientific. Both have their modern adherents and neither should be regarded as exclusive of the other.

At first, however, emphasis was placed on the collection and diffusion of information about the provision of public primary instruction. Jullien de Paris' famous *Esquisses et vues préliminaires d'un ouvrage sur l'éducation comparée* consists, after an introductory analysis of the purposes of comparative education, of a long list of questions about education. To many of them statistical answers were obviously intended; others were designed to elicit qualitative assessments. Some years later another Frenchman, Victor Cousin, stated a procedure to which many workers in comparative education have subscribed. 'I invariably followed one course,' he wrote, 'first, to procure the laws and regulations, and render myself perfect master of them; next to verify them by accurate and detailed inspection.'[14] Consequently his and many of the pioneering reports carried the full text of significant circulars, decrees, and laws relating to the provision of public instruction. Invariably through legislation the attention of the observers was turned to many other aspects of education, especially in countries like Prussia and France where comprehensive regulations existed. Inevitably, systems of administration were studied, but Cousin's account of Prussian education, for example, also dealt with the responsibilities of parents, the duties of local communities, the training, appointment, and salaries of teachers, the finance, control, and supervision of schools, and the actual content of the courses prescribed. In addition, as an appendix, he gave details of the Berlin plan for schools for the poor. This plan was symptomatic of a growing belief that primary instruction would ameliorate the lot of the poor and otherwise disadvantaged children. Many later comparative education reports give details of schools for the deaf, dumb, and mentally feeble as well as of orphanages and reformatories. While it is true that most legislation included broad statements about the objectives of national education, the interest of foreign observers centred on administration and the extent to which public instruction had been made available to the mass of the people.

Henry Barnard brought this approach to a fine art. As secretary of the Connecticut Board of Education he was required to make available all the documents and information he had regarding 'common school education in other states and countries'. He was quickly able to produce, as an appendix to his second annual report to the Board, lengthy accounts of education in foreign countries. Unquestionably this approach to comparative education was largely historical and descriptive, and his interest in the diffusion of such information continued throughout his life. Through the *Connecticut Common School Journal*, in which he published his Annual Reports, 'his own' *American Journal of Education*, he provided historical accounts of educational developments in many countries and kept his readers up-to-date with current issues and reform movements by publishing extracts from foreign reports and debates, details of legislation, and periodical articles. His aim to produce an encyclopaedia of education was, incidentally, virtually achieved in his collected works.

On the other hand the statistical approach was also developed. From the start of the United States Bureau of Education, Barnard hoped that he would be able to include statistical data. He realised the difficulties of getting complete returns even from the various states and cities of his own country—no two of them, he complained, included the same items. Under his immediate successors at the Bureau, Eaton and then N. H. R. Dawson, the size of the Annual Report and the mass of statistical data grew enormously. Most of them referred to American education, but a number of tables were included giving details of European and non-western schools. Salary schedules, teacher-pupil ratios, the proportion of females teaching, the per capita cost, the total national expenditure on education, and the percentage attendance were among the items listed. Comparative tables were sometimes given, but they were usually restricted to provinces within Germany. Nevertheless, Eaton's hope was that through statistics a science of education would emerge. 'Nor should it be forgotten', he wrote in his report for 1879, 'that the late increased attention to educational statistics in other countries, notably in France and Japan, indicates the possibility of certain agreements on at least a few points of nomenclature by which international com-

parisons may be made with greater satisfaction than hitherto
has been possible.'[15] The Bureau's statistician saw how difficult
it was to make valid statistical comparisons and emphasised in
the 1885–6 report that the figures for the proportion of children
attending school should be restricted to the pre-high-school (or
elementary) stage in countries where the age of leaving was
approximately the same.

Eaton's position, of course, implied that objective comparisons could be made by reaching agreement on points of
nomenclature. His view that a science of education could be
based on comparative statistics was not surprising since at that
time it was recognised that the quantification of procedures in
the natural sciences had contributed to their development.

Moreover, many philosophers accepted induction as the
basis of all scientific knowledge and held that initial observations should precede all hypotheses and statements of general
laws.

Against pure scholasticism there is, of course, much to be
said in favour of induction as an appropriate method in scientific enquiries. Certainly statistical information adds to details
of legislation by making possible some evaluation of the degree
to which particular countries had achieved their stated goals.
Eaton's demand for a science of education based upon apparently factual data in the form of statistics seemed to imply a
broader view of the purpose of comparative education than cultural borrowing. The question remained whether or not the
statistical approach was the most fruitful if the purpose was to
develop a science of education.

Already Matthew Arnold had made the point in his famous
report on the schools and universities on the Continent that
statistical data did not necessarily give precision to comparative
judgements. By way of illustration Arnold quoted an English-
man's defence of educational provision in his country by noting
that, according to the figures, only in Prussia was the proportion of 'scholars' higher than that of England and Wales.
Against the easy optimism aroused by such comparisons,
Arnold advanced several objections. The first related to the
machinery for the collection of data: in England no such formal
machinery existed—in France and Prussia it did. The second
weakness concerned nomenclature. For the continental nations

the word 'scholar' had a precise meaning in terms of the type of school attended and the qualifications of teachers. A third objection arose from the possible differences in the distribution of age groups from country to country. His reservations about the use of illiteracy figures as a way of evaluating educational systems were also very percipient. Clearly some knowledge of the criteria used by each nation to judge its own level of literacy is of fundamental importance when national comparisons are made. For example at the turn of the nineteenth century the United States authorities merely asked immigrants if they could read and write. In fine, the definitions of literacy are themselves objects of comparative study. The conclusion reached by Arnold in the face of these difficulties was that if people were going to make a case either for or against an educational system on the basis of facts, they should know the facts. On the whole he rejected the view that evaluations of educational systems should be made—and certainly not on the evidence of statistics.

The warning against the reliability of statistical data was repeated by William Torrey Harris. Under his guidance the U.S. Bureau of Education continued to provide an impressive number of statistical tables. Important items included school enrolment and attendance figures. These surely would provide an index of the universality of public instruction. But at that time Harris had doubts about nomenclature and the methods used to collect data. He commented in an Annual Report: 'It must be borne in mind that these comparative statistics are only approximately correct. There are many obstacles in the way besides inaccurate local records. The technical terms used by one nation do not have precisely the same import as words used by another nation to translate those terms. We are not yet sure that the item we call "enrolment" corresponds precisely to what the French and Germans express by the words *inscrit* and *eingeschrieben*.'[16] He went on to show how misleading certain methods of calculating 'average attendance' were.

Sadler appreciated that it was not only a question of nomenclature and methods of compiling statistics. Arguing against 'purely statistical enquiries' in the subject of education he saw how necessary it was to interpret data in the light of the value system of each country. He disapproved, for example, of evaluating an educational system on the basis of the amount of money spent on it. The return on this investment should also be considered. 'One country', he wrote, 'may pay for something called "primary education" which is intended to produce results that in another would be regarded as reactionary and objectionable.'[17] He raised a fundamental issue for comparative educationists. Can statistical information alone, even when collected with the greatest care and on the basis of agreed and standardised items, provide a basis for valid comparative evaluations? Even if such comparisons are desirable it seems evident that all the social consequences of policy should be considered and evaluated. These may or may not be capable of quantitative treatment. Yet it is difficult for assessors to dismiss them as unimportant. Statistical comparisons of secondary educational provision are more complicated even than these dealing with primary schools. A multiplicity of aims for it are advanced by each nation, and perhaps no objective yardstick exists.

Finally another important limitation should be placed on comparisons based on the evidence of documents and statistics. The existence of legislation does not mean, *ipso facto*, that it has been implemented. Certainly Matthew Arnold was not convinced of the need for compulsory education laws, but more significantly he realised that they were not always effective. His visit to France convinced him of this particularly when he discovered how easily manufacturers got round the child labour laws, and how regularly children deserted the schools during the summer and autumn in the rural areas of France. He took care to interpret the efficacy of legislation and to state how he thought it had influenced learning in France. Surprisingly he concluded that it was through the excellence of the language used. At the same time he uttered a word of caution against evaluating one educational system against the criteria appropriate to another. To understand rather than to judge was his aim. 'To treat this comparative study with proper respect,' he wrote, 'not to wrest it to the requirements of our inclinations or prejudices, but to try simply and seriously to find what it teaches us, is perhaps the lesson which we have most need to inculcate upon ourselves at present.'[18]

These objections, together with the desire to understand educational processes better, combine to give importance to the second of Cousin's dicta—verification of such evidence as was

available by 'an accurate and detailed inspection'. Few reformers used this technique more effectively than Horace
Mann as Secretary to the Massachusetts Board of Education.
When he visited Europe his interest in foreign systems of education, as revealed in his *Seventh Annual Report to the Board of
Education*, was restricted to those aspects of instruction he wished
to see improved in Massachusetts. Although he paid some
attention to the wider implication of a 'nation's failure to establish a national system', he was chiefly concerned with what went
on in the classroom. He went into the schools of Europe and
described what he saw: he was impressed by some methods of
teaching, the attitude and enthusiasm of teachers, and in
Prussia with the humaneness of the discipline. One example
will perhaps suffice to illustrate a general principle. He described at length the phonetic method of teaching reading in
the Prussian schools, and sought to impress on the teachers of
Massachusetts the need for reform in their methods. He urged
the adoption of the Prussian approach to reading, adding, 'And
I despair of any effective improvement in the teaching of young
children to read, until they shall *qualify* themselves to teach in
this manner;—I say until they shall *qualify* themselves, for they
may attempt it in such a rude and awkward way as will infal-
libly incur a failure.'[19] Neither recommendation was taken
kindly by the Boston schoolmasters. They questioned his competence to judge such matters and the yardsticks he used. And
in principle they were right to do so, for these judgements were
largely subjective. One observer using certain criteria of evaluation might arrive at an entirely different assessment of quality
from another with different criteria. Nevertheless, the vehe-
mence of the Boston schoolmasters' reply indicated that Mann's
criticism had struck home in spite of what they termed 'his
unjust comparisons between them and teachers in some countries of Europe'. They were unimpressed by Mann's original
disclaimer that in praising the Prussian teachers he did not
mean to disparage those of Massachusetts.

The Historical Approach

The incident serves to illustrate the need in comparative study
for acceptable principles of educational evaluation. Assessments

on the basis of personal observations, although useful, are not by themselves adequate. Of the two approaches to explanation —the search for historical causes and the pragmatists' attempt to predict consequences—it was probably inevitable that the former should be developed first in comparative education. The concepts of 'cause' and 'effect' in education had been used, perhaps rather crudely, by some of the earlier workers in the field. Joseph Kay, to mention but one of them, commissioned to study the condition of the poorer classes on the continent of Europe, concluded that their improved position in Germany and Switzerland since 1800 'was the result of two causes: first the admirable and long continued education given to *all* the children; and second the division of the land among the peasants'.[20] By implication this kind of assessment may be taken as empirical evidence in support of the general claims made for education by such men as Owen. The historical approach to comparative education—acknowledged by all the pioneers as important—tended to direct attention to the antecedent 'causes' of educational policy. Educational traditions and those of the nation they served, it was thought, should be carefully examined in order to understand why things were as they were. This implied a belief in the existence of direct causal relationships between certain determining 'factors' and actual policy and practice. There was, consequently, a desire through the discovery of universal 'causes' to establish laws of education and thus a science of education.

The historical method was developed in the twentieth century by a number of eminent scholars. Using it they identified the significant factors influencing educational policy. I. L. Kandel, whose emphasis on historical analyses was responsible as much as anything for its being accepted as the basis of academic studies, stated that: 'The chief aim of the comparative approach to such problems [previously listed] lies in an analysis of the causes which have produced them, in a comparison between the various systems and the reasons underlying them.'[21] These causes were to be found in the 'forces and attitudes governing social organisation, of the political and economic conditions that determine its development'. Another distinguished pioneer, Nicholas Hans,[22] identified the religious, the linguistic, the geographical, the racial, and the political factors as the most important. Friedrich Schneider[23] in similar manner dealt with national character, the formative influence of geographical space, culture, history, foreign influences, and the immanent development of pedagogy itself.

Invaluable as historical research and related analyses are, educational reformers are primarily interested in the consequences of their actions, not in the causes of their present dissatisfaction. Horace Mann, indeed, gave a valuable clue to the possible reconciliation of the two approaches. Reflecting on the object of his visit to Europe he concluded that history provided an explanation of the conditions and diversities he found there. But he was conscious of the fact that the future, whether 'glorious' or 'debased', would be caused by the activities of his generation. The past could not be changed but the future held infinite possibilities. 'The future, then, is our field of action; the past is only valuable as furnishing lights by which that field can be more successfully entered and cultivated.'[24] This pragmatic concept of history as illuminating present problems can, undoubtedly, contribute to that practical knowledge which gives directive or predictive power—namely science.

The Sociological Approach

In their more sophisticated sociological approach Harris and Sadler pointed to the possibilities of this kind of development. It was already clear to them that for the practical purposes of reforming their own systems of education through borrowing from others they really wanted to be able to predict all the consequences of educational change. Because they appreciated that education should be regarded as one of many closely related aspects of any culture, they were aware that educational innovation would have wide social implications. They needed instruments of prediction—theories which would enable them to anticipate events.

This introduced new and important considerations of methodology. Comparative education could not remain a descriptive study, a survey of documents and statistics. While certainly not antithetical to the historical method, the new approach to comparative education implied that emphasis should be placed on the possibilities of prediction rather than on the search for antecedent causes. This in turn implied that comparative education should be a study of the dynamics of an education system and of its relationships with other aspects of society. It meant, in fact, that comparative educationists were, broadly speaking, committed to processes of enquiry grouped under the term 'social science'.

The signal contribution made by Sadler and Harris to the science of education and to the methodology of comparative studies was the explicit manner in which they added a sociological dimension to the historical perspective of the earlier pioneers. Sadler expressed his position succinctly. 'In the study of education at the present time in this country, in America, in Germany, and in France', he wrote, 'there is an evident growth of feeling that school problems, though of course in some respects a special subject by themselves, are only seen in their true perspective when they are regarded as being in necessary and constant relation to other forms of social culture. The educational question is not a question by itself. It is part of the social question. And the social question is at bottom largely an ethical question.'[25]

Harris, too, had recognised the close relationships between the ethos of a country and its educational system. 'Doubtless', he argued, 'each nation has devised some kind of discipline, some course of study which will train the children of its schools into habits in harmony with its laws.' An investigation of these relationships would, he thought, form the basis of 'a science of comparative pedagogy'. Since he recognised that a multiplicity of 'educative values' and 'special fruits' grow out of any educational system he hoped that, before assessing relative merit, 'a more discriminating comparison may be made in regard to the methods of education abroad, so that we may know the entire scope of the problem. We must count in without omission all the educative values before we weigh the products of our own schools against those of other nations.'[26] This stress on the need to know, or anticipate, all the 'special fruits'—or consequences—of educational policy anticipates in some way the principles of explanation accepted by the pragmatists.

Methodology

Cultural Borrowing Today

Perhaps Sadler's concern with the reorganisation and expansion of secondary education made him less sanguine than some of his predecessors about the possibilities of cultural borrowing and more interested in the development of realistic theories on which policy could be based. The wider provision of post-primary education, hotly debated in Europe and North America during the second half of the nineteenth century, raised many issues of policy. Its aims, for example, should be distinguished from those of public primary instruction. If at the secondary stage some attempt was made to educate young people for adult life, what kind of life and social order should the system prepare them for? Should they be educated together in one school? Should boys and girls be educated together? Should there be a common course of instruction for all pupils? Who should decide its content? And how long should it last? What were the possibilities of training young people for commercial and industrial life when there were so many forms of it? These questions were asked by Sadler, who appreciated how many things had to be taken into account in forming judgements about the 'hygiene of education'. The questions are, of course, equally valid today. In short there are problems about secondary education of organisation and content which have little meaning for the promoters of primary or elementary instruction.

For this reason, no doubt, several nineteenth-century reformers were less reluctant to use the early comparative education reports to arouse influential leaders and the public to the deficiencies of their own elementary school systems. Cousin's report was, to take one instance, published in Albany, New York, in 1836, and Mrs Sarah Austin translated the report on primary education in Prussia to draw attention in England to the 'subject of Primary instruction, i.e. that education which is absolutely necessary to the moral and intellectual well-being of the mass of the people'.[27] A fellow countryman, Leonard Horner, translated Cousin's report on education in Holland for the same reason, urging that England should, in essence, 'take a lesson from a neighbour'.[28] Certainly not everyone was invited to undertake 'impartial reflection upon the subject' of popular education. It was a burning issue and the ardent reformers made what use they could of comparative studies.

Today the forces of expansion in education are again very actively at work all over the world. At one level the newly independent nations, many of them economically underdeveloped, wish to provide universal primary instruction. At another the expansion and extension of secondary education is urged in most of the industrialised countries. In the richer parts of the world, and even in some of those which are not so wealthy, the expansion of higher education either as a basic human right or in the interests of economic development is hotly debated. In their attempts to improve their own systems educational statesmen and administrators have taken a renewed interest in the schools of other countries. Cultural borrowing has again captured the imagination of many reformers and since the war there has been a revival of interest in the study of comparative education as an instrument of educational reform.

The problems which faced the nineteenth-century pioneers are still largely unsolved. A number of developments have improved the possibility of using comparative studies more effectively. For example, several agencies collect and disseminate information about education. The establishment of such institutions was proposed long ago. Jullien de Paris hoped, for example, to set up such an agency through which data on educational systems throughout the world could be widely diffused. As the first United States Commissioner of Education, Henry Barnard partially realised these hopes when his office continued the work he had begun in Connecticut. Later Jules Ferry[29] used arguments already advanced by Buisson. The latter had referred to the number of institutions which had been developed in Europe and North America for the exposition of educational works and materials. In particular he mentioned the Bureau of Education in Washington and Commissioner John Eaton Jr.'s work and the latter's comments on the desirability of founding an international museum for education. The creation of the International Bureau of Education in Geneva together with the work of UNESCO should be regarded as logical extensions of Jullien's concept. Moreover, many national governments now maintain research departments one of whose tasks is to study education in foreign countries.

Methodology

The information gathered in a variety of ways and by numerous agencies is all extremely valuable. But the search for a method in comparative education which will, as Harris hoped, give 'directive power', continues. It is with this consideration in mind that the subsequent attempts to give some precision to the problem approach in comparative education are undertaken.

Chapter II

A SCIENCE OF EDUCATION AND PLANNING

IN seeking to establish a science of education the pioneers of comparative education were attempting in a modest way to accomplish what many social philosophers were saying was possible; namely, the discovery of laws related to man's social environment in the same way as the laws of physics and chemistry were related to his physical environment. Some philosophers held that there were basic laws of society; others favoured laws of the mind. Some used models of scientific method drawn from physics; others biological prototypes. But most of them hoped to discover a few laws of historical development which would reveal to them how society would move towards its final glorious destiny.

This nineteenth-century optimism can be regarded as stemming from two, not unrelated, sources. There was, first of all, a faith in progress based upon scientific knowledge as envisaged by Francis Bacon and on education as conceived by Comenius. Confidence had been strengthened throughout the seventeenth century by many scientific discoveries which culminated in Newton's laws of motion. So successfully were these then used in astronomy, for example, that it is hardly surprising that the men of the Enlightenment felt assured that in their search for knowledge progress was inevitable. The second reason for optimism was the further pragmatic proof of the power of applied science in the achievements of the industrial revolution. It encouraged social thinkers to hope that by using similar methods they could gain control of their social environment and thus improve it.

The poverty, lawlessness, and misery of the industrialising societies served only to intensify the search by such men as

Methodology

Owen and Marx for scientific laws of society on which could be based reforms to ameliorate the lot of the masses. Out of beliefs like these grew concepts of social planning which contrasted sharply with a prevailing laisser faire liberalism of non-interference by government in the economic, social and political life of individuals. Major exceptions to this rule, however, were national defence and education. The provision of schools was too important to be left entirely to private enterprise or philanthropy. Some kind of national planning, however crude, was regarded as necessary. And for this, at least so several comparative educationists maintained, a science of education was needed.

In the modern world attitudes towards planning fall on an extended continuum. At one extreme left-wing governments are committed to social and economic development in accordance with overall plans. At the other end of the scale, some governments completely reject the notion of social planning as neither desirable nor possible. Somewhere between these two positions are those who accept the need for some form of piecemeal social engineering. In fact, at the operational level the argument turns on the issue of who should plan;—the representatives of national governments or the directors of private firms? At the theoretical level debates about planning often flounder because no unambiguous verbal definition of the term 'social planning' has yet been given (or generally accepted). Consequently an analysis of the mechanics of the process would help to clarify the issues. Until the constituents of planning are known it is impossible to say to what extent it is possible in practice. Such a breakdown would also help to answer the question of who should be responsible for each of its aspects. Of these, three processes are integral parts of planning, namely policy formulation, policy adoption, and the implementation of policy.

Attitudes towards the possibilities of planning often derive from political theories and views about the nature of knowledge. Many present-day approaches are founded in one or other of several important nineteenth-century schools of thought. Among them Hegelianism, Marxism, liberalism, and positivism competed for adherents, and towards the end of the century pragmatism was to become an important contender. Today the historicism of Hegel and Marx has been used to justify planning in fascist and communist societies respectively. Positivism has given support to those who believe in a democratically 'planned society'. Through pragmatism, social Darwinism became a twentieth-century American rationale of the Jeffersonian dream. Between these schools of thought there were considerable differences of opinion about methods of acquiring knowledge of society and about the nature of the millennium.

For example, Marx—perhaps the most influential materialist —prophesied a classless society. He maintained that his method was scientific, and postulated efficient (economic) 'causes' of social change. Hegel, on the other hand, had conceived progress as towards the realisation of the ideal state. His personification of the Nation made social development purposive, and causal explanation teleological. Both men applied dialectics— of different kinds—to arrive at the truth. Both of them 'knew' the final and absolute goal of social development. Such is the thorough-going determinism of both theories that the role of individuals is not clear. Apparently they cannot materially change the course of history although they might hasten progress.

Positivism represents another nineteenth-century school of social determinism. Empiricists like J. S. Mill and Comte were not sure they knew the ultimate character of society, but they had a positive view on the inevitable increase in man's knowledge about it. Mill's *A System of Logic* was intended as a contribution to the discussion of whether or not social phenomena were exceptions to the uniformity of nature principle and to see 'how far the methods by which so many of the laws of the physical world have been numbered among truths irrevocably acquired and universally assented to, can be made instrumental to the formation of a similar body of received doctrine in moral and political science'.[1] Having stated what he conceived to be the methods of the physical sciences Mill quickly saw that the complexity of society made their use in this sphere extremely difficult. Nevertheless he felt that sociologists would finally 'succeed not only in looking far forward into the future history of the human race, but in determining what artificial means may be used, and to what extent, to accelerate the natural progress in and so far as it is beneficial'.[2]

At the close of the century a similar case was stated with reservations by Lester F. Ward, a distinguished American sociologist. Nature, he maintained, was 'the domain of rigid law' and man was a product of it. But, he went on, man 'has reached a stage on which he can comprehend the law'. His destiny was therefore in his own hands to the extent that, whilst unable to change nature, he could guide its powers. Man's ability perpetually to better his estate—the aim of rational men —was possible in 'precise proportion to man's knowledge of nature'.[3] Ward was, however, less optimistic than Mill about the inevitable accumulation of knowledge. Indeed, he thought it unlikely, and consequently social change would be erratic— sometimes moving forward, sometimes slipping back.

Deterministic in a somewhat different way were the founders of nineteenth-century social evolutionism. In the hands of Herbert Spencer, for example, Darwinism became a theory of social movement towards the millennium. It was, according to Richard Hofstadter, a mechanical process which promised 'that whatever the immediate hardships for a large portion of mankind, evolution meant progress, and this assured that the whole process was tending towards some remote but altogether glorious consummation'.[4] Thus armed, Spencer was able to agree with laisser faire liberals that the amount of government interference should be reduced in future societies. Some modern pragmatists, however, undoubtedly support the concept of a planned society.

This classification of social philosophies takes no account of important differences of detail and emphasis among various schools. It points to four major positions which have been influential in Europe and North America, in forming attitudes towards, and providing justification for, social planning.

In general historicism and positivism imply that not only is overall planning possible, but that certain policies will be universally applicable. The argument is that since laws of nature and society can be discovered and since social change necessarily occurs in accordance with them, they can form the basis of plans which meet the interests of all mankind. The second claim, that certain policies can be applied with equal success everywhere, rests upon the philosophical assumption that the laws either of nature or of society are unconditionally valid.

Pragmatism, on the other hand, in spite of the claims of some of its adherents, provides little theoretical support for total planning. Furthermore, it suggests that while intelligent men may reconstruct society they can do so only in piecemeal fashion, and in the light of specific circumstances. Thus for the consistent pragmatist there are unlikely to be available any educational panaceas—a view, as will be seen, which accords well with modern philosophies of science.

Some understanding of these views is desirable, since it is as an instrument of reform or planned development, and as a method of enquiry leading to theoretical understanding that comparative education is viewed in this book. In short, it is assumed that a 'science of education giving directive power' can be developed through comparative studies, and that the search for the 'underlying principles which govern the development of all national systems of education' is important. Some of the assumptions consequent upon an acceptance of this position are examined and an attempt is made to show how the 'problem approach' can serve both ends in comparative education.

Comparative Education and Post-relativity Science

First of all, for social scientists who seek to apply modern methods, the implications of the late nineteenth-century revolution in science are important. A number of events occurred which raised fundamental issues. Advances in physics and chemistry made inadequate the theories which had served so well for so long. Electromagnetic phenomena, line spectra, the thermodynamics of radiation, threw increasing strain upon Newtonian concepts, and finally compelled Einstein to search for radically different theories.

In practice, of course, under certain conditions Newton's laws continue to be extremely useful. But theoretically the science of relativity which replaced them at the turn of the twentieth century is not, according to Herbert Dingle, 'a trifling change, touching only the latest refinements of physics; it affects the very foundation, the primary definitions and concepts, on which the whole science is built'. In pre-relativity days, he argues, 'it was possible for the physicist to be a naif realist— as, in fact, most physicists consciously or unconsciously, were.

29

He could believe that he was discovering laws of the world of matter which was external to himself—laws which had nothing to do with his own thoughts and which simply described relations between objective qualities of matter which he could discover but could not create or destroy.'[5]

Since Einstein advanced his theory of relativity philosophers have discussed with renewed vigour that which constitutes 'scientific method'. The debates continue. In general, however, there has been a movement away from the view that scientific laws are unconditionally valid. Nor are they regarded as irrefutably true or false. They are now generally regarded as necessarily hypothetical; statements from which future events can be deductively inferred. They enable us, A. J. Ayer writes, 'to anticipate the course of our sensations', and the laws of nature, 'if they are not merely definitions, are simply hypotheses which may be confuted by experience'.[6] They are judged by their usefulness, not their truth or correspondence with reality. Explanation is provided by the processes of prediction and verification. In order to make predictions, however, it is necessary to specify as fully as possible the circumstances or initial conditions under which the predicted event is to take place. Verification or confutation of the hypothesis depends on whether or not the predicted event corresponds to the observed event. Understanding therefore comes through successful prediction rather than through the discovery of antecedent causes. Verification depends upon experimental procedures. The tests in science frequently take on a common-sense appearance—it is easy for people to agree that a car is moving or an aircraft is flying, difficult for them to agree on speeds without the aid of instruments of measurement—the metre rule, the swinging pendulum, the arbitrary unit of mass. Crude sense impressions are converted into meter readings. This kind of test is also applied in cases where deductions take the scientist away from highly speculative hypotheses which cannot be tested directly to events which can be so tested. Agreements on the basis of meter readings is usually possible. But the objectivity of the scientist is not a psychological trait; it is the result of the public nature of his testing procedures. In short, the authority of the scientist does not rest upon him as a person, or on the authority of a group, nor is it an appeal to reason, logic, or truth alone, but to procedures which can be repeated by everyone and which finally lead to sense impressions and so in a crude way to 'common' sense.

These then are some of the implications of post-relativity views of scientific method. Similar conclusions emerged at the end of the century in the United States out of the ferment of discussion about Spencer's evolutionary theories. Within pragmatism many strands can doubtless be distinguished, but the fact that its main assumptions became part of the American climate of opinion is extremely important when attempting to understand some of the basic ideological differences between the U.S.A. and Europe. Philip P. Wiener has summarised its main implications for social thought. One was the idea of pluralistic empiricism—'the piecemeal analysis of the diverse issues pertaining to physical, biological, psychological, linguistic and social problems, which resist resolution by a single metaphysical formula'. Another consequence was the introduction of a temporalism which 'leads to a more empirical view of history and knowledge than that which finds eternal laws of development in social change and science'. Infallible rules of behaviour were 'replaced by contextual empirically tested generalisations as probable guides'.[7]

If, as K. R. Popper maintains, there is a complete unity of method among the natural and social sciences, these opinions have important implications for the comparative educationist who wishes to make his study scientific. Brought into question, for example, are basic assumptions about the universality of social laws, the objectivity of social 'facts' and of 'cause' and 'effect' as useful concepts. New theories of measurement are implied; and the whole belief in induction as *the* method of discovery is questioned. Consequently new roles have to be given to observation, the collection of data (social 'facts'), hypotheses, prediction, and experiment. The implications of post-relativity views about physical science are not, however, always appreciated. According to Otto Neurath,[8] 'Social scientists sometimes think of physics and astronomy as an El Dorado of exactness and definiteness', and think that contradictions are fatal to any theory. Neither, Neurath writes, is the case; the laws of physics are much less certain than was once thought. And as for the social sciences, Neurath felt that we have to 'expect gulfs and gaps everywhere, together with unpredictability, incompleteness, and onesidedness of our arguing, wherever we may start'.

Neurath's assessment of the position of the social sciences certainly seems applicable to comparative education in its present stage of development. Few practitioners would claim that reliable predictions are yet possible in the field of education—a *sine qua non* of reliable planning; but if the study is to become increasingly scientific, attempts to formulate theories giving directive power are necessary. The 'problem approach' which has been widely used in comparative education seems well designed to meet the requirements of those who wish to make the study scientific and at the same time use it as an instrument of reform. Stemming as it does from pragmatism, the assumptions within it are certainly not incompatible with those twentieth-century views about scientific method previously outlined. Not all comparative educationists are prepared to accept pragmatism and the arguments of men like Ayer and Popper. It is desirable, therefore, to make more explicit the theoretical basis of the 'problem approach' and comment on the tasks it demands of scholars and research workers in the field of comparative education.

Assumptions of the Problem Approach

The philosophical assumptions behind the 'problem approach' have been stated too frequently to warrant lengthy analysis here. A representative and well-known statement of the stages in the complete act of reflective thinking, on which the present formulation of the problem approach is based, can be found in John Dewey's *How We Think*;[9] he there maintained, of course, that the processes of reflection were scientific.

According to Dewey the function of reflective thinking is to clear up a confused situation, i.e. to solve a problem. Between the pre-reflective situation (confusion or perplexity) and the post-reflective situation (perplexity resolved), a number of reflective processes take place. These may be grouped under (i) hypothesis or solution formulation, (ii) problem intellectualisation or analysis, (iii) analysis and specification of context, (iv) logical deduction of consequences, and (v) practical verification. In the face of a perplexing situation possible solutions may immediately spring to mind. Further reflection involves a process of intellectualisation out of which the problem to be solved becomes clearly formulated. This stage directs attention to data of a certain kind, namely those which are relevant to the problem. Out of it emerge refined or new possible solutions which are then put forward as hypotheses to be tested one after the other. Testing involves making logical deductions from the hypotheses within the context of relevant factors and then (ideally) comparing the predicted events with the actual events which are observed to flow from a selected course of action. Agreement between predicted and observed events provides verification of a hypothesis, an explanation of the events, and constitutes a successful resolution of the confused situation. It also provides a springboard for further action. Disagreement between the two types of event (predicted and observed) constitutes a refutation of the hypothesis, but should lead to a re-examination of the degree to which all the stages of reflective thinking have been satisfactorily completed.

Several general features of Dewey's analysis should perhaps be emphasised. First, although a confused situation promotes thinking, subsequent intellectualisation is necessary in order to sharpen the foci of an investigation. In practice, the problem approach leads to the formulation of very specific questions about selected social relationships. Its use also directs attention to certain relevant factors within a general context or set of circumstances. As a result the scope of any comparative enquiry based upon it will be narrowed, and some, and not other, data and questions will be considered. It is important to note that such limitations do not mean that some data are inherently more important than others. Furthermore no *a priori* restriction is placed on the type of question posed, or on the kind of enquiry undertaken. Nor are the possibilities reduced of a multitude of social factors being relevant. The problem itself, however, determines what is relevant and what is not. It also helps to determine the relative importance of each of the factors contributing to the problem and its solution.

Second, the hypotheses or proposed solutions to any problem correspond to the scientists' laws from which future events may be deductively inferred, and which enable us 'to anticipate the course of our sensations'. To almost any problem—particularly if it is social in origin—there are several possible solutions. In practice each represents a policy choice and persons responsible for the adoption of policy are invariably faced with the necessity of making such a choice. It is at this stage that the authority and limitations of scientific procedures need to be known and taken into account when decisions are taken.

It should be appreciated, for example, that the two scientific processes on which choices are realistically based—(a) the logical deduction of future events, and (b) experimental verification of them—are extremely difficult to perform in the case of social issues. In particular verification presents real problems. All the relevant factors in the light of which deductions are made may be hard to identify and weigh. Secondly, even when this is possible, it is unlikely that the relevant context can be adequately controlled. For social and political reasons experiments, except on a very limited scale, are rare in the social sciences. Even ruthless governments, which may be more successful than those committed to persuasion rather than coercion in ordering human affairs, cannot entirely overcome this obstacle. Thirdly, many hoped-for outcomes of social policy occur after many years have elapsed, and for this reason rigorous experimentation is virtually impossible. To be sure, in historical perspective policies can be seen either to have worked or to have failed. The problem approach implies that understanding of social and educational processes comes from successful prediction rather than, as in some epistemologies, through the discovery of antecedent causes. Historical evidence should, therefore, be used pragmatically to illuminate present problems rather than to establish antecedent cause-effect relationships.

The explicit adoption of the problem approach and its methodological implications involves the comparative educationist in all, or some, of the phases of reflective thinking. The four main aspects of the approach are (a) problem analysis; (b) policy formulation; (c) the identification, description, and weighting of relevant factors within a given context; and (d) the anticipation or prediction of the outcomes of policies.

A Science of Education and Planning

Problem Selection and Analysis

The choice of problem will depend upon the investigator—his own experience, background of knowledge, and awareness of current educational discussion and debate, will focus his attention either on issues which appear important in his own culture, or on questions which have international significance. The fact that recognisable problems in his own culture seem to be universal makes them attractive bases for comparison. Indeed, the supposition is that the 'same problem' exists everywhere. Further and deeper analysis certainly may reveal important differences in its national characteristics which may be as much of kind as of degree. One task the comparative educationist should, therefore, undertake is, having once identified the universal, vaguely perceived problem, to intellectualise (or analyse) it in general terms, and then to reveal its specific features in selected contexts. The result may be to show that what appear to be common problems are in some respects not. Such clarification lends support to the belief that the comparative educationist may profitably assume that many problems (in their generalised form) appear in a number of different countries.

Of these, comparative educationists who wish to use their studies for the purpose of reform will be primarily interested in present-day issues. Broadly one group of them can be classified as basically educational: for example, those which are connected with the reorganisation of the curriculum, with teaching methods and with changes in the system, to name but a few. Other problems are basically socio-economic or political. For example, questions of educational control are intrinsically political in character. Then there are economic problems associated with investment in educational services. Others may be regarded as fundamentally psychological, and some as having their origin in the social class structure of a society.

Of course every educational issue has its socio-economic and political dimensions; and the reverse is equally true. Either kind of question—socio-economic or educational—can, as Sadler suggested, usefully serve as a point of departure for research in comparative education. The choice of starting-point will inevitably promote an investigation of selected questions and relationships. Such limitations do not imply that the other, loftier, aspects of education can be ignored. They simply mean a restriction of interest.

The selection for study of problems of pressing importance does not render the historical perspective valueless. Clearly most modern problems have roots in the past and as stated previously the pragmatic use of historical evidence can throw light on present-day questions. Indeed a deliberate attempt to investigate a problem in a selected historical setting may well serve the same purpose. If justification is needed for such studies in comparative education it is that they are case studies based on the general assumption that confused situations arise from the prior introduction into a society of innovations whose effects have been more or less traumatic. One advantage is that an historical context is obviously more manageable than a contemporary setting.

Methodologically J. S. Mill's suggestion that for the purposes of analysis it is desirable to assume that the innovation was introduced into a static society is very valuable. The choice of starting-point (the historical context into which the innovation was introduced) is thus important because it gives a certain perspective to the problem under consideration. For example, some of the difficulties facing French educators today may be regarded as having their origins in the traumatic impact of the Revolution on eighteenth century France. On the other hand some aspects of these and other problems may be considered to arise from events during the second world war. Doubtless, debatable issues tend to persist, and may, in fact, be analysed by reference to more than one starting-point, thus providing for one country a useful kind of historical comparative study. Having said this, it is worth repeating that contemporary issues and their immediate determinants are of particular interest to the comparative educationist who sees his study as an instrument of reform.

It is, of course, a truism that the modern world is one of change and abounds with problems. Evidently some of them can be viewed as having been created by processes either initiated or accelerated by the second world war. Few societies were unaffected by it. But three major changes may be regarded as particularly significant. Each, because of its dramatic impact, has been described as an explosion.

First there has been an *explosion of expectations*. The peoples of Asia and Africa demanded and were promised political independence and higher standards of living. The norms were generally those of Europe and North America. A concerted attack, so it seemed, was to be made upon imperialism, poverty, disease, and ignorance. Thus among the aspirations aroused almost immediately after the war was access to education. In the economically underdeveloped countries it meant, for the most part, universal primary education. In Europe and elsewhere it meant far greater opportunities than heretofore for secondary and higher education. Education and health, indeed, have come to be regarded as basic human rights, but in many countries the lack of resources and available institutions has made these widespread expectations unattainable.

The *explosion of population* has accentuated the difficulties of an already formidable task. The very success of improved medical services has created major educational difficulties. Infant mortality rates have everywhere been reduced. High birth rates and low death rates have resulted in rates of growth in population which are staggering, reaching percentages per annum as high as 2·8 in some African countries. These increases have made remote the prospects of satisfying some of the heightened aspirations. In particular low birth rates and higher death rates in the thirties have resulted in the proportion of school age children to the total population becoming alarmingly high, reaching some 40 per cent in India, for example.

The third major change has created problems of a somewhat different kind. The *explosion of knowledge* has profound political, economic, and cultural implications. The war accelerated the process of applying science to the affairs of men. Every medium of communication was improved from a technical viewpoint. New media were invented. Economically the effect has been to make automation more than an idle dream. With it will come a shorter working week, temporary unemployment perhaps, and the need for industrial re-training. The problem of educating youth for a leisure dominated by mass-media entertainment is very real in many technologically advanced countries. Politically the extensive use of mass media of communication has created unprecedented opportunities for the demagogue. In some countries these media were introduced to a literate population. In many others with high illiteracy rates the new media bypassed literacy in the sense of ability to read and write. These improvements in communication media have been matched by technical advances in every field, including the weapons of mass annihilation, against the use of which even the amazing advances of medicine appear powerless. Thus the explosion of knowledge has created serious problems in the social, economic, political, and educational realms. The simple literacy of the nineteenth century—the three R's—is now outmoded, and the growth of scientific knowledge has made imperative in education qualitative changes which would result in the development of scientific literacy on a wide scale.

Turning from the sources of common problems, it is evident that these overriding changes were accompanied by others which affected the nations of the world in various and different ways. Economically, both victor and vanquished, with the possible exception of the U.S.A., suffered greatly. Losses in manpower were accompanied by devastation and the destruction of material resources. The U.S.S.R. alone probably lost some 20,000,000 persons; France's economy was virtually destroyed by a ruthless occupation; and Great Britain's vast overseas credits were dissipated. The defeated nations, Germany, Italy, and Japan, suffered grievously too. Yet in spite of the destruction of their real resources the economic potential of Europe and Japan in terms of recovery and growth remained greater by far than those of most of the nations of Africa and Asia which did not feel so directly the impact of war. The gap between the economic potential of these countries and that of Europe and North America is still enormous; yet the expectations of peoples everywhere are no longer dissimilar.

Major political changes left the European nations, with long imperial traditions, with much less power than formerly. The United States, previously isolationist towards Europe, moved into the centre of world affairs and was soon to be joined there by the Soviet Union. In the subsequent struggle for independence by former colonies a new battle for the minds of men was joined. Both the U.S.A. and the U.S.S.R. tried to influence the newly independent nations. These changes demanded of individuals everywhere new attitudes towards world politics. Evidently an analysis of the precise problems in selected regions or nations raised by these explosions would constitute a major comparative study. In particular, of course, their implications for educational policy would be of special significance to the comparative educationist. Undoubtedly acceptance that these changes have initiated problems of educational significance is useful, but it should be noted that it constitutes a choice and represents only one of many possible general starting-points of analysis.

Formulation of Policy Proposals

Just as many common problems exist in the world today, so there is no shortage of proposed solutions in the form of policies. A survey of intentions—often, as Cousin realised, expressed in legislation—reveals that similar educational policies have been widely accepted. In economically under-developed countries one of two policies has been adopted to meet raised expectations. On the one hand many governments have stated their intention to establish universal primary education as a human right; on the other, 'fundamental', 'basic', or 'community' education has been regarded in some quarters as a panacea. In Europe the strong pressures to re-organise secondary education have been designed to extend opportunities and make them less dependent than previously on the accident of birth or wealth. In some countries too, notably the U.S.A., policies to expand higher education have been accepted (see Chapters VI and IX).

Again, where the promotion of political democracy has been regarded as important, attempts have been made to decentralise systems of administration. This policy was, for example, accepted by newly independent India. The Allied Powers tried to impose it in Japan and encouraged it in Germany. Communist governments, too, recognise the desirability of decentralising some aspects of educational control. Such policies are invariably justified on the grounds that they

39

are democratic. In the event practice sometimes—as in post-war Japan—reveals the dangers of assuming that forms of control which work well in one country will lead to the same results elsewhere (see Chapter XI).

There is perhaps less agreement about the ways in which the explosion of knowledge should be handled. The demand for scientists and technologists appears to be insatiable in spite of some manpower estimates. It has been met in Communist countries, as well as in others, by the establishment of technological universities and technical schools. Yet solutions to the problem of providing a sound general education through science and vocational studies are difficult to devise, although vigorous attempts to do so have been made in the Soviet Union and other Communist countries (see Chapter X).

Awareness of the fact that the same policies are widely proclaimed should not, however, lead the comparative educationist to suppose that they will be equally effective wherever they are applied. On the contrary one task of comparative analysis is to make clear the range of policy choices available, and another is to propose more realistic solutions through refinements in the processes of analysis.

Identification of Relevant Factors

Choice implies the necessity of making decisions and of adopting one policy rather than another. Inevitably policy is to some extent goal-directed—a reflection, that is to say, of social aspirations and expectations. Obviously sound planning should not deny such aims and objectives. Its technical role should be to make them attainable and to ensure at the same time that undesirable and unexpected results do not occur when a choice of policies is made. The planners' task is to formulate policy (or policies) in such a way that those whose duty it is to adopt it can, if they wish, make a rational decision based on predicted outcomes.

Modern concepts of science suggest that the logical deduction of outcomes (consequences) from suggested solutions (policies) is possible only if the specific circumstances in which the solution is to be introduced are known. Consequently the task of identifying all the factors or determinants which influence the outcomes of policy is crucial to the process of social planning. It is, moreover, an extremely complex operation demanding insight, critical analysis, and rigorous description.

Comparative educationists have, of course, located the major areas of the social context which bear on the outcomes of educational policy. Before the predictive element in social planning can be perfected, not only is a detailed analysis necessary of the educational structure itself, but also specific features of its infrastructure—economic, political, class structure and so on—have to be identified. The number of such possible variables, even in each of the major sectors, is large, and associated with the task of identifying them is that of reducing them to manageable proportions. Two approaches to this problem should be mentioned. An Aristotelian may suggest that there is, in fact, a limited number of universal and essential factors which when discovered and described enable the relevant context to be fully known. Similar in intention would be an attempt to reduce, by the process of logical factor analysis, a vast number of variables to the minimum required to enable a social context to be adequately described and understood. In the problem approach, however, the problem itself determines what degree of importance should be attached to each of the identified contextual factors. In practice, some kind of reduction is based upon a selection of factors using directing problems and hypotheses.

In summary, a specification of the circumstances under which predictions are to be made involves three operations. First, the contextual determinants or initial conditions should be identified and analysed in detail. Second, those relevant to the problem under consideration should be selected, thus reducing the total number of variables to manageable proportions. Finally, in order to make logical deductions each of the factors (variables) should be weighted relative to the others. Hence, for example, to anticipate the consequences of introducing comprehensive schools in any country, among other factors account should be taken of the aspirations of its people and the degree of industrialisation. Each should be further analysed to show by which group aspirations associated with the establishment of the comprehensive schools are most strongly held. Moreover, what degree of urbanisation and

geographical mobility is implied by the degree of industrialisation? When such very dissimilar but not unrelated factors
have been selected as relevant, the way in which and the
relative force with which they will act should be assessed and,
ideally, expressed mathematically.

There is danger in assuming that only those variables to
which a quantitative or statistical index can be given are
important. Certainly correlations between variables and outcomes established on the basis of quantification give an
impression of rigour and precision. Both in the economic and
in the psychological fields indices of this kind have been devised.
It is possible to give the percentage distribution within a country
of the working population in terms of primary, secondary, and
tertiary occupations; similarly figures for per capita income and
per capita productivity can be worked out; and per capita
educational costs. Correlations between various economic
indices can be established on a national basis. In the same way,
some of the variables regarded as contributing to examination
success, intelligence, parental income and occupation, length
of school life, can be quantified and correlations established.
In other spheres, such as politics, quantification is not so
readily achieved. Evidently the honesty of a government is an
important determinant of the outcome of policy; to identify
it and recognise its relevance is straightforward, but to accord
to it in numerical terms a weight relative to and compared
with, say, degree of industrialisation is extremely difficult.

If the tasks imposed on the social planner by the need to
specify the initial conditions within a national social context
are great, the difficulties when attempting international comparisons of contexts are much more formidable. The processes
of identification, selection for relevance, and weighting should
be carried out for each of the countries compared. Each
item should be capable of cross-cultural comparison. Having
satisfied himself on this score, the investigator may well find
that the factors considered relevant in one country are not so
regarded in another. Moreover the relative weighting accorded
to factors accepted as important may also vary very considerably. The order of difficulty will depend on which particular
set of factors is being considered. Certainly, ease of identification
and quantification should not be taken as the sole criteria of

relevance for the purposes of weighting. This warning leads to the need to consider whether or not it is desirable to classify factors, either on the basis of the documentary sources and methods through which they are investigated or in accordance with certain of their characteristics. These two principles of classification are not entirely antithetical, as will be made clear in the next chapter, where it is assumed that a useful distinction can be made between (*a*) ideological factors—norms, attitudes or values; (*b*) institutional forces represented by organisations and practices within the various sectors of the social context; and (*c*) those factors, such as terrain, climate, the availability of natural resources, and population statistics, which are less directly, or not at all, under the control of men. Evidently the major sectors, economic, political, educational, religious, and so on cut across this system of classification; but more about this later. At the moment it is sufficient to indicate that a complete description of a social context would, working on this assumption, involve a statement of all the social norms; an analysis of the functioning of all the social institutions: and an account of all the geographical and demographic features of that society. It seems hardly necessary to say that such a task is impossible, but selection and weighting of factors within the social context are facilitated by the distinctions suggested here.

Finally, in view of what has just been said, it is perhaps appropriate here to comment on so-called descriptive studies and some explanatory studies in comparative education. It is sometimes assumed that the former are intrinsically different from accounts based upon an explicit acceptance of the problem approach. This argument implies that information can be collected without the aid of a directing problem and hypothesis, and, pushing it a little further, that the data are not 'selected'. Investigators accepting induction as *the* method of science would go further and claim that careful observations of all data are a prerequisite of descriptive studies and say that total descriptions were possible. Essentialists would probably argue that the observations of 'essentials' of an educational system do not involve arbitrary selection. Certainly in the Kandel-Hans-Schneider tradition explanations of present educational systems are available in terms of essential determining factors. There is much to be gained from these and similar comparative studies, but the logic of the problem or reflective thinking approach to the acquisition of knowledge and the search for explanation makes any description selective and any explanation hypothetical and partial.

Prediction: an Ingredient of Science and Planned Reform

The final phases of reflective thinking are prediction and verification. Comparative educationists interested in the planned development of education should be particularly anxious to improve techniques of establishing causal relations. Even at the level of attempting to explain 'why things are as they are' in different countries the situation is far from satisfactory.

From the viewpoint of social planning and cultural borrowing a most important type of study is that which endeavours to anticipate and compare events in a number of given situations. It is perfectly possible to make international comparisons of educational achievements using certain criteria of success. It may be possible to explain the differences noted in terms of existing school systems. A more difficult and yet more rewarding study would be one which attempted to predict and compare cross-culturally the educational consequences of a reform: for example, the effects on achievement of the introduction of grouping 'gifted children' for instruction. Too frequently arguments for or against reform are based upon naive comparisons and on prophecies which are often a direct reflection of prejudice or faith, rather than on conclusions reached by careful deductions from hypotheses and against a background of specified initial conditions.

The difficulties associated with this formidable task give rise to several temptations, all of which in the interest of sound planning should be eschewed or at least be noted in investigations intended to contribute to policy formulation. The first danger, that no attempt will be made to predict all the consequences of innovation, has been mentioned. In these circumstances most probably the outcomes considered will be those which seem easiest to predict: the crude costs of the change in policy, for example, or its effects on academic standards. Evidently the extent to which it may contribute to personal happiness will be infinitely more difficult to predict with any certainty. Should it be ignored because criteria of happiness are difficult to establish so as to command general acceptance? Again is it impossible to decide, except completely arbitrarily, at what point in a person's life happiness should be measured? Yet such an outcome is no less difficult to assess than, say, 'sound moral character'. And both may be legitimate aims of education. To ignore them by restricting predictions to those which appear easy because they are quantifiable, illustrates in somewhat exaggerated form this particular danger and dilemma.

A second closely related temptation when making choices is that of paying attention to the predicted short-term consequences, to the detriment of long-term results. Doubtless of the two sets some, if not all, of the short-term immediate outcomes of an educational policy are more accurately predictable. Yet again it would be unwise to assume that choices based upon them, even if the accuracy is considerable, are necessarily sounder than those which take into account the less tangible longer-term results.

In general it is important to establish criteria of success. Among these accorded to education by philosophers and statesmen are individual development, social justice, political stability, and economic growth. These represent long-term objectives and are directly related to the highest ideals of a national educational policy. On the other hand, many of the aims which act most powerfully on educational practice reflect short-term outcomes and expediency. National studies would reveal the extent to which long- and short-term objectives are compatible. In comparative studies it is important that criteria of success should be comparable. That is to say, higher aims in a society should be compared with similar objectives elsewhere and not with the lower level operating aims or, still worse, with practice.

Two principles of classifying outcomes should perhaps be noted. First, there are those which can be regarded as measurable in terms of either social returns or the benefits (or losses) sustained by individuals. Secondly, in either case returns can be classified as economic, social class, political, educational and so on. Care should be taken to establish appropriate criteria of evaluation for each of these various categories. Similar care should be taken not to assume that apparent correlations between indices necessarily mean that direct causal relations exist between the factors. Some measurable outcomes are bound to be more closely related than others to a particular educational policy, but the latter is likely to have some effect in all the areas mentioned, and both on individuals and on national institutions. Apparent correlations should be regarded as starting points of more thorough studies of interrelated factors and not as final answers. Economists, for example, have had some success in relating personal investment in education to the individual's subsequent salary. Societal returns in terms of per capita income have also been related to national investment in education. There is an obvious temptation to draw from these figures the conclusion that, whatever the other circumstances, a higher investment in education will result in rises in per capita income in low-income countries. Such a conclusion, however, may give far too much weight to the role of education in economic development. A more balanced approach is needed which takes account of other relevant contextual factors and which pays attention to other possible consequences.

Interdisciplinary Co-operation

To achieve this balance demands that comparative studies designed to contribute the formulation of educational policy should be interdisciplinary in character. Evidently at each stage in the process of reflective thinking (the problem approach) the co-operation of economists, political scientists, sociologists, philosophers, anthropologists, and comparative educationists is desirable. Jointly they should proceed to analyse or intellectualise the problems under examination by formulating relevant questions. Each, of course, should be free to propose possible solutions. The contextual background would consist of data drawn from all or most of the social sciences, and each participating member would help to identify, select, and weight the relevant background factors. Each could no doubt contribute techniques by which the number of variables are reduced to manageable proportions. Finally each discipline might suggest techniques appropriate to the task of logically deducing consequences or outcomes in the light of specified initial conditions.

In interdisciplinary studies the comparative educationist has a particular role to play. His duty is to ensure that the difficulties of comparing educational systems and ideas are not overlooked. His task is to compare only what is comparable by making sure that educational terms, contextual variables, and criteria of success are stated unambiguously and in a manner which makes them meaningful across the cultural boundaries of comparison. A further role for him is to insist, with Sadler and other pioneers, that research should be well balanced and should take account of the implications of cultural borrowing. In these ways greater rigour can be introduced into comparative studies and into the use made of them to plan the reform and development of education.

Chapter III

CRITICAL DUALISM AS A CONCEPTUAL FRAMEWORK

THE 'problem approach' is only one of several in comparative education—a reflection on the state of development of the discipline. Thus today in discussions among comparative educationists attempts are still made to contrast the historical and the scientific approaches. Of course it has been noted that the first tradition has within it two branches. The one favoured by Cousin and Barnard, for example, gave rise to studies which were largely *descriptive*; the other, developed by such pioneers as Hans, Kandel, and Schneider, aimed at *explanation*. They were concerned with the discovery of antecedent 'causes' or determining 'factors'. In the same way so-called scientific studies have been classified either as *descriptive* or *explanatory*. Thus on the one hand the importance of collecting statistical data has been emphasised. Explanatory studies which aim at being scientific are of two kinds. Some seek to identify the present-day determinants of educational policy, such as social class, industrialisation, urbanisation, and so on. Other scientific studies of the kind envisaged by Harris and Sadler aim at *prediction*, and are thus particularly relevant in planning educational development. Certainly for Dewey the 'problem approach' was scientific and was designed to help men order their lives by controlling the forces of change.

Each methodology has its present-day exponents. It is perhaps true to say that before World War II the historical-explanatory and the descriptive approaches were pursued with most vigour. Kandel's *Comparative Education* published in 1933 is an example of the first type of study; later Hans' *Comparative Education* and Schneider's *Triebkräfte der Pädagogik der Völker* were in the same tradition. Between the wars excellent descriptive studies were, and still are, provided in publications from the International Bureau of Education in Geneva, Kandel's *Education Year Book*, and *The Year Book of Education* published between 1932 and 1934 by Evans Brothers in London, and then under the auspices of the University of London Institute of Education. Over the years these studies gave some indication of comparative trends of development throughout the world. Post-war interest has, however, turned increasingly to the role of comparative education in the reform of education.

From their different viewpoints, comparative educationists everywhere have accepted the challenge of helping to advise on the formulation of educational policy. At an expert's meeting in Hamburg UNESCO Institute for Education in 1955 the role of comparative education in the planned reform of education emerged as a topic of considerable interest. It served as the theme of a conference organised jointly by the Hamburg Institute and the University of London Institute of Education in London, 1961, when the Comparative Education Society in Europe was launched. It was taken up again at an expert meeting of invited comparative educationists and social scientists at the UNESCO Institute in Hamburg in March, 1963,[1] and was also strongly emphasised in the first general meeting of the Comparative Education Society in Europe's Conference in June, 1963, at Amsterdam.[2]

A common purpose has not yet made possible reconciliation of the different viewpoints. Perhaps there is no need for consensus. Each comparative educationist wishes no doubt to work within his own conceptual framework and at the moment no one method seems likely to gain universal acceptance. But the perennial problems associated with the study of comparative education should not be ignored, and any conceptual model or framework should facilitate and help to make more rigorous comparative studies whatever the set of assumptions on which they are based. A useful framework should not be restrictive but should suggest possible solutions to frequently stated methodological dilemmas. It should help the initiation of various kinds of enquiry and make it possible for the investigator to sharpen and make more precise the techniques of research at each stage or phase of his work.

The conceptual framework based on Popper's critical dualism is presented here with these objectives in mind. Naturally it is primarily intended for use with the 'problem approach', but it should also strengthen descriptive and explanatory studies in the statics and the dynamics of comparative education. It should moreover indicate that the historical and scientific approaches are complementary rather than antithetical and that in rigorous comparative studies not only are data needed from the various social sciences but the techniques of the philosopher, historian, economist, sociologist, political scientist, among others are essential ingredients. For increasingly, as in many scientific investigations today, research in comparative education should, for reasons already mentioned, ideally be undertaken by interdisciplinary teams, rather than by individuals however gifted.

This framework is basically an attempt to classify data of different kinds in a way which will enable various kinds of comparative study to be made more rigorous.

Critical Dualism

First of all it is perhaps important to note that it was with the philosophical assumptions behind social planning that Popper was concerned when, during World War II, he wrote *The Open Society and its Enemies*.[3] Against the total planners of that period Popper argues in favour of piecemeal social engineering. Against the out-and-out determinists on the one hand and the laisser faire non-interventionists he advances arguments of critical dualism, thus effectively avoiding the pitfalls both of historicism and cultural relativism. Against nineteenth-century concepts of natural and social laws Popper takes a post-relativity view of science, thus making it impossible for social planners who accept this view to ignore the relevance of initial conditions. In fact, while attacking some contemporary views about planning he illuminates many of its important problems and thus contributes to a theory of planning quite different from those of either the Marxists or the Fascists.

According to my understanding of Popper, then, critical dualism asserts that in any society there can be identified and distinguished two types of law—the normative and the sociological.

This distinction, Popper maintains, is a consequence of another (carefully made by Protagoras), namely that between man's physical and social environments. The important characteristic of norms and normative laws is that they can be either accepted, rejected, or changed by men. Men are responsible for them, and can blame neither God nor nature for them. But at any point in history men are responsible not so much for the norms they find to exist when they study the matter, as for those norms they are prepared to retain once they realise that they can do something about them. Rejecting or changing normative laws should not be confused with disobeying civil laws. Certainly legislation and the consequences imposed when laws are broken represent normative laws. The rejection of or disregard for any of these by an individual may well have well-defined consequences for him. He may be subjected to legal action and then thrown into jail. Nevertheless the argument is that in principle man is intellectually *free* to reject norms even if legal and other restraints are placed upon his actions. Of course this very feature—man's freedom overtly to challenge the norms of his society—is an assumption, and could be used to categorise or classify societies throughout the world. In short the degree to which such freedom is allowed to the individual is itself a measure of the 'open society'.

In practice normative laws find most obvious expression in a legal code or a written constitution like those of the U.S.A., France, and the U.S.S.R. They are statements of what 'ought to be the case'. But innumerable codes of behaviour, taboos, values, beliefs, ideas are more or less formalised by rules of behaviour or commands, and are accepted (or challenged) by individual members of a society in which they are found. The processes of evaluating these statements of intentions are complex—emotion, reason, conscience are among the personal motivating forces which contribute to individuals' decision to accept or reject any norm. Evidently from time to time in any society some members of it decisively reject certain of these standards of behaviour. In an 'open society' it is their privilege, provided they do not break the law: in a closed society they may do so openly only at their peril. There is enough evidence to show that social norms do change and can be changed by processes which are themselves important subjects of sociological enquiry. Such changes are one source of social problems, as will be made clear later.

The outside observer, naturally, should be in a position to identify the norms and normative laws by which a society lives. He may also be able to recognise the problems arising from the changing attitudes within that society. As an observer he should not uncritically use criteria on the basis of which he evaluates the norms of his own society to discriminate between the norms of all other societies. Indeed it is questionable whether or not he should attempt such evaluations; but more about criteria of assessment later.

If normative laws represent an area in man's social environment in which he is able to choose freely, some changes in society are less under his direct control—or rather can be controlled only by using scientific techniques. These changes occur in accordance with sociological laws. Critical dualism, in fact, assumes that there are operating within any social environment a number of regularities which are similar to those found to apply to man's physical surroundings—in physics, chemistry, and biology. Such sequences of social events can be stated in sociological laws which bear to man's social environment the same kind of relationship that natural laws bear to his physical environment. They can be used to explain the operation of social institutions or organisations such as schools, insurance companies, industrial concerns, trade unions, and so on. They make predictions possible in the social sciences. Examples of such laws or hypotheses in the sphere of economics are those which form the basis of Keynesian economic theory.

Sociological laws enable selected institutions to be understood, and make it possible to predict chain reactions resulting from the interaction of institutions, and regularly repeated sequences of events. The establishment of a pattern of sociological laws provides, therefore, a basis for understanding not only the operation of selected institutions but in addition some of the processes of transformation within a society. Prediction, however, does not necessarily mean social control is possible for reasons already given. In short, contrary to his freedom, *vis-à-vis* normative laws, man's ability directly to control certain processes of social transformation is theoretically as restricted as in, say, a chemical reaction which he sets in motion. Indeed he has less power because it is less feasible in social affairs to control the initial conditions.

Nevertheless, it should be repeated, an important assumption of critical dualism is that within any society there are causal relations whose operation can be understood through the establishment of sociological laws. These relationships are functional and constitute a deterministic element. It is the study of the relevant sociological laws that constitutes the science of education, or if preferred, the scientific study of education. It is these laws which give predictive power and, could they be established firmly, provide the scientific basis of planning. This assertion should not be taken to mean that the other elements are unimportant; quite the contrary.

In fact, the distinction between normative and sociological laws suggests that a useful model for the study of society should take account of both. It should be based on the construction of at least two important social patterns or configurations. One of these—the *Normative Pattern*—would comprise norms and normative laws; the other—the *Institutional Pattern*—institutions and their associated sociological laws.

A third important pattern, which does not arise directly from the assumptions of critical dualism, may be constructed from data relating rather particularly to the natural resources of a country, its demographic features, terrain, climate and so on; in fact, by using information drawn from man's physical rather than his social environment. To be sure, demographic data may be held to come within another category and for certain purposes can be taken to do so. In this respect, however, as in others the value of the conceptual framework should be judged not because of its correspondence with reality, but on the ground of its usefulness.

Evidently the data and techniques needed in order to establish each of these three patterns vary considerably, as do the sources from which relevant information is derived. The stated characteristics of the two types of law distinguished in critical dualism provide criteria for classifying sociological data. Into the third pattern, data drawn largely, but not

53

exclusively, from the natural sciences should be collected. In this chapter more attention will be paid to the two patterns which arise logically from an acceptance of critical dualism. The construction of normative patterns presents the most serious difficulties and these will consequently be discussed first and at greatest length. It should not therefore be supposed that this kind of pattern (or the techniques needed to establish it) is considered to be the most important of the three—all of them are integral parts of the model.

Another cautionary note should be sounded. It is not to be supposed that useful patterns for any society can be constructed *in vacuo*. The purpose which the composite picture of information is to serve is important. Already descriptive studies have been distinguished from those which attempt to provide explanations, and naturally of primary interest is the use to which the model can be put in conjunction with the problem approach.

The Construction of Normative Patterns

In general two methods of establishing a normative pattern recommend themselves. An empirical approach would involve collecting information by the use of opinion polls, attitude tests, questionnaires, and similar techniques largely developed by psychologists and sociologists. Derived in this manner the pattern could be termed an *empirical construct*. Statistical validity would depend upon technical criteria of sampling. Qualitatively, however, the assumptions on which the information-collecting techniques are based should be closely examined where such patterns are to be used in cross-cultural studies, when the difficulties of avoiding misinterpretations are considerable. A good example of the use of empirical techniques to compare attitudes is provided by the work of a team of research workers from the Institute of Comparative Education and Culture of Kyushu University, Japan, who visited Europe in order to compare important moral attitudes of French, German, English, and Japanese children of a similar age. The battery of tests used yielded valuable information, but revealed specific rather than more general attitudes and beliefs, by probing the views of testees or interviewees in selected situations. From information acquired by such techniques a pattern of more general norms could, of course, be induced and the development and refinement of them are of great importance in comparative education.

The second method in which philosophical techniques and sources (particularly the writings of representative thinkers) are employed has the advantage of reversing the emphasis from the specific to the most general statements of norms. A pattern resulting from this approach could be described as a *rational construct* of the Weberian type. Doubtless the empirical and the philosophical approaches are complementary and a well devised rational construct should reflect norms established by empirical techniques. It is however with problems of constructing normative patterns using philosophical sources and techniques, i.e. rational constructs, that this discussion is concerned.

Obviously, a normative pattern cannot include all the norms by which members of a society live. Nor if established philosophically can it include everything a chosen philosopher (or his followers) has written. Rational constructs are designed, as Weber said, to 'facilitate the presentation of an otherwise immensely multifarious subject matter'.[4] Hence the pattern should simplify rather than complicate. Consequently having selected a philosopher as providing material for a rational construct the investigator then selects data from among the writer's various works or from among the ideas he expresses. The criteria on which this selection is based should be made explicit. No choice is ever either entirely arbitrary or objective. In this presentation it is based upon a particular analysis and evaluation of some features of philosophical discussion. Three issues have been debated at length by western philosophers— the *nature of man*, the *nature of society*, and the *nature of knowledge* and methods of acquiring it. Through the ages philosophers have attempted to say what man and society are like, have sought to justify their findings, and have laid down rules of conduct in accordance with them. They have postulated what constitutes knowledge and reflected on how men may acquire it.

Because of the difficulties of decisive evaluation in philosophy, there have been endless debates which will continue.

Conflicting theories of what constitutes the good society have been advanced; different opinions have been held about the unique characteristics of individuals and the extent to which these qualities are possessed by all men; and finally the nature of knowledge has constantly been in dispute. Frequently philosophers have stated their views as matters of incontrovertible fact, adduced by entirely reliable methods of enquiry. Often their aim has been social reform, and they have attempted to persuade people of the truth of their opinions. It may be argued, however, that most philosophers have been presenting certain norms in statements not of what is, but of what ought to be, and challenging others. The empirical evidence for and against the major social and psychological theories is inconclusive, just as the assumptions on which this analysis is based cannot be either decisively refuted or confirmed.

What can be said, however, is that most philosophers have attempted using the tools of analysis, logic, synthesis, and even intuition, to give clarity, coherence, and logical consistency to the complexity of beliefs about man and his environment. To be sure, formal methods of philosophical discussion have been devised, and from time to time professional discussion has become extremely esoteric and specialised. Nevertheless, philosophers have provided the synthesised patterns against which the norms of any society can be viewed. And in education it is useful to accept the general themes—man, society, and knowledge—as persisting criteria on the basis of which data can be selected.

For the purpose of rigorous study these large categories need to be broken down. The class and power structures of society, for example, have always interested philosophers; so too have its economic bases. Norms associated with religious life and with education have also been identified and discussed. In each sphere, concepts of the nature of man have been presented. Thus for example it has often been argued that all men are (or should be) before the law and in politics equal, but less often that all men are intellectually equal. The point is that norms have been advanced, challenged, and rejected in all the spheres of man's life, and one task philosophers have accepted has been that of finding relationships between the parts of the total pattern and between specific theories and general concepts. They have used prevailing systems of logic, or developed new ones, to establish consistency between, and coherence among, the more specific theories—psychological, economic, political and social. Logical consistency and coherence, it is true, may be achieved only in the writings of philosophers (and not all philosophers accept the same standards of consistency or achieve those they themselves accept). An empirical survey would surely reveal an even greater degree of inconsistency among a population.

A significant analysis of the type of norms that are found in a society and the kind of inconsistency which may exist is made by Gunnar Myrdal in *An American Dilemma*.[5] He makes a valuable distinction between the norms which relate directly to certain aspects of an individual's daily life—for example politics, occupation, education, social class, and religion. These he describes as 'lower valuations'. Norms of more general application are termed 'higher valuations' and may or may not be consistent with the 'lower valuations'. Naturally, a philosopher may be the source of knowledge of social norms at both these levels, and only careful analysis will reveal the extent to which in his writings he achieves logical consistency. At another level, Myrdal points out that an individual is likely to accept the 'higher valuations' at the verbal and emotional level. Yet the more restricted theories and beliefs are more likely to determine his actual behaviour. Hence an individual's pattern of beliefs is not necessarily consistent. In establishing normative patterns it is, therefore, desirable to take account of norms at both these levels. Inconsistency, as we shall see, may be a source of serious social problems.

'Ideal' and 'Actual' Constructs

The assumption that men can challenge and reject norms and normative laws implies that no single philosopher can be the source of a permanently satisfactory normative pattern for any society. The investigator has, therefore, to consider the stage of a society's history or evolution for which he needs a construct in order to decide which philosophical views or combination of views he should select as useful. Evidently the features of a normative pattern are bound to change over the years, and techniques of construction are needed which will take account of modifications. The principle adopted here is that a number of basic sources should be recognised and amalgams appropriate to the period being considered should be constructed from these. The basic sources may be regarded as providing 'ideal' patterns, the modification of them as being 'actual' patterns. The source of an 'ideal' pattern is almost certainly one philosopher or school of philosophy, and is likely to be historically prior to those sources from which modifications are derived. Another way of looking at the distinction being drawn is to regard 'actual' patterns as compounded of ingredients from a number of different (and historically separated) 'ideals'. There can be no guarantee, of course, which elements will predominate; and the result must be regarded as hypothetical.

The choice of writer to provide the material for an 'ideal' pattern is obviously based upon the investigator's evaluation of the historical influence a philosopher has had on the evolution of a particular society and the degree to which he continues to be referred to. Likewise selection of appropriate sources for 'actual' patterns implies similar evaluations. However, the assumption that this or that philosopher has been influential places no obligation on the investigator to demonstrate this relationship by careful historical and sociological studies. One purpose of a rational construct is to provide a framework in which ongoing debates can be understood and placed in perspective. Historical judgement is not decisive in determining the extent to which a selected source may be useful. For instance few scholars would dispute that for European societies either Plato or Aristotle could provide the bases of a useful 'ideal' pattern. A decision about which is better is not crucial, since it could be argued that one would simply be a modification of the other, at least in some respects, and in any case each forms a basis for understanding many of the other's views. An alternative could of course be taken from Plato's opponents, the Sophists, whose arguments he strongly challenges.

Another problem turns on the geographical or cultural complex for which the patterns are intended. A distinction may be made between regions which share at least some important common norms—such as Europe—and the individual nations within the region which have unique features. A common 'ideal' pattern may well be the basis of useful national constructs or 'actual' patterns. But the views of Locke are important in England and those of Descartes in France. Again, it would be unwise to ignore the historical dimension and the investigation itself will help to decide the appropriateness of possible philosophical sources.

A further point is that cross-cultural contacts between members of different societies often mean that an 'actual' pattern for one of them should be drawn from vastly different 'ideal' patterns. Sociologically the situation is rather one-sided. For western societies with their rich literature and imperial histories it is easier to construct a few major 'actual' patterns, than for non-western countries. Even for those such as India and Japan, with long literary traditions, the whole operation of constructing patterns useful today is complicated by the strong admixture of norms from foreign and radically different philosophical sources. Indeed simple translations of statements of some norms from one language to another may fail to convey accurate meaning. The need, incidentally, to give philosophical terms unambiguous meaning across cultural boundaries is of immense importance to comparative education.

Nevertheless the interaction, however it has occurred, between members of one culture and those of another has often left the norms accepted in at least one of them a complicated mixture of both. In these circumstances an attempt should be made to build up an 'ideal' pattern for both types of society before considering the possibilities of amalgamating certain features of them. For this task men are needed who are deeply conversant with the philosophical climate in both countries, and the integration of the two sets of norms into a satisfactory 'actual' pattern calls for intercultural co-operation of a high order.

Possible sources of major 'ideal' patterns are not difficult to find. The great religions of the world—Buddhism, Christianity, Islam, and Judaism—represent clear choices. The secular writings of Confucius and of the ancient Greeks and Romans are further examples which spring readily to mind. Nor is it difficult, in a general way, to select from among these sources one which appears appropriate to a major region of the world. In the case of Europe, for instance, an obvious basis of a rational construct is Plato's *Republic*. Here are found stated political, psychological, and economic theories together with an epistemology which form a clear, coherent and (on certain criteria) consistent whole. Whatever starting-point is taken—man, society, or knowledge—*views* about the others fit in logically. These relationships are logical rather than functional, and naturally the opinions expressed may be, and certainly have been, challenged.

Modifications to this 'ideal' provide 'actual' constructs. The choice of components will depend upon the period of European history for which the pattern is intended, and upon the particular nation for which it is designed. A distinction should be made between elements which may be regarded as important in an evolving European pattern and those features which relate to individual nations. For example, at times the differences between Platonists and Aristotelians were sufficiently sharp to make it necessary for any 'actual' pattern for Europe to take account of them. At other times the differences between them relative to others which existed are much less significant. If in some respects the mid twentieth century is such a period, emphasis should be given in a general pattern to features common to both these classical schools of thought.

At least three other sources should be included in a construct for modern Europe. In the first place account should be taken of the common features of the Judaic-Christian traditions. A second important source could be found in the works of the Enlightenment. For the third modifying source writings would be taken from the nineteenth-century social philosophers. The elements from within these 'ideals' common to the whole of Europe reflect, when comparisons with other cultural areas are made, the unity of Europe.

From another viewpoint, however, each European nation should have its own 'actual' pattern. Each of the three modifying traditions contained a number of interpretations. In the Christian tradition the Roman and the Orthodox schism has to be recognised; and then the Reformation and the Counter-Reformation. In a similar way while the writings of the men of the Enlightenment show many common features, nevertheless somewhat different interpretations of important points were made by philosophers from different countries. At this stage perhaps there begin to emerge more strongly than before uniquely national viewpoints. Again during the nineteenth century several social theories found general acceptance among some sections of the peoples of Europe. The writings of certain authors were taken up more readily in some countries than in others. National traditions and nationalism began to reflect more divergent viewpoints than previously so that although the 'actual' pattern for each European nation should contain elements from the four major 'ideals'—the classical Greek, the Judaic-Christian, the Enlightenment—it should also include one or other of the nineteenth-century utopias.

Complicated as the construction of 'ideal' or 'actual' constructs for Europe is, in areas where European views about man, society, and knowledge have impinged upon non-western cultures the contrasts between chosen 'ideals' may be profound, so that reconciliation of them in one 'actual' pattern is difficult. It may be maintained in theory that through selective cultural borrowing a viable normative mixture is possible, but in practice, the problems associated with the process are formidable. Japan provides a particularly significant example, because in many ways the attempt by a few leaders to westernise their society was remarkably successful. The power structure within their own society helped them to influence the attitudes of a great many people. At the same time in Japan a great many very ancient traditions persist which stem from very different roots from those of the west.

Some of the difficulties which arise where there is such a clash of cultural values are well known. Attempts to construct 'actual' normative patterns on the lines suggested would have the advantage of helping to clarify some of the problems already vaguely perceived, and may in addition help to reveal new ones.

The arbitrary features of constructing Weberian normative patterns for the purposes of description should now be apparent. Why this piece of information rather than that? Evidently they are designed, as Weber says, to bring order into the difficult task of presenting a great deal of varied subject matter. As we shall see, however, the type of enquiry undertaken will determine how data are selected and arranged. Descriptions of normative patterns are likely to be so complex that they are bound to be based upon certain criteria of selection. As the context is extended to include the institutional pattern and the physical environment, the problems of describing *in toto* the social context assume overwhelming proportions.

Institutional Patterns

Description and explanation enter into the establishment of institutional patterns. Naturally, certain institutions have first to be selected before they can either be described or included in explanatory studies. The most significant of the organisations relevant to an understanding of education are well known. Methods of describing them in static terms are also readily available. Critical dualism implies, however, that it is also desirable to discover the sociological laws in accordance with which selected institutions operate.

First, consider how a description of an educational system in its social context could be attempted. Classification of the major spheres within the pattern is straightforward. Impinging on the school systems are *political* institutions such as the agencies of national and local government, political parties, pressure groups, and so on. *Economic* institutions are also functionally connected with the schools, since from the schools and universities young people enter the world of industry and commerce. In the *social* sphere there exist institutions which are closely related to education, such as the family, social class, and other cultural organisations. A more detailed classification of each of these major spheres could and should go on if the social institutional context in which an educational system operates is to be described.

Formal *educational* institutions constitute a sphere of their own. Comparative educationists have frequently attempted to describe and compare them. Identifying relevant details is consequently important, then an orderly grouping is desirable. A distinction should be made for example between institutional arrangements throughout the system as a whole, and those which operate in individual schools, or in other words there are institutions which are *national*, then there are those which are *regional* and *local*, and finally those connected with the *internal* running of a school. A second kind of criteria is also useful in classifying these institutions. These criteria are functional, that is to say some institutions perform similar functions at all three levels in many cases.

For example, there are elements of *administration* and *finance* at the national and regional levels and within individual schools. Again within an educational system different school types are related in ways which constitute the *structure of the system*. The articulation between levels or stages of education provides vertical relations; those between school types at the various levels, horizontal articulation. This structure is often maintained by processes of *selection* based upon *examinations* and other procedures of evaluation and certification. These, or similar, techniques are also found within each school, so that for example it is important to appreciate what *guidance* and *psychological services* are available in any school. The *curriculum* and *methods of teaching* are also important institutions through which the work of a school is conducted. So too are its methods of maintaining *discipline* and the organisations through which students are encouraged to participate in the running of the school. Classification of various institutions in terms of function enables refined descriptions to be made.

Outside the formal part of an educational system there are a number of ancillary services. Some of them are organised by the school itself in *out of school* or *extracurricular* activities. Further classification could draw together institutions which provide for (a) leisure time activities, (b) intellectual demands, (c) vocational aspirations of children, or (d) aspects of their moral training. Several other agencies not necessarily directly connected with the school can be regarded as falling inside the educational sphere, although their functions are not as formal as those of the school; such institutions would include youth clubs, parents' organisations, former pupils' clubs, and religious institutions.

Other *ancillary services* provide for welfare, scholarships, allowances for school meals, dental and medical care, libraries, and museums. There are also institutions associated with the selection, recruitment, training, and certification of teachers. It is advantageous to break down these fairly large categories into more manageable units for the purpose of description.

Methodology

In order to describe the operation of an institution it is important to pay attention to the *legal framework*. The extent to which each of the institutions identified is regulated by law should be known. Distinctions should also be drawn between types of legislation, the relative exactness of the provisions, and the degree to which they are enforceable. It would be well, for example, to distinguish rather carefully between statements of intention—invariably open to different interpretations—and exact regulations applied to finance, inspection, curriculum, and planning procedures. A great deal of work has, in fact, been done on the legal basis of education, but there is scope for further comparative studies in this area. Parenthetically it should be reiterated that the legal basis—often in written constitutions—frequently provides an excellent source of the norms or objectives of a national system of education.

A second approach to description is through *statistical* enquiries. As many aspects as possible of a school system and school life itself should be given a statistical base. The number of children attending various kinds of school, pupil-teacher ratios, per capita costs of education, pass rates in examinations, and wastage rates throughout the period of schooling are obviously capable of statistical treatment. There are, however, a number of other ways of looking at institutions within an educational system. The political scientist will use indices for institutions different from those used by the sociologist or the psychologist or the administrator. For this reason descriptive comparative education is bound to be a synoptic study drawing techniques and data from the social sciences.

In the same way the comparative educationist will also have to rely heavily upon information from social scientists about institutions in the wider social context of the educational system. The political scientists will be primarily concerned with agencies of government, the sociologists with social classes, family groups, industrialisation and urbanisation among other things. The economist will be interested in describing the operation of economic institutions. From all this evidence a composite but partial picture of the infra-structure can be acquired.

Finally in order to describe the social context in which an educational system operates it is desirable to give some account of the *physical or material* circumstances. Such features as terrain, climate, and natural resources are described by geographers and geologists. Demographers have built up population studies which show the distribution of population, rates of increase, proportion of school age children, and so on. They have, of course, also projected their figures to show future trends in population. Again since these data are relevant to the working of educational institutions they are necessary to the comparative educationist. Vast though the accumulation of data is there is need for more information of direct relevance to the problems under consideration. Even so, demographic, geological, and economic surveys of many parts of the world provide a great deal of relevant material.

The impossibility of providing a complete description of an educational system within its total social context should be apparent. The establishment of three patterns, the *normative*, the *institutional*, and the *material circumstances*, offers an approach to the establishment of a fairly systematic picture which is nevertheless only partial.

The view that a reduction of the number of factors to the *essential* minimum would give an adequate description of any educational system in its social context and make cross-cultural comparisons meaningful has been rejected. The framework based on critical dualism really does little more than suggest possible criteria for selection of data from the mass that is available and makes possible a useful classification of them, thus suggesting in addition possible sources of information.

Relationships and Explanatory Studies

Comparative educationists have rarely been content merely to describe a system or systems; they have wished also to explain and interpret. In attempting to explain why things are as they are, and why different systems reveal similar features as well as differences, they have sought to discover 'causes'. The scholars who tend to stress the importance of historical factors or causes can be compared with those who feel that ongoing processes of industrialisation and urbanisation exert more power. Again some comparative educationists stress the power of ideas, such as Hans, of whom J. A. Lauwery writes: 'His factors represent immanent and permanent forces in a sense more real and lasting than the phenomena observed and described.'⁶ Schneider's approach is similar. On the other hand C. A. Anderson and others tend to give greater weight to economic and sociological forces. The more materialistic approach has not, however, been developed as systematically as the ideological one.

The framework based on critical dualism, in fact, offers scope for all these attempts to find the determinants of educational policy. Obviously a normative pattern enables special studies of the influence of ideas to be made either in a historical context or in the present day. In the same way the institutional pattern offers opportunities of investigating the relationships between economic political and social institutional forces, either historically or at present. In any of these approaches, however, the appropriate weight each factor which has been identified as relevant should be given is important when deciding the extent of its influence on educational policy.

Against these introductory remarks it is worth considering the kinds of relationship which should be investigated in comparative education. The framework based upon critical dualism clearly offers several possible choices. Two main types of relationship can be studied comparatively. First there are relationships within one or other of the main patterns, i.e. normative or institutional. The former are logical: and the relationships between institutions form the basis of sociological laws. The second type of relationships are those which link together aspects of different patterns.

In the first group fall the type of relationships already mentioned when the construction of normative patterns was reviewed. Comparative studies could seek, for example, to reveal the relationships which exist in various countries between political theory and educational aims; or between the latter and prevailing psychological theories. It is apparent, for example, that most if not all the major political theories of Europe (at least) have within them the seeds of pedagogical theories. An earlier suggestion was that attempts should be made in these studies to assess consistency of coherence using one or a number of 'ideal' patterns as yardsticks.

Studies of functional relationships within institutional patterns have attracted considerable attention, among them are those carried out by social scientists which have dealt with social class and education. Church–state relations and their impact on education have interested comparative educators. More recently attention has been paid to the relationships between economic occupations and education; between fiscal management and the schools; and between political institutions and education. Many other similar studies could be undertaken with advantage. The list of possible relationships within the institutional pattern is almost endless. In the educational sector itself a study of the influence on curriculum flexibility of the type of administration was, for example, carried out, in many ways quite brilliantly, by F. S. Cillié.[7] The impact of universities through their examination systems on the organisation of the school system offers equally important possibilities for comparative analysis.

Inevitably some of the relationships within each major pattern and any sub-section of it will be very tight; others much looser. Some will be more obvious than others. It may be that the former are on analysis less fruitful than those which, because they are less apparent, are more subtle and important. This is saying no more than that truly important studies should aim at getting behind purely legalistic and verbal relationships to those which are sociologically significant. Indeed, it seems necessary to distinguish rather carefully between relationship studies which attempt both to correlate significant data into two areas of the pattern and to establish the mechanics of the relationship, and those in which the investigator is content to attempt only the first of these tasks.

This distinction has important implications. The discovery in one society of certain relationships does not mean that identical ones exist elsewhere. The detailed way in which the connexions are made is likely to differ from country to country. Another way of stating this assumption would be to repeat that even functional links of the kind under discussion are valid only within the context in which they are found. Thus simply to correlate per capita income and average length of school life on a comparative basis has little meaning unless other features of the context bearing on the relationships are examined.

In spite of these important reservations the development of

the scientific study of education will depend upon the accumulation of carefully conducted 'static' investigations. Success will depend very much on co-operation between social scientists such as anthropologists, sociologists, social psychologists, economists, and political scientists. More often than not their investigations will be unicultural, yet on the availability of the information they can provide for an ever-increasing number of societies will rest the possibility that comparative education may develop as a scientific study.

Another type of study would involve cross-relationships between the two major patterns—for example, between norms and institution, theory and practice, legislation and actual operation. The general societal norms about men, society, and knowledge (and the more specific economic, political, and social theories) undoubtedly play a considerable part in running educational institutions. Specific educational aims, theories of learning, and views on individual abilities, although derived from a more general social ideology, are more closely related than this last to the operation of the schools. Undoubtedly inconsistencies exist; educators frequently urge that theory should be made more relevant to practice—or the reverse. Nevertheless, powerful support is found in theory for the continuance of certain practices. The dominating theories in European educational history have been epistemological and psychological. Selective secondary schools have been justified on the view that 'real knowledge' could be acquired by only a small percentage of the population. No evidence adduced thus far is conclusive. Consequently there continue to be differences of opinion about it, and these rest, finally, on a particular philosophical position. But since there are differences of opinion at the level both of general philosophy and of specific theory, the possibility of educational change exists.

Finally, certain features of the material circumstances pattern can be related to aspects either of the institutional or normative patterns. Even non-environmentalists can hardly fail to recognise the force of circumstance in the organisation of man's life. The nomad is more likely to be found in a land with a low or intermittent rainfall and sparse vegetation than in a well-watered lush countryside. Coal-bearing countries were able to develop industrially, and today countries where oil has been discovered are potentially wealthy. The presence of mineral resources does not mean, of course, that they will be developed, or that the consequent riches will be wisely distributed or invested. Natural resources, nevertheless, constitute important elements of a framework within which man pursues his various activities. Who can doubt, for example, that the natural wealth of the United States has made some contribution to the enormous rise in personal wealth? On the other hand, few people would deny that this growth in prosperity has also been in part due to the energy and outlook of the American people. For this reason multi-relationship analyses are very important. Critical dualism also suggests ways of undertaking multiple relationship studies, although at present they may be analytical and qualitative rather than statistical.

Multi-Relationship Studies

An example of a multi-relationship study was provided by the *Year Book of Education 1959* under the title of *Higher Education*. It goes without saying that the universities have been, and are still, among the most important of all the institutions in Europe and copies of them have been established in practically every country of the world. Some of the relationships between the universities and other social institutions formed one basis of this comparative study. The position of universities within the institutional pattern is influenced by the climate of opinion about them, i.e. by aspects of the normative pattern. Since universities are expensive, their growth also depends upon the financial resources of a city, a private organisation, or a nation. Finally the links between the universities and other aspects of education are usually extremely close. Consequently a comparative study of the universities involves an analysis of the various types of relationships (both internal and between different patterns) previously outlined and specified more precisely in this paragraph.

A glance at some university norms immediately reveals important traditions. In Europe from the earliest times one of the most significant was the concept of academic freedom. To give it meaning some of the norms accepted by university men should be remembered. They ought, it was held, to be free to teach what they liked, in the manner they thought best, and only to students of their own choice. Moreover it was thought that university men ought to have the right to appoint their own confrères. Another set of norms related to the kind of work the universities should promote. Research and scholarship were of prime importance, on the principle that knowledge ought to be acquired for its own sake. In addition, there was established quite early in the European universities the view that the community of scholars should be international and that enquiries ought to range widely. This concept of universality is indeed deeply ingrained.

In spite of frequent attacks many of these traditions have been retained. Vigilance on the university's part has always been necessary, and particular circumstances have influenced the degree to which academic freedom has been maintained in practice. Evidently a mere statement of what ideally 'ought to be the case' does not ensure that it will be so. The practical autonomy enjoyed by a university depends upon the relationships it has with other social institutions. Where, in short, do the universities stand in the power structure of a particular society? Furthermore, what is the source of any power they enjoy?

One thing is clear: whatever the stated aims of university men their training has always prepared them for all walks of professional life—the Church, law, medicine, teaching, and positions in the government. During the nineteenth century they became administrators in the developing bureaucracies. In fact, at each phase of political change the universities provided political leaders with advisers and executive officers. The esoteric knowledge they possessed made them indispensable no matter what group was in power. As the temporal power of the Church declined in Europe, national governments found that they needed lawyers as civil administrators. The rise in power of medical doctors is closely correlated with the growth in scientific knowledge. The constant demand for one or other of the several professional groups within the larger community of scholars helped the universities to maintain their autonomy and that of the individual professors.

These generalisations or hypotheses should be examined more closely within specific contexts. Changes in the finance of universities have affected their autonomy in some areas more than in others. State legislation and the growth of mass education at the secondary level have created pressures on the universities which in some countries have been difficult to resist. To the vocal demands of a few carefully selected students have been added in recent years the demands of an articulate public. A comparative study would seek to reveal the power relationships within selected countries between the universities and other institutions.

Relationships within education are, of course, important. For example in Europe at least the universities have tended to dominate the rest of the educational sector. Not only have they helped to establish and maintain the aims of secondary schooling, but they have powerfully influenced what has been taught and how. For many centuries they formed a closely integrated system with the academic secondary schools of Europe. Since the schools feeding the universities enjoy the highest prestige, attempts have been made by other schools to copy them. Of course, university domination should not be accepted simply as a fact under all circumstances, but should be regarded as a possibility for detailed investigation.

Clearly, numerous institutions could be studied in this multi-relationship manner. In all cases, certain principles of operation can be established, although the details will vary from one country to another. Clearly important features of the three societal patterns should be similar if direct comparison between the operation of an institution in one country and a like named one elsewhere is to be made. Criteria of grouping can be taken from any of the three patterns. Countries ideologically committed to democracy are comparable, even if the institutional arrangements designed to achieve this aim vary. The relationships between education and industry would be similar in two countries of comparable technological development, even if their normative patterns show considerable differences. Finally, criteria of grouping are to be found in the pattern of material circumstances. Attempts to show that there are universal relationships between geographical conditions (such as latitude) and educational policy (such as the age of compulsory attendance) should not ignore features of the institutional and normative patterns which affect policy.

Evidently when considering the possibilities of comparing the operation of like-named institutions certain features of nations or regions may conveniently be emphasised. On other occasions different criteria of grouping should be used. For example, many basic comparative studies have been concerned with European countries. The diversities among them, particularly as regards Church and State, language, and 'national character', have made for fruitful comparisons, but these have been possible because of a common heritage. Because there is a common tradition western European education can be compared with the systems in U.S.A. and U.S.S.R., whose societal patterns are derived from Europe. On the other hand it is doubtful whether reliable comparisons can be made between areas where a great many aspects of the social configurations are vastly different. It is, therefore, necessary to identify what elements make a basis for meaningful comparative studies. In summary, the principal importance of static studies is in the extent to which they contribute to an understanding of relationships within and between societal patterns. Relationships, rather than the institutions themselves, form the basis of useful comparisons. Such studies in the statics of education are often descriptive and analytic and not only statistical, and give the details of the articulation in a given context.

These concluding remarks emphasise the fundamental purpose of the model as far as the statics of education are concerned. A complete description of a society or nation is regarded as impossible even if desirable. The concept of various patterns should, however, help to direct attention to certain relationships which contribute to an understanding of an educational system. Generally speaking it is assumed that critical dualism makes it possible to embark upon such comparative studies of relationships between, say, education and occupation, education and social class, and education and the Church with more confidence and rigour. It also suggests relationship studies between the education sectors of the two major patterns and between theory and practice in education. The main criteria of classification in the normative pattern are theories of *man*, *society*, and *knowledge* in relation to politics, economics, social class, religion, and education. Selected organisations within these specific spheres obviously form the basis of institutional studies.

Chapter IV

CRITICAL DUALISM AND THE
PROBLEM APPROACH

CRITICAL dualism can be used in conjunction with the problem approach at each of the stages of reflective thinking. It provides a framework in which problems may be identified and intellectualised. It reduces the difficulties of identifying relevant background factors by providing criteria of classification. It also facilitates weighting, and suggests the range of consequences that should be considered when attempts are made to predict the outcomes of educational policy.

These stages are integral parts of dynamic studies based upon Dewey's epistemological assumptions. In order to show how they may be performed two other assumptions should be re-affirmed. First, various aspects of any social system are closely interrelated either logically or functionally. Next, changes are asynchronous in a society. These in turn give rise to inconsistencies (the source of problems) which can be identified by reference to the social patterns constructed for the society in question. Various types of inconsistency are possible, and hence different kinds of social problem can be identified. In general, however, a sharp distinction should not be drawn between changes regarded as evolutionary and those described as revolutionary. The processes are similar, differing in degree rather than in kind.

The view that social problems or, to use Dewey's terminology, perplexed, troubled, or confused situations result from asynchronous changes in society is not novel. Some philosophers, however, have given to it a somewhat restricted meaning. Here an attempt is made to show how different types of inconsistency create social problems. The model based on critical dualism can be employed to analyse these processes of change in society and

73

thus to clarify the characteristics of various kinds of socio-economic and educational problems.

Here social change is considered to be the sequences of events initiated by an innovation in any one of the three social configurations. For example, an existing norm or norms may be rejected; a new institution set up; or a new source of wealth discovered. Evidently more than one innovation may occur simultaneously in one pattern, in two, or in all three. Historical support for these statements can easily be provided. In this analysis it is argued that during major wars changes occur on a very broad front. Hence the starting point in the later discussion of the various types of problems is taken to be World War II.

Each type, or combination, of innovation may form the basis of a useful comparative study. The characteristics of subsequent problems will depend in large measure on the kind of innovation and the way in which it occurs. Three general types can be distinguished. All stem from the fact that, according to critical dualism, some changes in society take place according to sociological laws and others do not; so that at any time human freedom and a measure of inevitable institutional change coexist. Thus on the one hand innovations in the institutional pattern lead to sequences of events within that pattern in accordance with sociological laws. Normative innovations, on the other hand, set up no 'necessary' sequence of events, although, logically, changes in one sector of the normative pattern make adjustments in other sectors of it desirable; but man is free to accept or reject them.

For example, reformers usually select for attack those norms which they find most distasteful, and philosophers rarely question all the assumptions of their predecessors or contemporaries. Major transformations in philosophy occur when most of the prevailing assumptions about man, society, and knowledge are challenged and rejected. The sociological impact of these processes is slow to take effect. But combined with the retention in unmodified form of other norms serious normative inconsistency occurs and results in a certain kind of social problem.

A successful normative challenge implies a change of policy, which finds expression in attempts to establish new institutions. Failure to achieve in practice what is intended in theory constitutes another kind of inconsistency. A third kind of problem arises when, whether by intention or not, a new institution is created. This kind of innovation implies not only that certain other institutional changes will follow but that problems of normative adjustment will arise. In short, institutional innovation means that new attitudes or norms are needed in order to run the institutions affected by the innovation. A new rationale for them is required.

Each of these three types of inconsistency will be considered in turn in a little more detail.

Normative Inconsistencies

Consider first the mechanics of a normative challenge. It often occurs principally in the political sphere. Tom Paine's attack on the aristocracy, and the concept of inherited power in *The Rights of Man*, is a typical historical example. Other reformers, e.g. Luther and Calvin, attacked selected religious theories. Again Marx concentrated his attack on the ownership of the means of production. And of course many men like Owen spoke out against accepted views on education. Obviously few of these philosopher reformers restricted their challenge to a single one of many sectors of the normative pattern. Yet, in general, seen against a Platonic rationale for example, it is apparent that, in Europe at least, political normative challenges have been more successful than attempts to modify his fundamental psychological and educational theories. For example, the principle of inherited political power and leadership has been abandoned in many countries, to be replaced by a belief in democratic elections. Yet confidence in an aristocracy of talent based upon innate abilities remains. The difficulties of reconciling modern democratic political theories with an élitist psychology become increasingly apparent, nevertheless there is a reluctance on the part of many people to abandon either.

Normative inconsistencies find expression in other kinds of psychological and sociological phenomena. By way of illustration Myrdal's analysis of a basically psychological problem in *An American Dilemma* (and he is referring particularly to the racial problem in the U.S.A.) is that in many situations 'the assumption should be that *people's beliefs are not necessarily*

75

consistent,[1] and furthermore that Americans (and doubtless most individuals to a greater or lesser extent) hold simultaneously valuations on two important planes. The higher one is represented by the American Creed; the lower plane is characterised by valuations less general in their applicability but exerting a greater force when applied to day-to-day judgements on which individual behaviour is based. Frequently the higher and lower valuations virtually contradict each other, which accounts for one form of inconsistency in an individual's belief patterns. This phenomenon is present not only among the outcasts of a society, but is shared by respected and esteemed citizens. Most of them, for example, readily accept the 'higher' valuations derived from the most general statements about the nature of the individual, society, and knowledge made by a philosopher or school of philosophers. The distinction previously made between 'ideal' and 'actual' patterns means, of course, that even this pattern may not be consistent. But it is more likely that the more specific rules on which people tend to base their behaviour, and which apply rather directly to the economic, political, and social class aspects of it, will lack inherent consistency. Since these rules represent 'lower' valuations, an individual's day-to-day thinking and behaviour tend to be highly inconsistent. Several possible types of inconsistency of belief exist; recognition of them enables many of the attitude and behaviour patterns of individuals to be better understood.

At the same time this kind of psychological problem has sociological implications. The inconsistencies of thought and behaviour in individuals are carried over into group action. Group policies may reflect the simultaneous acceptance of beliefs, either at the higher or lower levels, which are not wholly consistent in themselves and may show that the principles of policy have not been applied consistently in every sphere of social activity with which the group is concerned. The situation becomes more complicated when, with a number of patterns from which to choose, individuals and groups engage in social debates. The value of constructed normative patterns is that they provide a framework against which ongoing debates can be understood. They facilitate the identification of ideologically opposed groups and enhance understanding of their relative positions. For example, they permit certain aspects of the political scene to be more readily understood, and in these and other respects they enable national comparisons to be made.

Consider the level of higher valuations: in many countries it is evident that all, or most, of the political parties overtly subscribe to and recognise a commitment to certain beliefs. Certainly, in the United States none of the great questions which were political party issues in Europe entered into the debates of the American parties during the nineteenth century. Then and now it could be argued that the American people accept without question the higher valuations contained in the Constitution and, to some extent, in the Bill of Rights. Where there is consensus of this kind, debate takes place at the level of specific regulating theories. In many countries, for example, democracy is accepted by all political parties, but each of several groups advances its own views about how it should operate. Again there are debates about economic policies against an accepted view that progress is desirable. In each case an assessment of the degree to which, in various spheres, there is joint commitment to very general ideas should be made. At the same time conflicts at the level of specific regulating theories should be analysed; where reconciliation is not possible problems appear. Internal inconsistency should be examined by looking, for example, at each party's manifesto to see how far, against an accepted philosophical rationale, each possesses a consistency and coherence at both levels—general ideas and regulating theories—and what contradictions between the two levels exist.

Evidently logical inconsistency finds expression in a number of ways in a society and leads to certain problems. On the other hand it may contribute to social growth and dynamism. Freedom to disagree, even if it leads to inconsistency, is often regarded as necessary to the health of a political democracy. If so, it is well to distinguish between awareness of disagreement within a society and an assessment of its seriousness. The object of comparative research is not simply to arrange social and human problems on a scale, but to study those that appear to be serious in order to help in the formulation of policy designed to solve them.

It is improbable that empirical technique indices can be assigned to normative factors in order to measure ideological inconsistencies and place them on a scale. But in a changing society their number (and the extent of each of them) is constantly in the process of being increased or reduced. Under certain circumstances and as the result of certain innovations, normative inconsistencies may be radical and fairly obvious. At other times there may be an accumulation of less serious inconsistencies. It would be useful to give quantitative precision to these situations. Even if this is not possible, both represent, for the purpose of analysis, a transitional stage in the development of a society. The first type of situation may be termed revolutionary, the second evolutionary. In either case some reconsideration of the constructed 'ideal' pattern is needed with a view to establishing a more viable 'actual' pattern. The presence either of radical inconsistencies or of an accumulation of several, even of a relatively minor nature, should be regarded as the possible source of a serious ideological problem whose solution would involve some readjustment of attitudes and outlook on the part of individuals within the society.

However lacking in quantitative precision this approach is, Myrdal's analysis shows how valuable it is in attempts to identify and intellectualise a variety of ideological problems.

Theory and Practice

Of course new norms rarely, if ever, become effective unless accompanied by institutional innovation. Lewis Mumford maintains for example: 'New changes in our conceptual apparatus are rarely important or influential unless they are accompanied, more or less independently, by parallel changes in personal habits and social institutions.' And again, 'New ideas do not take possession of a society by mere literary dissemination: . . . to be socially operative, ideas must be incorporated in institutions and laws. . . .'[2] This extends the analysis of normative inconsistency to make plain how somewhat different kinds of problems may arise. There is a sense in which no norm or normative law becomes effective unless it is institutionalised. In other words normative innovations are only successful when accompanied by effective organisations. The problem is sometimes referred to as the relationship between 'theory and practice'—a particular aspect of the general problem of putting philosophical aims into practice which was analysed in the *Year*

Book of Education 1957—Education and Philosophy. A fundamental task of would-be reformers or educational planners is to establish institutions which will operate according to their sociological laws in such a way as to achieve stated aims.

The mechanics of successful normative challenge will vary in detail, but a few general suggestions indicate how they occur. In the first place, as mentioned, a normative challenge is usually selective. Made initially by relatively few individuals within the society—a leader and his immediate followers—their object is to win general support for their aims and for the stated reforms they propose. Success will depend upon the media of communication at their disposal, and upon the institutions they can create or capture for their own use. Mass media have improved the possibilities of wide acceptance at the verbal level of new or anti-traditional norms which can lead to an explosion of aspirations or expectations. There is abundant evidence in the postwar world that to this extent at least a great many normative challenges have been successful. The second feature of success—institutional control—may or may not be preceded by general acceptance of the new aims. Political revolution may be the work of a minority group. But on the other hand an enlightened minority may succeed in having its aims widely accepted prior to the enactment of policies in accordance with their views.

Another way in which reformers may influence events in a modest degree is through the establishment of experimental institutions. These may be copied, making the influence of new ideas more widely spread. But in such cases, as in other assessments of successful normative innovations, the political framework (in the most general sense of the term) will be in one respect decisive. In another sense material circumstances may seriously affect the translation of theory into practice. But the question of utilising whatever resources are available is, finally, a political one. When resources are very limited, however, the question of priorities is more relevant than when such a lack does not exist.

Another difficulty is unrelated to politics. It is frequently by no means easy to formulate in precise, operational terms, theories derived from 'higher' valuations which will make it possible for individuals to run institutions successfully. For example, in order to translate the ideal of universal primary education into efficient practice teachers are needed who have at their command a pattern of classroom techniques and attitudes which will enable them to perform effectively. With the best will in the world teachers cannot operate educational institutions satisfactorily unless there are available to them a set of realistic operating theories on which they can call. Frequently the gap between theory and practice is due to a shortage of these bridging theories. Too often radical changes are made in the 'higher' valuations and most general theories without enough attention being given to the development of their regulating or operational counterparts.

Institutional Innovation and Social Re-adjustment

A somewhat similar problem occurs when because of certain institutional innovations new policies and theories have to be devised for education. That is to say, changes in educational theory are sometimes necessary not because educational aims have changed, but because certain institutions have been modified either within the educational system or outside it. In either case the modified institution will operate according to appropriate sociological laws and will interact with other institutions. Attempts to change political institutions often achieve more rapid results than attempted modifications to schools. But in any case political changes will spill over into education and vice versa. Institutional innovations in either of these two areas will also affect the economy, the social class structure, and probably the position of religious organisations.

Different rates of change make institutional readjustment necessary. For example a political innovation will almost certainly have its most rapid and extensive effects on other political institutions. In the same way any institutional change within the educational sector will react most quickly and sharply on other parts of that system. The predetermined order in the response of various sectors can be drawn up. Generally speaking the impress of political innovation will appear to be more obvious. Perhaps changes brought about by educational reform, though slower, have more permanent effects. The point is that in order to clarify the problems of readjustment in the institutional pattern some assessment of the rates and directions of changes stemming from a particular innovation are necessary. In practical terms comparative assessments of the impact of a particular kind of innovation should be made by reference to a stated historical starting-point. In other words, it would be a mistake to affirm categorically which type of institutional innovation should or does precede others or is most important in understanding change. The decision to accept as a basis for study one rather than another innovation is methodological and makes a restriction of interest possible.

Take, for example, the establishment of a new school type. One of the most illuminating historical case studies is the American 'common school'—in important respects a unique institution. How it was established is the object of a special study. Here the impact of its creation on other institutions is considered; first on other educational institutions—the organisation of the system generally, examinations, promotion of pupils, teacher training, higher education, and the curricula of schools at various levels; then on other socio-economic and political institutions. In brief, what were the necessary consequences for the American institutional pattern of the firm establishment of 'common' schools in Massachusetts and elsewhere in the 1840s?

Even in retrospect assessment of the socio-economic and political consequences of the American common school movement is difficult. Certainly Horace Mann's aim was to improve social morale and by bringing the children of workers together in the same classroom with children from the upper classes reduce class differences. The evidence is not conclusive, but it seems probable that against the nineteenth-century background of uniquely American circumstances—mass immigration, the movement westward, and rapid urbanisation—the schools helped to reduce social class differences, and promoted co-operation between members of various echelons within industry and commerce. Dewey's purpose in much of his writing was in fact to make it possible for the schools to prepare young people for democracy and a changing economic order. Much present-day criticism of their own schools by Americans probably stems from the fact that in the post-war world their country has had to face quite different problems from those of the late nineteenth and early twentieth centuries. Schools which over a century were gradually modified to meet current needs are now thought to be failing to meet the economic needs of the country in the light of the international political situation. Under these circumstances J. B. Conant has pointed out in his *The Child, the Parent and the State* that a sequence of events initiated when a certain kind of school is set up cannot be checked or reversed simply by legislation. The American schools are, if anything, suffering today not from past failures but from past successes.

The educational impact of the common school is more obvious. Among others Harold Rugg has shown the inevitable experiments which were made during the second half of the nineteenth century in the U.S.A. to cope with the problems which arose in related educational fields as a result of introducing the common school. A number of Committees—the Committee of Ten on Secondary School Studies (1892), the Committee of Fifteen on the study of the elementary school (1893), and the Committee on College Entrance Requirements (1893)—were set up by the National Education Association to consider the problems of reform in American education. In a period of intense debate, inevitably not all the educational consequences flowing from an acceptance, first of a common elementary school and then of secondary education for all, were acceptable.

William Torrey Harris, a distinguished superintendent of schools and Commissioner of Education, is a good example of a man who, seeing changes going on around him, was able to accept some but not others. His views on the education of emancipated slaves, for example, were far ahead of his time. His appreciation of the forces of urbanisation, improved communications, and industrialisation on the educational system of America was first-class. At another level he recognised the need to improve systems of promotion within schools, and in fact proposed that changes should take place every two months. But at the same time and in spite of the fact that the high schools were enrolling a large and ever increasing proportion of the population he staunchly resisted the gradual disappearance of Latin teaching. His struggle was not entirely in vain, but in face of the radical changes in the schools of America there was little he could do to maintain important features of traditional policy.

In fact a Dewey was needed who could work out a new rationale appropriate to the new institutions which had evolved from the time the common school movement was initiated.

Concepts of Social Lag

The need for a new rationale in the light of major institutional changes has been analysed in great detail by sociologists. Critical dualism would suggest that it is due to the fact that institutional changes take place according to sociological laws and are therefore deterministic, whilst normative changes do not. No set of institutions can operate satisfactorily unless individuals possess, as stated previously, a pattern of appropriate theories or norms. There is a limit beyond which institutional change cannot proceed without creating serious problems unless appropriate attitude modifications occur fairly rapidly in the relevant sectors of the normative pattern. Unless this kind of adjustment takes place, individuals try to run new institutions with old theories. In a somewhat different, yet similar, manner William Ogburn[3] among other sociologists has analysed a social phenomenon which he named social or cultural lag.

According to Ogburn there is always a time interval between the initiation of change in one sphere of human activity and the adjustment to it of other parts of the culture. Different rates of change in the material and the non-material parts of any culture account for cultural lag. Like many other sociologists Ogburn was impressed by the changes brought about by the accumulation of scientific and technological invention. He thought of cultural lag as the failure of the ideas, attitudes, institutions, and customs to keep pace with changes in the material culture. Mumford, Mannheim, and of course Marx, stressed the significance of changes wrought by men's mechanical inventiveness. Technological changes proceed more rapidly than men's ability to make sense of them. Consequently men are constantly attempting to deal with new material conditions with outworn ideas, beliefs, and institutions. Mannheim, for example, writes that when '. . . in a given society technological and natural scientific knowledge has advanced beyond moral powers and insight into the working of social forces, we will speak of a *"general disproportion in the development* of human capacities".'[4]

Methodology

Attempts were made by Ogburn to give objective, quantitative meaning to his concept of 'lag'. It is measureable, according to him, as a period of time between a change's taking place in the material culture, and its adaptation in the non-material. The examples he used are open to objection. It is possible to argue that legislation does not satisfactorily complete the adaptation but only achieves a greater measure of normative consistency. Brought into question are the concepts of criteria of adaptation. Nevertheless, if no attempt is made to give quantitative precision to it, the analysis has methodological merit. It does suggest that technological change creates psychological and institutional problems, and that a reduction of cultural lag may call for the formulation of a rationale more appropriate to a new state of affairs, or for the establishment of new institutions, or for both.

In the light of this discussion it would appear that extended use may be made of the concept of 'lag' as a source of social problems. According to critical dualism several types of 'lag' are possible. Normative inconsistency may arise either because groups hold violently opposed views or because the beliefs of individuals are inconsistent. Secondly, there may be inconsistencies within the institutional pattern: e.g., because political institutions have changed more radically than the schools. Further, the relationships between theory and practice (norm and institution) may be weak and inconsistent. It should also be noted that any major change in the circumstantial pattern—for example the discovery of oil—will create its own problems either of institutional or of normative adjustment. Many problems can, in fact, be regarded as stemming from the circumstantial or environmental pattern in its relationships with the other two, or as a result of changes within it. The problems due to demographic changes, for example, are considerable today. Frequently the natural resources of a country are so limited that to satisfy the expectations of the population is virtually impossible. Gaps between expectations and resources, and between the latter and the institutions through which they may be exploited, constitute the origins of other significant types of 'lag'.

All these inconsistencies have to be judged against certain criteria, and basically these are constructed ideological patterns which are representative of the aspirations and hopes of individuals within a country. An accumulation of inconsistencies or the presence of radical unresolved 'social lags' (as judged in the light of stated criteria) constitute more or less serious social problems.

Evidently, given these possibilities, it is likely that throughout the world similar or common problems will be found which can form the first stage in comparative enquiries. Out of the rigorous analysis of a general problem solutions, in the form of hypotheses, will present themselves for consideration. Many years of patient endeavour often elapse before the imaginative hypothesis becomes useful operationally. The point is important because in the case of social problems imaginative solutions abound. There are far fewer realistic regulating theories which can successfully be applied under special circumstances. Policy, however, should always be functionally related to the special circumstances, whose identification and weighting constitute the basis of another type of comparative study.

Data Relevant to Problem Analysis and Proposed Solutions

Once the possible source of perplexed or confused situations has been identified and the problem to some extent intellectualised the next stage is to describe it in specific contexts. The patterns based on critical dualism are useful because they draw attention to kinds of data which should be taken into account when this more detailed analysis of a general problem is made. Possibly all the various kinds of data will always be relevant to some extent. Less certain is the chance that data from every sector of each of the three societal patterns will be needed in order to sketch in the background.

The selection of what is relevant and the rejection of what is not, in fact offers considerable scope for the employment of specialised social science techniques. Economists have developed methods of studying their own restricted problems; in a similar way sociologists have worked out their own approaches to sound investigations; and psychologists use their own techniques. Usually these procedures have been developed within a national framework, and they can no doubt be applied in their generalised form across cultural boundaries, but if so it should not be assumed that the relevant factors will be the same in every country. When common factors are selected the relative importance of each of them, in its own cultural context, should be assessed. How special circumstances affect the characteristics of the general problems outlined in Part II are illustrated in the case studies in Part III.

Consider, by reference to these, what is involved in the process of selecting data on the ground of their relevance to a problem. In western Europe a major practical problem has been the reorganisation of post-primary education. It has been the subject of heated political and educational debate. The impetus in favour of reform has included statements demanding (*a*) secondary education for all, and (*b*) some kind of common or comprehensive secondary school. Against traditional European normative patterns these proposals reflect new, and to certain groups unacceptable, aspirations. Ideologically the forces are primarily based on political and social rather than educational theories. Consequently in many countries policies regarding secondary school reorganisation have been debated by different political parties. At the same time many of the advocates of reform have retained traditional psychological theories so that when challenged they find certain arguments difficult to refute. Thus, at the level of political and educational debate, in few countries of western Europe has either policy been accepted widely enough to make general legislation possible.

Within the institutional framework one factor stands out. The inertia of traditional educational institutions inhibits the adoption and implementation of a policy of introducing common or comprehensive schools. Neither political power nor economic forces have succeeded in overcoming it even to the extent that it has been overcome (in this respect) in the United States. But viewed comparatively, proposed non-selective secondary education policies in western Europe differ; so does the extent to which they have been accepted. The institutional obstacles also differ. Yet many of these same nations have reached rather similar stages of industrial, technological, and urban developments. Since these are, it is often argued, potent forces making for educational change, a question of considerable comparative interest concerns the reasons why policies relating to secondary education in, say, England and Wales, France, the

Netherlands, and Sweden differ in detail as much as they do (see Chapter IX).

A somewhat different pattern of factors is relevant in the study of policy decisions about the provision of general and vocational education at all levels. The dichotomy itself has its ideological origins (in Europe at least) in Aristotle's distinction between the kind of education appropriate to a gentleman and that needed by the artisan. In practice, conditions of work, economic rewards, and social status have in the past confirmed opinion that mental work has more prestige than manual labour, and the types of education preparing individuals for the two branches of occupation have been placed in the same hierarchical order.

In this debate economic factors are certainly important and should be given considerable, but apparently not decisive, weight. Conditions of work have certainly improved enormously for manual workers. Moreover changes in the wage structure of industry and commerce throughout Europe have had some influence on the aspirations of youth. At the same time automation is creating a demand for personnel trained to a high level in science and technology. Manpower demands may be difficult to estimate with accuracy, but it is apparent that economic growth is related to the availability of trained personnel. But these powerful forces have not decisively altered policy. Again the power of established educational institutions makes difficult a movement away from the traditional liberal education, which once prepared young people for the learned professions. Even where there is some general acceptance of the need to combine liberal and vocational education in a way that will make the latter the core of the former (as in the U.S.A. and the U.S.S.R.), it seems hard to find suitable educational theories and appropriate institutional ways of achieving this aim in practice (see Chapter X).

Again, consider how the explosions of expectations and knowledge in the post-war world have affected teacher training. Everywhere the radical rise in the demand for education and the rapid growth in population have combined to create a demand for many more teachers, assuming certain pupil teacher ratios to be desirable. There is an unfulfilled demand practically everywhere. On the other hand, the explosion of knowledge has created a need for more teachers with special kinds of knowledge and skills. Of course the level at which these explosions find expression depends on the level of existing provision. In newly independent countries universal primary education is demanded. In Europe, as mentioned, until the late fifties agitation was for greater educational opportunities at the secondary level. By then a situation had been reached in the U.S.A. where higher education was regarded, like secondary education before it, as within the grasp of everyone. The possibilities of meeting these demands at various levels by creating new institutions or expanding existing ones depend upon a complex of factors whose relative weight will vary very considerably throughout the world. A general shortage of teachers, and an acute shortage of teachers with particular skills (in mathematics and science), cannot easily be overcome. The success of policies designed to do this will obviously depend on economic circumstances, the priority given by government to educational policy, and the professional power of teachers. Even a reduction of the gap between supply and demand in teacher recruitment and training depends heavily on economic and political factors.

But there are other difficulties too. At the ideological level there is the question of what role the teacher should play. Should he be the mediator between one generation and the next? The uncritical transmitter of cultural values? Or should he be an agent of change and social reconstruction? Both opinions are held and debated. Moreover what should be the source of his authority as a teacher? Is modern science to replace the authority of God or the state? In short the whole concept of the ideal teacher in a changing world is in dispute and inhibits change.

At the level of organisation prospects of change in teacher training frequently depend very much on the way in which it is related to the universities and their own propensity to alter. Traditionally these powerful institutions were responsible for the recruitment and training of intending teachers for the academic grammar schools. Mass education created demands for teacher-training institutions. By and large they were not initially the responsibility of the universities, which slowly, and often somewhat reluctantly, began to take more interest in teacher training generally. The prospects of autonomous devel-

opment and the re-professionalisation of education in the field
of teacher training depends practically everywhere to a very
large extent on policies adopted by the universities (see
Chapter IX).

Data relevant to yet another universal problem can be drawn
from both major patterns. The difficulties of finding a balance
between social conformity—without which no nation can survive—and individual freedom and responsibility are related to
concepts of authority and the social agencies through which it
is exercised. Thus, data needed before the lack of balance can
be assessed, and proposed solutions evaluated, should be sought
in the familial, social structure and political spheres of a society.
Under conditions of economic change the degree to which these
institutions are strengthened, or under pressure to change, is
important. Some of the relevant factors are concepts of knowledge, how it can be acquired and by whom. In a sense a lack of
balance, however measured, constitutes a moral problem of
very considerable dimensions (see Chapter XI).

These problems mentioned, the professionalisation of education, the reform of secondary education, the dichotomy between
liberal and vocational education, and the balance between
social conformity and individual responsibility are examined
with special reference to selected countries in Part III.

The Comparative Aspects of the Problem Approach

The comparative study of problems has its own fascination. In
the foregoing analysis an attempt was made to show the variety
of problems which could be treated comparatively. At the same
time it is apparent that case studies are needed to show how
different kinds of inconsistency find expression in selected
national contexts. Evidently these differ so widely that some
classification of areas is desirable before embarking on comparisons. For example, only at the level of very general theory
is it realistic to compare the economic problems (and their
educational implications) of Europe and, say, Baluchistan or
Ethiopia (see Chapter VI). Out of realistic case studies based
upon assessments of general problems may appear realistic
policy solutions which are likely to differ from region to region
and from nation to nation. In fact, apart from its theoretical

interest the comparative study of problems has an extremely important role to play in the planned development of education.

Unfortunately in the post-war world there has been a lack of such preliminary planning studies. Inevitably, as a result, government policy everywhere has been based on a combination of political faith, expediency, inadequate surveys, and defective research. The technical instruments of national planning are being developed slowly and national governments are increasingly aware of the need for special planning departments. Nevertheless policy formulation and adoption cannot await the preparation of perfect plans.

Comparison of national educational policies can be attempted through a careful analysis of legislation or policy statements. Among the aspects of education on which these are likely to occur are: (*a*) compulsory attendance, (*b*) levels and stages of education and their interrelationships, (*c*) functions of specified schools, e.g. vocational and general, and (*d*) administrative control and fiscal management. National policies can usually be ascribed and compared for each of these spheres of education. Parenthetically, the processes by which national policies are reached are also capable of fruitful comparative enquiry (see Chapter VII). Naturally the extent to which the identified aspects of an educational system are themselves capable of providing cross-cultural studies determines the degree to which policies relating to them can be compared.

Reference has already been made (Chapter III) to the possibilities of describing and comparing educational systems within their social context. Evidently studies of this kind based upon a selection of data are integral parts of problem approach comparative studies. The fact that data are often collected without direct reference to a stated problem does not necessarily reduce their value. Nevertheless, the development of area studies designed to contribute to an understanding of some major problems in education is urgently needed. National and international agencies, to be sure, are increasing the fund of information and statistics which facilitate the establishment of adequate comparable descriptive background studies. More needs to be done, perhaps, in the way of collecting data in the light of precisely defined educational or socio-economic problems.

The potentialities and inherent difficulties of attempting to incorporate all the aspects of the problem approach in one major comparative study can be found in the *Year Book of Education 1954: Education and Technological Development*. This volume, it is perhaps true to say, was based quite explicitly on the problem approach and can be seen as an application of a method previously attributed in this book to J. S. Mill. It attempted to analyse the implications of introducing new tools, machines, or modes of production into a number of societies. The problems created were identified and the proposed solutions compared. The agencies through which technological development is promoted were described and their success and failure assessed. The consequences of introducing new techniques and ideas were analysed in normative and institutional terms and in the economic, social, political, and educational spheres of life. In particular the educational contribution to the process received much attention. Finally, some indication was given of the various problems which were likely to arise in the future, and those which will remain, if the expectations raised in many countries during and after the war by the image of economic prosperity and technological development in Europe and North America are satisfied.

The growth of comparative education as a social science depends upon the accumulation of all these kinds of study: problem analysis, policy comparisons, descriptive studies of comparable educational data, forecasts of trends of development, and studies combining all the elements of reflective thinking. Each type may be more appropriately undertaken by a particular agency or agencies. Indeed in emphasis this distribution of function has already begun. The resources of UNESCO make it possible for its secretariat members concerned with comparative education to initiate various types of study, but perhaps the *World Surveys of Education* are the organisation's most noteworthy contribution. Over the years the International Bureau in Geneva has, on the basis of its annual conferences and special enquiries, provided invaluable surveys of government intentions and policies. The UNESCO Institute for Education in Hamburg has been able to study particular problems through international expert meetings and follow-ups. Individual institutions have conducted studies either of problems or of countries. Case studies of particular educational systems or of specific problems in particular areas—in spite of an apparent lack of a comparative element—should be seen as leading both to a greater understanding of that area and to the improvement of method. In particular, area and case studies as integral parts of comparative investigations based upon the problem approach should not be considered merely examples of *Auslandpädagogik*.

To conclude this section on methodology some important assumptions of the problem approach should, perhaps, be re-stated. First the problem approach is forward-looking. It implies that understanding comes, largely, through processes of prediction and verification, in contrast to an emphasis on antecedent causes. It was regarded by Dewey as a (if not *the*) scientific method of enquiry, and thus, when applied to education, represents an attempt to make that study scientific. In the same way it represents one way of making the study of comparative education scientific. The questions whether a science of education is possible and whether, if it is, comparative education is the discipline through which it could be achieved are debatable. What is apparent, however, is that because the problem approach is forward-looking it is well adapted for use in social planning or, to use Popper's phrase, 'piecemeal social engineering'.

Types of study within the problem approach are directly related to the phases of reflective thinking. Detailed comparative studies at each stage require skill and material drawn from all the social sciences, and particularly from history used pragmatically. For this reason practically every comparative study is to some degree based upon interdisciplinary co-operation or on literature and investigations in the various fields of specialised enquiry.

The approach is also evaluative; not in the sense that this system of education is judged to be better (or worse) than that, but in the sense that the predictive element requires first that goals should be recognised and then that choices of policy should be made. Judgement enters into all explanatory studies. The processes of identifying and weighting relevant data or 'factors' are among the most important in the work of the comparative educationist. Acceptance of the problem approach makes these tasks easier, but at the same time makes meaningless any harsh dichotomy between the relative importance of historical and present-day forces (determinants). All are relevant, but each has to be given a weight appropriate to the problem under investigation. Similarly the relative weight given to political, economic, religious, and social forces should not be prejudged. Likewise to stress, without reference to the problem, the importance either of ideological or of institutional forces runs counter to the principles of weighting implied by the problem approach. Critical dualism, of course, makes clear the difference between predictive generalisations and statements about widely accepted cultural premises. An understanding of both, and the role of each kind of statement in the processes of social change, are necessary if the problem approach is to be rigorously applied to the study of comparative education.

CLASSIFICATION SYSTEM FOR COMPARATIVE EDUCATION DATA

NORMATIVE PATTERN

Contents:

Normative statements and Normative Laws based on theories of:

1 knowledge
2 society and individuality

Techniques and Sources:

1 Philosophy
2 Legislation
3 Empirical tests

INSTITUTIONAL PATTERN

Contents:

Descriptions and Sociological Laws based on the operation of institutions within sectors of the pattern.

Techniques and Sources:

Those appropriate to the social sciences.

NATURAL ENVIRONMENT

Contents:

Aspects of man's physical environment beyond his immediate control, e.g. climate, geology, demography, location, natural resources.

Techniques and Sources:

Those appropriate in the main to the natural sciences.

PART TWO

SOCIO-ECONOMIC PROBLEMS AND EDUCATIONAL POLICY

INTRODUCTION

IN this part, selected socio-economic problems are taken as starting-points of comparative analysis. Major social changes brought about or accelerated by the second world war are assumed to have created or increased the gap between stated intentions or aspirations and the possibilities of meeting them in practice. The factors contributing to these situations have, in general terms, been identified and thus the nature of the problem clarified.

Related to these major issues are educational problems the solutions to which are regarded not as panaceas, but as making some contribution to the amelioration of the larger difficulties of policy formulation, adoption, and implementation. In each case an attempt has been made to show that educational statesmen are invariably faced with choices. Their decisions are often based, not on a careful assessment of the facts and anticipated outcomes, but on generous intentions. Too often results are less satisfactory than they might otherwise have been, through a failure to recognise in education that priorities have to be established and, apparently, harsh choices made. One object of these general comparative analyses is to show how the explosions identified in Part I give rise to problems in education and what kinds of choice present themselves.

The analyses are based on the assumption that the origins of the problems are universal and hence throughout the world show common features. At the same time a broad distinction has been made between the specific difficulties found in so-called economically underdeveloped and newly independent nations and those experienced in the high income regions of Europe, North America, and the English-speaking dominions.

Obviously two areas in which major problems are found are the political and the economic. Doubtless several ways of analysing these issues are possible. In Chapter V, Walter

Lippmann's approach in *The Public Philosophy* has been chosen as a useful starting-point. It is by no means the only one, and the limitations of the analysis in relation to educational policy should be appreciated. The point is that it is illustrative of the problem approach. Detailed case studies designed to reveal the specific features of the problem in various countries are needed. To a limited extent illustrations are provided in Part III.

The starting-point of Chapter VI is the analysis made in the *Year Book of Education 1956: Education and Economics.* Since that time there has been a rapid growth of interest in the economics of education, especially in relation to the planned development of education. Here no more is attempted than to review the conclusions reached by economists and at international conferences. The problem is seen as due to the gap between the demand for, and the supply of, education. Lack of real resources makes impossible the immediate satisfaction of expectations of higher living standards. The solution to the difficulty as far as education is concerned lies in the establishment of allocation priorities, and economists have urged that these should be based upon the concept of education as a form of investment. This theme is illustrated in a specific context in Part III.

Not everyone is prepared, of course, to accept this view, much less to accept the consequences of policies based upon it. In order to understand the nature of the problems of policy adoption facing educational planners it seems necessary to study the mechanics of decision-making in education. This task is attempted in Chapter VII, and the framework used is one outlined by Talcott Parsons in *Administrative Theory in Education.* Evidently to give details of the institutions involved in the formulation of education policy, even for a few selected countries, would require a separate book. What has been attempted is to illustrate the general principles of the analysis by reference to well-known practical examples in a number of countries. This theme, too, is taken up again in the national case studies presented in Part III.

Chapter V

THE POLITICAL PROBLEM AND THE EDUCATIONAL CHALLENGE

AMONG the strongest desires aroused by the war was the wish for peace. The victors were inclined to believe that it could be secured only by the introduction of democratic forms of government everywhere, for after all the dictators had been overthrown. The democracies had triumphed in spite of an uncertain beginning and the gloomy prognostications of commentators like Walter Lippmann[1] about their ineffectiveness. Among the agencies through which these desires were to be satisfied were the United Nations, the forces of occupation, and at a different but still important level, education.

The situation was, in fact, vastly different from that envisaged even by astute political scientists. To be sure, before the war several major powers had been able to maintain an uneasy peace. During the thirties the traditional dominance of Britain and France was once again being challenged in Europe by Germany and Italy. To the east the Soviet Union, concerned for so long with internal reorganisation, was emerging as a major economic and political power. In the west, the U.S.A. maintained its traditional policies of isolationism towards Europe, no doubt encouraged by the other great powers, and United States interests in the Pacific were increasingly threatened by the power of Japan.

The post-war situation was quite different. Europe was more exhausted than was at first apparent, and had suffered economically and psychologically. In particular the position of Britain and France had been undermined. In spite of enormous losses in men and materials the Soviet Union emerged as the most influential power in Europe, for the first time 'able to make itself heard in the councils of the world'. The United States,

99

still protected by an insularity which Britain no longer enjoyed and in possession of the most destructive weapon ever devised by man, was the most powerful nation in the world. At first, Wilson-like, she was seemingly reluctant to use this power, so was soon to be locked in a prolonged political stalemate with the U.S.S.R. Her international responsibilities increased enormously as the freedom of action and economic strength of the great imperial powers, France and Britain, waned.

One of the first consequential changes was in the power relationships between the major powers and less industrialised territories. New aspirations and expectations, both political and economic, were promoted throughout the world, although few of them, evidently, could be easily realised. Such new sources of wealth and industrial power as oil and uranium were rapidly exploited, partly as a result of the tremendous explosion of scientific knowledge both at the theoretical level in all the fundamental natural sciences and at the level of application. Man's power to control his physical environment increased apace, far outrunning his ability to establish institutions through which he could control his social and political environments. The atomic bomb, and later inter-continental missiles, added new dimensions to the problem. Dangerous, exceptionally destructive weapons had been given to an immature world, immature in the sense that the continuation of political and economic policies through acts of war had not been discounted despite the appalling and obvious consequences. Nor, in spite of optimism, had appropriate forms of world government been devised. These changes extended on an international scale the problem described before the war by Lippmann.

Lippmann's Analysis

The isolation of a problem, as previously stated, is methodologically important since on this basis data become relevant. Not everyone, of course, would accept Walter Lippmann's political analyses, but at least one political scientist, Hans J. Morgenthau, has lauded his political acumen. 'It is', he writes, 'the great contribution, one is almost tempted to say the historical contribution of Walter Lippmann's *The Public Philosophy* that it poses the fundamental problems of democracy again in terms relevant to the concrete political problems of the day.'² The general thesis can be stated simply. In *Phantom Public*, Lippmann argued that a problem is the result of change: 'In an absolutely static society there would be no problems.'³ He develops this theme with reference to the liberal western democracies. 'Over the years the most significant changes in those countries have led to a functional derangement of the relationship between the mass of the people and the government.'⁴ Whatever power the people have to elect or remove a government, to approve or disapprove legislation, they cannot, he argues, govern. That is to say, they cannot normally initiate legislation or administer it. Effective government depends on the kind of relationships between the executive, the representative assembly as a consenting power, and the electorate, and on the measure of authority each has. Lippmann's main point is that in the liberal democracies mass opinion has acquired so much power that it can paralyse executive action. The public can veto policy, but it is unable to formulate alternatives. His analysis is intended to show that at many critical junctures, and particularly in crises, prevailing mass opinion has been wrong.

Naturally the criterion on which this judgement is based should be examined. For one thing, the public is liable to sacrifice real long-term benefits for the present's apparent advantage. Veto action today may lead to consequences which the public neither expects nor wants. Its inability, either through lack of knowledge or sustained interest, to assess the result of its actions on its own long-term interests constitutes part of the problem. Conversely the ability of the executive to predict is questionable, and indeed few people would regard it as infallible. Moreover, the full implications of policy, as far as they are known, are not always made available to the public. Foreign policy particularly is often presented to the public in terms which will win support. An unhappy mixture of propaganda and traditional diplomacy informs the conduct of foreign policy. Without the detailed information possessed by the executive the public can hardly be expected to weigh the consequences of alternative political action. Yet revelation of all these details would restrict a government's freedom of action *vis-à-vis* other nations. The dilemma is apparent, and cannot be wished away, particularly since in so many countries the support of the masses has been evoked in the struggle for power. In democracies the power of the masses is a political fact; this together with the power of the representative assembly has brought the executive to the verge of impotence.

It is not enough to suppose that this dilemma can be resolved, as some of the contributors at the early UNESCO meetings seemed to think, simply by more and more education and more and more democracy. The faith in education stems from Protagoras, and was given new impetus by the eighteenth-century philosophers. As an ideal, based upon the assumption of man's inherent goodness and educability, it is one which democrats find hard to reject in spite of the evidence against the possibilities of achieving effective democratic government everywhere. Lippmann's indictment of educational trends initiated by the Jacobins is severe. The tenor of his remarks is that the public has never been prepared to pay what it would cost to provide this effective education. There are two aspects of politically effective education; one concerns the education of personnel for effective executive leadership, in which field the French and British have been notably successful, and the other concerns the possibilities of educating the masses in the kind of political discrimination regarded as necessary to weigh the consequences of alternative political action. Lippmann, it should be remembered, is speaking of the liberal western democracies with universal educational systems going back almost a hundred years and with even longer democratic traditions. The most serious problem for them appears to lie in the realm of foreign policy, although few countries, with the possible exceptions of the U.S.A. and U.S.S.R., can pursue domestic policies independent of foreign policy. But what of the new liberal democracies whose base of literacy is so thin and whose experience of western-type political institutions is so recent? These two aspects of the general problem were vastly complicated by the war.

The Educational Solution

The political role of education in the post World War II era was soon restated. Even before UNESCO[5] was established in November 1945, some educators were convinced that in order to 'lay a firm basis for democracy', depth and breadth must be given to the education of the common people. Moreover, the preamble to the organisation maintained that 'since wars begin in the minds of men, it is in the minds of men that the defences of peace must be constructed', a view of the cause of war which calls for universal mass education as an antidote. Only this could promote a lasting peace. Yet another task for education was introduced; that of raising the economic and social conditions of all peoples through mass or fundamental education.

The basic step in this ambitious programme was at first thought to be the removal of illiteracy, a gigantic task, since in 1946 more than half the world was known to be illiterate. As soon as the organisation was set up, the acting Executive Secretary, Sir Alfred Zimmern, urged that a world campaign should receive first priority. This was soon realised to be beyond its resources. In 1951 the Director General of UNESCO, James Torres Bodet, acknowledged this, adding that of direct concern to him was the training of fundamental education leaders. There had also been a shift of emphasis about the importance of literacy. The view that it was not an end in itself had gained ground, so that it was then regarded as one 'part of a tragic circle of underproduction, malnutrition and endemic disease'.[6] Nevertheless in its modified form—community development—universal education still seemed crucial to many educators.

Even during the early UNESCO sessions voices protested against education as a panacea which would promote democracy and secure world peace. Literacy was no guarantee of either peace or democracy. Education, it was argued, had not always been a liberating force. Nazi Germany was cited by Julian Huxley as an example of a highly literate nation where democracy had failed. Indeed, J. A. Lauwerys, commenting on a paper by C. K. Ogden, remarked that literacy simply increased the possibilities of political exploitation: 'Those who cannot read are the victims of some form of verbal illusion. Merely teaching them to read does not free them from verbal illusions, but in addition makes them more liable to exploitation through print.'[7] Mass media of communication considerably complicated the situation.

A basic question is whether or not educational solutions can be found for political problems. Writing on the philosophy of UNESCO, H. L. Elvin sharply contrasts two ideological approaches. The first is 'education in the service of peace', and the other, 'peace in the service of education, science, and culture'.[8] One position implies a very positive crusade for education, the other that the resolution, or partial resolution, of political problems depends on political action, and not on good intentions. Certainly some political scientists like Hans J. Morgenthau argue that political problems are not capable of final solution but can only be restated, manipulated, and transformed, so that each epoch has to deal with them afresh. He has also drawn the distinction between political realism and the approach to political questions which assumes universal principles about the essential goodness and infinite malleability of individuals. His position of political realism implies that education should not be looked at as a solution to political problems, but only as one among many sources of power for its individual recipients, groups within a nation, and the nation as a whole.

Precisely for these reasons is it important in comparative studies to state or redefine major socio-political problems as clearly as can be done so that the possible roles of education as it relates to major problems may become apparent. Acceptance of the problem approach in comparative education places upon the investigator an obligation of this kind. General educational proposals should be considered as making some contribution to the transformation of political problems. The outcomes of similar policies will depend upon circumstances. Here a very general distinction is made between the general situation in newly independent nations and that more typical of Europe and the United States. It should be obvious that the generalisations serve only to reveal the general features of the problem. The social context of each nation will show marked differences from that of any other country, and a more detailed comparative analysis would reveal them.

Newly Independent Nations

The decline of Britain and France as imperial powers was soon apparent. Mounting pressure, first in Lebanon and Syria and ter in Asia, meant that in many cases independence could not be long delayed. The speed of transition caused apprehension. Some Indian national leaders at least were as concerned as the British about the probable effects on the country of the hasty withdrawal of a powerful executive. The consequences of the sudden acceleration of a process which had been for many years a matter of affirmed policy ought to be weighed very carefully. Certainly some of the techniques used in the understandable fight for independence left national leaders in some countries at least with considerable problems of orderly independent government. Nationalism as a political ideal mounted everywhere. Independence and democracy were preached simultaneously in colonial territories. Some leaders incited the masses to ugly shows of violence and bloody revolution. To do this is no doubt one of the arts of politics, which is, it has been said, always in part a process of influencing, manipulating, and controlling group and individual behaviour. New media of communication have improved the effectiveness of many of the devices outlined by Quincy Wright in *The Study of International Relations*.[9] Among these, the use of propaganda, patronage, and force, e.g. rioting, political strikes, and so on, should be contrasted with the dissemination of knowledge through education, the bestowal of honour and prestige for long and meritorious service, and the invocation of civil law. A wise choice of methods is not always possible. Demagogues are not afraid to use unscrupulous methods whatever the consequences; today a large audience is quickly available. By whatever means, the process of emancipation from colonial rule has accelerated greatly. Within years rather than centuries, the 'new' masses have been given a position of power which signifies nothing less than political domination by them.

After independence, by no means all the norms essential to honest non-violent democratic government are accepted by the inhabitants of newly freed countries; nor are readily adaptable institutions of democratic government available. Notably many of the emergent countries lack a substantial middle class and a well-developed educational system. A sudden successful reversal after independence from the cruder but effective methods of persuasion to non-violent processes of education may be extremely difficult. Independence does not

105

necessarily solve the problem of democracy; in many cases, the removal of a powerful executive renders the solution, at least temporarily, more difficult.

The power of the 'new' masses, then, does not depend upon literacy but on the use made of them by political leaders in a struggle for power. A new struggle is likely to develop after independence, when the removal of colonialism leaves competing groups within a country jockeying for supreme power. The cold war between the U.S.A. and the U.S.S.R. has complicated the picture. The competition between these two countries is frequently couched in ideological terms as liberal democracy versus communism. To distinguish between the two requires a degree of literacy and a level of political sophistication and discrimination which simple forms of literacy certainly cannot give. In such struggles for power the masses are pawns. Indeed, literacy may extend the opportunities of exploitation, for even a 'free' press is often controlled by interest groups competing for popular support. Nevertheless, literacy can be regarded as one index of a nation's political power. A spectacular rise in literacy rates within a country would strengthen its international power as a developing nation. The twin considerations of national unity and international power have doubtless been kept in mind by the leaders of those countries, like India, whose avowed intention, on becoming independent, was the maintenance of democratic forms of government and the adoption of a policy of neutrality among the major power groups. These aims, together with the recognition in the constitution of education as a basic human right, gave high priority to universal education. According to the Secondary Education Commission's report the 'educational system must make its contribution to the development habits, attitudes and qualities of character which will enable its citizens to bear worthily the responsibilities of democratic citizenship and to counteract all these fissiparous tendencies which hinder the emergence of a broad, national and secular outlook'.[10] Optimism at first ran high. Soon after independence the forty years suggested by Sir John Sargent as necessary to achieve universal primary education in India were quickly reduced to fifteen. In view of the very high percentage illiteracy in 1947 in a population of millions the magnitude of the task is apparent.

It has been immensely complicated by the variety of languages which are spoken within the country and by the belief generally held by many leaders that a single national language, preferably Hindi, was necessary to national unity—a belief which, translated into policy, has perhaps led to more political problems than it solved.

Education has, of course, another important political role. It is an instrument of selection and training for political leaders. The leaders of independence movements have frequently been western- or European-educated men; members of a tiny new élite. On the other hand, and this is well illustrated by the pre-1947 situation in the Indian subcontinent, leadership groups before independence, and consequently to a greater extent afterwards, have been divided over educational policy. One group has usually associated itself closely with European type education. Another group has stressed the need to maintain in their purest form ancient indigenous traditions through the educational system. But education has been recognised as a source of political power. Minority groups, such as the Tamils in Ceylon, sought education as a way of improving their position in society, often thereby occupying far more administrative posts than their sheer numbers might appear to justify. In India, one of the expressed purposes behind the foundation of Aligarh Moslem University was to redress the balance between educated Moslems and Hindus. Its political influence has been considerable and perhaps contributed to the partition of the subcontinent. Before independence, in spite of the fact that within both parties were advocates of non-European education, the incentives to learn English were great. English-medium schools were more popular than the vernacular schools, and attempts made by the government to replace British and European with Indian history were interpreted as a way of keeping students ignorant of the liberal ideas of the West.

Divisions based on educational background meant very often that independence from foreign control did not necessarily result in political unity. Many of the colonial territories had been fashioned into political units by imperial powers. One factor in their remaining so was the presence of foreign administrators and officials. Independence meant that after the first flush of victory, there were serious problems of creating political units out of areas in which great diversity existed. Europe is really no more diverse than the subcontinent of India; it is certainly less so than the huge African continent. Geographical boundaries whilst giving some colonial territories a measure of unity are no longer as important as they once were in moulding communities into political units. Social factors are among the most diversifying elements. Among these tribal, caste, linguistic, and religious loyalties are very important. Distribution of population (and other demographic data) enters into this problem, as does the general distribution of wealth among the various groups. All these aspects of the societal patterns (institutional and circumstantial) are related to the power structure within a society. In specifying the problem in terms of individual countries a different weighting should be given to the various factors. In some cases religious differences contribute more than social structure to the political problem. No one factor should, however, be taken either as the most important or the only one. Nor should it be assumed that these factors are distinct. Religious, linguistic, and occupational activities are often closely related. Members of one religious organisation speaking the same language and having similar economic standards of living become a small power group. Any of the symbols, religion, language, occupation, or educational background, can therefore be taken as an index of power. The divisions within an élite may be grounded on any of them. Comparative 'sociograms' of the composition of and relationships within an élite would be very enlightening. At present in many countries the power struggle is still within the leadership group, either between ideological factions or between the traditional leaders and the younger men. The outcome may ultimately depend a great deal on the kind of education the young leaders have had both at home and abroad.

The Role of Education and Political Unity

Education, therefore, plays a considerable part in the maintenance or disruption of the power structure of society. The political position of the first recipients of a European or American type of education helps to determine the transition from colonial status to independence. In any case, the struggle between the old and new generation of leaders will be severe. In many parts of Africa, tribal diversity shows itself in differences not only of language and religion but in power structures. One group within a political unit has perhaps a monarchical system operated by patronage; another a lineage system by which power is widely dispersed. Apart from the intertribal hostilities, which in the fight for independence are to some extent concealed, the reconstruction of power to meet the requirements of western type democratic institutions presents considerable difficulties. Old leadership patterns are badly distorted by selective education. Some of these effects have been shown by O. F. Raum in 1955 and 1956 *Year Book of Education* articles. If this process selects traditional leaders or their heirs, the prospects of maintaining community stability may be fairly good. The educational policies of the colonial powers have varied considerably, but always great attention has been paid to the education of future leaders. Mass literacy and universal primary schooling have hardly as yet been considered in many African territories. The demand for it on the part of African leaders does not seem, thus far, as vociferous as in many parts of Asia. Proposals to introduce it into Eastern Nigeria before resources were available, however, gave rise to a great deal of unrest and dissatisfaction.

Linguistic differences within a country enter into the struggle for political power and raise serious additional educational questions as far as literacy is concerned. Reference to some of the features of European developments should throw light, by analogy, on problems in India, for example. Through the temporal and spiritual power of the church, Latin became the language of a small élite in Europe. After the printing press improved the means of communication between large masses of the people the vernaculars began to be used, which contributed to the rise of nationalism and the division of Europe on new criteria, i.e. national rather than religious. If literacy is one of the instruments through which a sense of nationality can be achieved, then the decision of the Indian leaders to make Hindi the national language was wise. But if language is so important in the development of national sentiments, it is equally a powerful preserver of regional loyalties. The prospect of increasing communication by the use of regional languages and hence of mobilising a greater proportion of the population than hitherto has to be weighed against the possible disintegration of national unity. Needless to say, Soviet, Swiss, and Belgian language policies have shown that linguistic diversity does not preclude political unity. A feeling of nationality is, however, only one of the ways of preserving this unity.

Unfortunately nationalism and nationality have been confused with political unity which depends on the power of the central executive to pursue policies often irrespective of the support of major linguistic groups. Unity based on a national culture requires a degree of social communication as regards language, ideology, common interests, psychological behaviour, and the acceptance of a common heritage, which is difficult to achieve through language policy if Europe's experience has any meaning.

Religious differences enter deeply into the political problem if they happen to be institutionalised because a religious institution wields power, although ideology may direct its action. A comparative analysis would necessarily include a study of religious organisations as power institutions, e.g. the position of the Roman Catholic Church in Italy and France. Overemphasis on this source of conflict would be a mistake where the institutional power of religious groups is not great. Even so political power is to some extent being restructured round religious affiliations in some parts of Africa, where the European missionaries have been particularly successful in making converts. This should be contrasted with the relative lack of success in Moslem areas where political considerations often made the colonial powers discourage missionary activity. There has been considerable competition in Africa between the various churches, resulting in the breakdown to some extent of tribal, clan, and in some cases family unity. Denominational affiliations, based on missionary education, sometimes form the nuclei of new political power groups in African society.

Further detailed analyses of the other divisions within a country are necessary if the problem of political unification is to be understood and its educational implications recognised. Conflicts occur between urban and rural groups, between landowners and commercial people, and between the majority racial groups and the minorities. The relative strengths of the various groups complicate the political structure picture. Clusters of characteristics—ideological, social, and economic— identify each of the groups. Language is often associated with religion and both with particular types of occupation. A power élite is frequently identifiable by a whole cluster of character- istics, of which only one or two are possessed by other societal groups. The different ways in which these factors are combined means that many different societal types exist. Perhaps none of them should be classified as simple or complex before criteria of simplicity have been drawn up. If cultural diversity is one criterion, then many African societies are as complex as English or Danish society.

It follows that no one educational policy can serve all countries. A realistic one cannot be based merely on peda- gogical theories of learning and innate abilities, or yet on a single political or social theory. Local control, for example, will not necessarily promote under all circumstances political unity. Nor should it be assumed that the adoption of the mother tongue as the medium of instruction in all primary schools will have the same political consequences in the United Kingdom and in India. In some countries the retention of a foreign language as the medium of official communication, rather than as an agent of national unity, may promote political unity. In other countries quite contrary results will flow from such a policy. Similarly the designation of one of many indi- genous languages will not everywhere solve the political problem. Where only two main languages are found, as in Ceylon, such a solution may be virtually unworkable politi- cally. Where more languages exist the political problem may not be so great. Yet each of these principles has, at one time or another, been accepted as the basis of educational policy, and the consequences in one country have been very different from those occurring in another because the contexts or initial circumstances have been different. The comparative task is to identify all the factors militating against political unification and weigh each of them in specific case studies. Only then can the likely consequences of educational policy be appreci- ated. This does not imply that the political problem can be finally solved through education. Educational policy is one of many factors which contribute towards the transformation of the political problem and should be given its appropriate weight relative to the other diversifying features.

Europe and the U.S.A.

The political problem in western Europe and the U.S.A. is somewhat different. In spite of great internal diversities each of the European countries has a considerable sense of nationality and political unity. Literate populations have had considerable experience in managing their domestic affairs, although, if democratic forms of government are to be criteria, not all with the same success. France, intensely democratic in outlook and constitution, continued until recently to suffer after the war as she did before it from lack of permanence of executive power. Changed world conditions and the even balance in parliamentary membership of the two major British political parties has made the pursuit of consistent policies there difficult. This has been made worse by the apparent inconsistencies between domestic and foreign policy. Only recently has this problem become acute. Absolute monarchs did not need to distinguish between international and national affairs. Democratic governments have increasingly had to allow national traditions and public opinion to operate freely in domestic matters. Until relatively recently the executive has reserved the right to pursue foreign policy in comparative independence of public opinion. This has been true even of France, despite the constitutional weakness of the executive. In Britain the freedom of the Crown and government in foreign policy was not radically affected until the Labour party became powerful. Subsequently, domestic politics coloured foreign policy debate. Labour's power became truly effective when in the immediate post-war election it was swept into power with support from all sections of the community as well as from its traditional sources of strength—organised labour and the co-operative movement. In power the emphasis in its programme was, it should be conceded, on social domestic reform. The country's economic position vitally affected her ability to have an independent foreign policy, as the distinguished Labour Foreign Secretary, Ernest Bevin, knew. Bitter memories of the pre-war depressions doubtless made it difficult for trade unionists to adopt wage and work policies appropriate to the country's new economic and political position in the world. The diffidence shown by political leaders to make this clear to the rank and file meant that, in the opinion of some observers, quite inconsistent domestic and foreign policies were advocated.

With the Conservative government in power so fine was the balance of world power that it, too, seemed unable to pursue consistent foreign and domestic policies. There was lack of national unity about the economic necessity of maintaining Britain's imperial lines of communication and about the contribution of the empire to her economy. At the same time organised labour demanded reduced hours of work and increased social benefits, and was awarded higher wages without committing itself to higher productivity. Managements, be it said, seemed equally oblivious to the fact that pre-war industrial policies were neither economically appropriate nor politically possible in the post-war era. The failure to pay much attention to industrial relations, as reported by the Advisory Council on Industrial Relations, may be said to have had an indirect bearing on British foreign policy.

One educational task, then, is to wean a population generally away from conceptions of personal and national interest more appropriate to a previous epoch. The transformation of attitudes is seldom easy. Deep-seated prejudices enter deeply into the political problem, and these have tended to make foreign policy in Britain a question of party politics to be debated not on its merits but as a way of embarrassing the incumbent government. Divisions in the representative assembly have been matched by similar differences among the population generally; a highly articulate press, radio, and television have introduced new dimensions into foreign policy debates. The educational system, as in most European countries, acts as a means of selecting political leaders. Only one member of the Macmillan Conservative cabinet in March, 1959, had attended neither one of the 'public' schools nor Oxford or Cambridge university. The leader of the Labour party at that time was Hugh Gaitskell, a product of Winchester College and Oxford University. Even the membership of the House of Commons was still heavily representative of the 'public' schools, the publicly financed academic high schools, and the universities. Similarly in France, attendance either at a *lycée* or *collège* (both academic secondary schools) is almost a *sine qua non* for entry into the House of Assembly. The intellectual emphasis on rationalism inculcated at these schools makes realistic compromise difficult between groups starting out from different premises. Particularly in Britain, party lines tend to be drawn in terms of educational background, but many leaders on both sides are products of the same kind of public-school education.

This policy, one may say, was certainly not inappropriate to the traditional methods of conducting foreign policy. European secondary school and university systems generally speaking take care to train statesmen, diplomats, and administrators. The last serve at home and abroad and are not political appointees. They have considerable responsibility, power, and prestige. While the manner of training varies from country to country, most of these men are intellectuals who have distinguished themselves at one or other of the universities of Europe, as indeed have many of the elected officers. Even if the high quality of these men be admitted, the usefulness of retaining such highly selective systems of secondary and university education may be questioned. Labour party and socialist documents in England show how deeply the lack of educational opportunity as a source of political power is resented. The system restricts entry into positions of leadership no less than it reduces occupational choice and provides a criterion of social class. The 'public' school leadership of the Labour party is embarrassed by the suspicion of its educationally less privileged members. Under the new circumstances of considerably reduced international power, effective co-operation within and between the various national groups seems vital to Britain's national interest.

The situation in the U.S.A. shows marked differences. The educational task has been changed by the sudden thrust of the country into the centre of the international stage. Under difficult circumstances the U.S.A. has been called upon in the post-war era to exercise the kind of leadership in world affairs that Britain and France previously undertook.

Her educational system has not been geared to this. Although John Dewey was constantly analysing the role of education in a democracy his concern was primarily domestic rather than international. Over the years, the system has served this purpose well. Many of the unfortunate consequences which have flowed from the highly selective and highly academic education of Europe have been avoided by the establishment in the U.S.A. of the common high school and the lack of snobbishness about non-academic studies. Moreover, political rather than educational considerations are extremely important in the selection of executive officers. Unlike the situation in Europe, many of them are political appointees with no security of tenure beyond the lifetime of a political party's pre-eminence. This system also means that many able men have few opportunities to exercise responsible leadership in political life. A further consequence is that the permanent appointees have much less responsibility and power than their European counterparts. Thus, perhaps relatively fewer of the first-class men, using criteria of education and intellect, have been recruited to the civil and diplomatic services of the U.S.A. than in Europe. If this be true some consideration should be given to the effects of the educational system on the recruitment and training of these men. Already considerable interest has been shown by political scientists in America in the public's role in the conduct of foreign affairs. The evidence quoted by one author suggests two things: first, that the opinion and policy leadership group is small—about 1 per cent of the total population; second, a large proportion of the U.S.A. is neither informed nor interested in foreign policy—another study placed this figure as high as 80 per cent. Data are given in Buck and Travis' *Control of Foreign Relations in Modern Nations*,[11] a useful comparison dealing with the four major powers and other areas.

This apparent lack of interest may be no accident since isolationism is not quite dead. And indeed fears have been expressed that foreign policy may become too much a matter for public debate. Educational discussion of the problem has been rather limited. The N.E.A. policies commission reports published in the immediate post-war period have little to say about the role of the school in the conduct of American foreign policy and international relations. The compilers of President

Truman's commission report on higher education spent some time on America's responsibility in an atomic age. Conant's report on the American high school makes but brief mention of the political problem as discussed by Lippmann, although amongst political scientists it has received a great deal of attention. In the N.E.A. pamphlet *American Education and International Tensions*[12] the potential influence of American citizens on world affairs is recognised. The questions it raises about the responsibility of the schools are germane to this discussion. The proposals the report makes would hardly meet the criteria of political realism advanced by Morgenthau.

The other contribution made by the educational system to the political problem relates to what is taught in the schools. If the public are to participate in foreign affairs (and its determination to do so at times of crisis is a *fait accompli*) then perhaps the systematic teaching of political science is a necessary corollary. It could be argued that school-age children have neither the maturity nor the intellectual competence to study such subjects. When else will they be trained in the methods of political analysis and the principles of weighing the possible consequences of alternative political action? One approach to a solution would be to extend considerably the scope of post-secondary school education in the colleges, placing emphasis on political science in teacher-training programmes and in institutes of technology and the like. Against this approach may be advanced the view that through history, general social studies, geography, science, and so on, the basic principles on which political decisions should be made could be drawn out. Then the whole question of how the subject matter or data should be treated arises.

The Explosion of Scientific Knowledge

If Lippmann is stating one of the basic problems of our time, then every subject in the curriculum should be assessed in the light of its possible contribution to the transformation of the impasse he outlines. Thus history should be taught, as John Dewey suggested, for the light it can throw on present social and political questions. The issue arises in its most acute form in the natural sciences.

The explosion of scientific knowledge during the war was quite startling. Before the war it was possible for a university-trained scientist to be familiar with most of the work in his own field, e.g. physics or chemistry. Increasingly since the war few, if any, men can have a detailed knowledge of more than a fraction of any major field in the natural sciences; even to keep up with the literature is an almost impossible task. The general scientist, let alone the layman, is hardly competent to enter into informed discussion of any of the special fields. The post-war era has become one of extreme specialisation and has revived in acute form questions about secondary school and university education. The pursuit of a scientific career requires a high degree of specialisation somewhere along the educational line. But the danger of specialisation, as Frederic Lilge, drawing his illustration from Germany, points out, is in the domination of such education by the 'utilitarian concepts of science to the exclusion of its basic humanistic elements'.[13]

Other speakers at the Massachusetts Institute of Technology meeting to discuss the social implications of scientific progress revealed their own fears. Among these was the view that the advance of knowledge had led to a decay of morals and a sense of insecurity. Two reactions to this state of affairs seem possible. Science can become either a god, a symbol of unchallengeable power, or a scapegoat. The fact remains that since the war governments have increasingly had to rely on the judgement of scientific 'experts' about the consequences of policy. This is nowhere more starkly revealed than in the debates on the testing of atomic bombs. Apparently the 'experts' disagree. Cynics may assume that the disagreement is basically political rather than scientific. Other observers may argue that predictions in the sciences are in any case never certain, and the inevitable margin for error gives rise to real differences of opinion between scientists who advise governments. Because political decisions rest with statesmen, the scientist's responsibility is considerably reduced. The public has to take on trust both its political leaders and their scientific experts. There is no guarantee that scientists as such are politically more responsible than statesmen. Scientific demagoguery becomes a possibility. Neither the public nor the executive is in a position to question the scientific arguments advanced. All either can do is to take into account all the scientific arguments which bear on political and moral judgements.

There is a sense in which scientific literacy has become critical in liberal democracies. If members of the public are expected to weigh the consequences of alternative political action, then they should be able to weigh those consequences which are regarded as scientific. Scientific literacy means that the public can at least weigh the evidence, as presented by scientists, bearing on such issues. The magnitude of the task, even in countries whose populations are generally literate, is enormous. Yet how can the public participate in debates on the control and use of atomic energy and pass judgement on proposed action unless it has access to all the evidence available and is able to assess its validity? How can it decide which parts of the conflicting evidence to accept? The decisions involved are basically political, and should be debated as such. Moral issues also loom large. Individuals will make their judgements on whatever basis they are able. Scientific literacy implies that individuals before passing judgement are familiar with certain short- and long-term implications of a decision; for example, the effects on the health of the present generation and on the lives of future generations. This degree of scientific literacy is out of the question.

Not all the issues on which the public will be expected to pass judgement are so dramatic. Nor are the scientific aspects of them as difficult to assess. Some of the social consequences and paradoxes of technological progress will be mentioned in a later chapter. The educational questions concern what is appropriate training for future scientific specialists and for all youth. Adequate measures may entail a further extension of schooling, but in any case, as theory both in the U.S.A. and in the U.S.S.R. suggests, there is need to study the social implications of science with the object of achieving some measure of scientific literacy. Overemphasis on scientific training for industry is dangerous because it diverts attention from the more crucial political question posed by Lippmann. Some of the detailed proposals are considered more fully in Chapter X.

The kind of revolution in curriculum required by such a change of emphasis is apparent when it is realised that science courses in Europe, and to a large extent in the U.S.A., are still organised on a subject basis and follow the lines of historical development. The criterion here advanced is that scientific data should be selected and organised for the purpose of illuminating major social problems. This implies that data are drawn from a number of traditional subjects and organised in terms of social relevance. In terms of the political problem some criteria of selection emerge quite clearly from the identification of atomic energy control, space travel, and improved health services throughout the world as of major concern in the post-war era.

Even brief reference to the problem of scientific literacy throws into sharp relief the enormous educational task of preparing the public to participate effectively in the democratic process of weighing the consequences of alternative political action. Some implications of taking this task seriously should now be evident.

Democratic Participation and the Schools

The political problem is not transformed by stating it. Lack of sustained interest in foreign affairs does not prevent the public from taking decisive action in moments of starkly revealed crisis. Evidently this kind of crisis action makes the worst of both worlds. The executive is prevented from conducting a consistent policy but at the same time is not prevented by the public from getting into a crisis. Constant day to day contact with the progress of foreign policy seems necessary if the public is to act as more than a guide in the statement of broad goals. In the western liberal democracies the tradition that the public cannot be expected to understand world affairs has been abandoned along with secret diplomacy. Educators, aware of the problem, are hardly provided with a free choice of alternatives. If the challenge is taken seriously they are faced with the task of reorganising the curriculum and perhaps the structure of the secondary schools. One of the main difficulties is to develop qualities of leadership in young people who will occupy positions of political authority responsibly and honestly without at the same time creating a self-perpetuating power élite. To achieve this end in the U.S.A. may mean that more power should be accorded to a federal agency to promote educational policies as much in the diplomatic and administrative fields as in technology and science. Though the objections to greater Federal control of educational policy have been well stated in the U.S.A., some of its advantages cannot be overlooked. The new responsibilities placed on the country by changes wrought by the war should direct attention to them.

In western Europe, on the contrary, the continuation of highly selective secondary schools, especially in France and Britain, seems bound to exacerbate the political problem as defined by Lippmann. The future of the comprehensive school in England is largely in the hands of the political parties. Reasons for rejecting it by educators and political parties have been couched in educational terms in lowered standards, loss of educational purpose, and disintegration of the curriculum. Some attention has also been paid to its effect on the development of the gifted or talented children and on the quality of national leadership. These consequences should be weighed against the other possible outcomes of the establishment of more comprehensive secondary schools.

The problem in the 'new' democracies has very different dimensions. A basic choice lies between the concentration of resources in the education of leaders and the wide dispersal of resources in an attempt to establish universal literacy.

In practice, governments frequently have no choice. Political pressures make it impossible to deny educational provision as a human right in the interests of training future leaders. Ideally the choice should be based upon an assessment of outcomes in the light of particular political circumstances. At the moment comparative educationists are not in a position to offer very positive advice. Obviously faith in the short-term effectiveness of education in the promotion of political democracy has been shaken by events. Democratic governments can hardly deny to large numbers of people basic educational opportunities. The cautionary note introduced into the early UNESCO discussions illustrates the negative role of the comparative educationist. It reflects, however, the limitations of the methods of prediction now available to him. It is noticeable, for example, that where economic arguments have been used more attention has been given to the value of concentrating resources in education although the political dangers of doing so may be considerable. Some aspects of the economic question will be considered in the next chapter.

Chapter VI

ECONOMIC PROBLEMS AND EDUCATIONAL POLICY

THE war transformed the world economic scene as radically as it upset international politics. The gap between the demand for goods and services and available resources widened. On the one hand aspirations were considerably heightened but shortages were everywhere apparent. The balance of economic power shifted. Europe lost heavily through the destruction of equipment and buildings, the loss of men, and because foreign investments were liquidated in order to prosecute the war. The U.S.A. suffered no material damage and gained relatively, and so did the U.S.S.R. in spite of enormous losses. Nevertheless the rich countries became richer and the poor countries poorer. Karl W. Deutsch[1] has illustrated this by giving per capita income data for a number of countries for the periods 1925–34 and 1949. Comparisons reveal that over this period of time the differences between per capita incomes of the industrialised countries and those of the semi- or non-industrialised nations increased considerably. The lack of balance between demand and supply was much more acute than before in these countries because expectations had been raised enormously.

A number of agencies helped to change world and national attitudes towards standards of living. Global warfare gave many soldiers from impoverished lands a glimpse of some of the material comforts of the western countries. Emulation forced up the demand for consumer goods. Better transport increased cross-cultural economic comparisons. A greater proportion of the world's population than ever before was made aware of the possibilities of material goods. Empirical studies such as those of I. Schapera, Sol Tax, the U.K. Board of Trade,[2] and others reveal the growth of consumer awareness in parts of Africa and elsewhere.

Encouragement to expect better social services was also given. In many colonial territories, of course, educational provision either by missionaries or later by the secular authorities has a long history. But in the thirties the welfare and development policies of some imperial powers gave further impetus to the desire of colonial peoples to raise their living standards. Even if none of these policies need be regarded as entirely altruistic, modest aspirations were aroused. Indeed British Welfare and Development plans originally stressed the economic objectives of colonial planning, one of which was the establishment of overseas markets for British goods. The returns were much less than is often supposed, and certainly after 1940 and until the economic crisis of 1947 social welfare tended to receive most attention. After several disastrous experiments policy reverted. Barbu Niculescu[3] considers that French policy followed rather similar lines but that strategic considerations played a greater role in planning than with the British. Inevitably over the years the choice between welfare and economic development presented itself. The final outcome of colonial policy is difficult to assess, but one way of doing so would be to consider the extent and level of educational provision. The records of the various European powers in this regard would be found to differ considerably. Nevertheless their policies contributed in some measure to a growth of demand not only for consumer goods but for improved social services.

At the same time the improvement of living standards was a theme taken up by leaders in colonial areas approaching independence. Even before 1947 an Indian advisory planning board stated categorically: 'The general objectives of planning, as the board envisaged them, were "to raise the general standards of living of the people as a whole and to ensure useful employment for all".'[4] Parenthetically, national leaders promising improved conditions after independence sometimes inferred that the removal of colonialism would automatically make this possible. In the course of a fierce debate on colonial policy Pierre M. J. Ryckmans, a former governor of the Belgian Congo, ventured to point out the fallacy of this inference. 'Let me first dispose of the assertion that political dependence, *as such*, is bound to hamper economic development. There is an obvious fallacy. Political status, *as such*, has nothing to do with economic advancement. Stable and efficient government has; but stable and efficient government is not synonymous with self-government.' Sir Ramaswami Mudiliar's eloquent and impassioned reply was that, on the contrary, if development were left to colonial powers progress would be delayed for a long long time. The solution, he thought, lay in 'the organised collective effort either of the United Nations or a group of nations together'.[5]

Certainly powerful ideological support was given to this kind of international participation. According to its Charter, 'We the peoples of the United Nations determined . . . to promote social progress and better standards of life'. Through its numerous technical agencies the United Nations has tried to meet the challenge. Conferences and seminars have been sponsored, fellowships and scholarships awarded, and training centres set up to promote higher living standards through the sharing of skills and techniques. The aid of experts has been enlisted to advise governments on development plans. A small but important percentage of the resources of the United Nations has been used to carry out preparatory surveys to determine economic and social potentialities. Direct teaching, advisory services, and pilot projects have been among the techniques used. Finally the United Nations technical agencies have undertaken research work in many parts of the world.

Wealthier nations, too, have made their own contribution either through their own aid programmes or through bilateral agreements. Colonial powers such as France and Britain have continued to provide loans on a large scale. Generous support for development schemes was promised by President Truman in his inaugural address (January 20, 1949). The Point Four programme was initiated in these words: 'Fourth, we must embark on a bold new programme for making the benefits of our scientific advances and industrial progress available for the improvement and growth of underdeveloped areas.' The original programme has been extended and now includes the Peace Corps. Into this situation the political cold war between the U.S.A. and her allies and the Communist nations introduced an element of competition for the allegiance of the uncommitted third of the world's population. Lippmann states the challenge succinctly. 'The Communists are expanding in Asia because they are demonstrating a way, at present the only effective way, of raising quickly the power and standard of living of a backward people. Our only convincing answer to that must be a demonstration by the non-Communist nations that there is another and more humane way of overcoming the immemorial poverty and weakness of the Asian peoples.'[6]

In short, economic, political, and humanitarian motives combined in the post-war era to produce throughout the world a climate of opinion summarised by Philip M. Hauser as follows: 'Toynbee has said that our generation will be best known by future generations for having achieved, for the first time in human history, an aspiration to high living standards. There are virtually no areas left in the globe, with the possible exception of middle Africa and isolated tribal spots in Asia, where the population does not aspire to levels of living equivalent to that enjoyed in the West.'[7] If this does not represent a statement of empirical fact, at least it throws into sharp relief the nature of the post-war economic problem: that of raising the level of production throughout the world in order to meet the increasing demand for 'better standards of living'. The phrase means many things to many people, but closer contacts of non-western peoples with America and Europe and the assumption by western experts that their own way of life is best, have combined to identify 'better standards of living' as Hauser says, with those enjoyed in the U.S.A. and western Europe. Doubtless Communist achievements are increasingly regarded as desirable objectives.

In addition to the explosion of aspirations the explosion of population has intensified the problem by enormously raising the total number of persons who wish to enjoy the improved standards of living. Data are available which show how populations are rising and at what rates. Broad distinctions can be made between the western European nations, the U.S.A., U.S.S.R., Latin America, and the Asian countries. These trends have been summarised and classified in Hauser's *Population and World Politics*. The accelerated tempo of population increase is greatest in Latin America with an estimated growth of between 2 and 3 per cent per annum. But such are the differences between the various countries of this sub-continent that the economic problem in each has its own special features. The growth in India is variously estimated as being between 1 and 1·5 per cent or even higher—or between 4 and 6 million more people each year. China's population is thought to be growing at the rate of 2 per cent per annum. In European countries this rate is in the region of 1·5, and a little higher in the U.S.A. The reasons are that everywhere crude death rates have been reduced by improved medical services. Infant mortality rates have dropped, endemic and epidemic diseases brought under control. Moreover, such social customs as infanticide and widow burning have continued to decline. Birth rates, on the other hand, have not declined and in some cases have increased. Voluntary control of family size has hardly been as effective as the determined implementation of national birth-control policies. In this respect Communist policy should be contrasted with the attitudes of some non-Communist governments where population growth presents an acute problem. In any case, in most areas the number of deaths per year has become considerably less than the number of births with a consequent, but differentiated, growth of population. Gloomy Malthusian predictions are again advanced when productivity increases barely match rates of population growth.

Another feature of population change is in-and-out migration. Generally speaking, restrictions are placed on immigration by the governments through quota systems in countries like the U.S.A., Australia, and Canada. Britain exercises considerable control over entry into the country and members of the Commonwealth cannot, as once, enter freely as British citizens. Apart from the consequent gross increase (or decline) in population, which may be quite small, the process affects the supply-demand position in another way. The expectations of the newcomers obviously swell the demand for goods and services. But the level of education of the immigrants influences the labour market and production. Highly skilled workers and technologists are usually acceptable, frequently the best unskilled workers from low-income countries are also welcomed. The latter take up jobs no longer regarded as desirable by their hosts. The effect, of course, is to denude the struggling countries of some of their best personnel since a similar transfer of population does not take place in the opposite direction. Rather sensitive newly independent territories may even be unprepared to take in highly skilled workers. Certainly few semi- or unskilled workers are likely to be attracted to the low income countries. This process is thus bound to operate constantly in favour of the highly developed regions and against the underdeveloped ones.

Scales of Preference

The precise nature of the post-war demand for better living standards, although perhaps vaguely 'western', has been by no means the same everywhere. Actual scales of preference differ widely, not only between the peoples of different nations but within each nation between members of different social groups. In short, in their hierarchy of preferences in what order do people place food, housing, automobiles, clothes, medical services, wage packets, shorter working hours, television, beer, tobacco, and of course education? In his *The Theory of the Leisure Class*[8] Veblen brilliantly describes the mechanics of emulation, conspicuous leisure, conspicuous consumption, and the complementary attitudes to labour. These processes are likely to occur everywhere, but only careful comparative studies would enable realistic cross-cultural scales of preference to be drawn up. Even then two caveats should be noted. Paradoxes are likely to exist in any constructed scale. André Siegfried has, for example, contrasted the enduring spirit of thrift among the French people in their private affairs with their apparent extravagance in public matters. Again other social taboos may restrict the expression of personal desire. Consider India; the per capita food deficit is estimated as 550 calories per day and is also lacking in variety. The achievement of a balanced diet, however, is gravely handicapped by the Hindu's deeply religious attitude towards the eating of meat and particularly beef. However high on the stated scale of preference something may be, there is no guarantee that in practice real sacrifice will be made to acquire it. In other words empirically determined preference scales should be regarded as guiding hypotheses rather than as matters of fact.

Of particular interest on the various scales of preference is the position accorded to education. All the agencies promoting demand have proclaimed education as a human right. Superficially it should be placed high on the list of priorities in most countries today. Certainly post-war legislation has acknowledged

128

the political force of this demand. At one level parental demand frequently lacks discrimination. Whatever education is available regardless of its content is, initially at least, thought to be desirable. In India the primary schools in many areas are overwhelmed by applications and entrants. Soon other pressures begin to operate and wastage and stagnation become serious problems. Many children leave after one year of schooling, or never advance beyond the first grade, so that impossibly large numbers of children have to be handled at that level. Unrealistic curricula, the growing usefulness of children in the fields, and the difficulties of visualising what advantages education will bring help to account for this fall in enthusiasm.

A more sophisticated demand is for a particular kind of education usually provided in certain kinds of schools. Then individual parents are frequently prepared to pay tuition fees which apart from any income from endowments represent the full cost of their children's education. They pay for a very specific service which may be entrance to further education, ultimate access to positions of political power and social prestige, or a well-paid job. Provided they can meet parental demand such schools will stay in business. But as the pattern of parental demand changes features of the schools are likely to change too. A variety of considerations will, therefore, influence parents in their choice of school and in the amount of money they are prepared to invest in education. Studies by American economists at Chicago tend to show that in economic terms the personal financial profits from investment in higher education are very considerable in the United States. They are certainly higher in low-income countries.

In the case of State or publicly financed schools the operation of this sophisticated demand for education is much more complicated. A whole pattern of relationships is involved in the control of education, some general features of which will be considered in a later chapter. Here it should be noted that the degree to which consumer rather than social demand (as defined by members of some group) is allowed to determine the extent and type of education provided in a country has a considerable bearing on the economic problem. Parents and pressure groups can, in fact, raise the level of the demand for education as a consumer commodity, and if at the same time they are in a position to determine the type of education provided may well reduce the contribution it could otherwise make to increased production.

Immediately after the war, in Europe at least one feature of the situation made a great difference. Many Europeans were led to expect higher standards of living, and while resources were very scarce, the European nations, unlike the low-income regions, had human resources unsurpassed anywhere in skill and education. Long experience of industrial and commercial organisation made the problems of recovery less severe than in the non-industrial areas. Moreover universal elementary education lasting for at least seven or eight years was a reality. The demand for education in Europe therefore was for an extension of compulsory schooling, for a new kind of secondary education, and for higher education.

The differences between both the nature of the demand and the supply positions in high and low income countries are so vast that direct comparisons appear meaningless. Nowhere, for example, has the margin between the two been greater than in south-east Asia, where demand was quickly raised yet levels of production, in many cases, remained little above those of a subsistence economy. The provision of educational services was extremely limited and the level of literacy was invariably low (Japan and the English-speaking dominions being exceptions). But high expectations were in some cases given official sanction. Compulsory free and universal primary education was promised to all Indians under section 45 of the constitution. The resources of manpower and capital have proved grossly inadequate and the target has not yet been achieved. Yet the Indian government has courageously maintained its policy of allowing consumer preferences to operate over a wide field of choice. Perhaps the best contrast is with China, where by government decree compulsory investment in basic industries and in productive education has received more attention than the production of consumer goods.

The Allocation of Resources

In spite of these profound differences between northern Europe and the economically underdeveloped regions elsewhere a basic economic issue makes comparisons meaningful. Faced with an imbalance between demand and supply, and indeed with absolute shortages of trained manpower, material, and capital, choices are necessary. The problem is more poignant where the margin between supply and demand is greatest. But Mendes-France and Ardant maintain that choice is one of the basic problems of economic life. And, they continue, 'Man does not make the best choice as naturally as certain philosophies would have us believe. Unconsidered decisions, excessive pre-occupation with the present, and failure to draw comparison between possible solutions are more frequent than any other kind of behaviour. The same is true to an even more marked degree of communities, or if we prefer it, of their rulers. To engage in the simultaneous pursuit of contradictory aims is doubtless the most natural way for statesmen to behave.'[9] If true, this assessment of statesmen suggests a serious state of affairs, because since the war emphasis has been placed to a greater extent than before on government planning. One aspect of planning is the allocation of resources, a process which, according to M. J. Bowman and G. L. Bach, is one of economising 'scarce resources in order to produce the various goods ultimately desired by the consumer'.[10] On the other hand others would argue that in allocating resources more attention should be paid to national and social needs than to consumer preferences.

The dilemma is a real one. Planning *per se* has sometimes been regarded as the solution. The complexity of relationships between personal and group attitudes, power groups within society, and the availability of resources, however, have frustrated many hopes of achieving a democratically 'planned society'. Planning there has been, but it has been essentially piecemeal in nature. The crux of the allocation problem has been well stated by F. A. Hayek, whose attitude of 'total planning' is well known. It is more than the problem of allocating 'given' resources known to a single mind. 'It is rather', he continues, 'a problem of how to secure the best use of resources known to any of the members of society, for ends whose relative importance only these individuals know. Or, to put it briefly, it is a problem of the utilisation of knowledge which is not given to anyone in its totality.'[11]

Today education enters into the allocation problem in a very real way. It accounts for a sizeable proportion of a nation's expenditure. As much as 30 per cent of the annual national budget of the Philippines is spent on education, and in Laos teachers' salaries account for 13 per cent of the national budget. Frequently in the Asian countries the figure is well over 10 per cent. Education makes heavy demands on manpower, equipment, and capital. Consequently the economic returns on any investment in it become extremely important where resources are limited. Since the early fifties more and more attention has been given to this problem. Some studies have attributed in some cases a 44 per cent increase in labour productivity to primary education and higher yields to secondary and higher education. Even in high income regions—Europe and U.S.A.—studies give great weight to the role of the educational system in the growth of production. Consequently some economists have argued that a higher proportion than at present of the gross national product should, in most countries, be allocated to education. This conclusion is based upon an assessment of the relative weight which should be given to investment in education compared with investment in other sectors of the economy. In the early sixties a figure of between 4 and 5 per cent of the gross national product was regarded as desirable and possible for the nations of Africa, Asia, and South America. In Asia it was not anticipated that this rate of investment would be reached until 1980. Of course, in spite of the heavy expenditure on education these proposals imply great sacrifices and can hardly be achieved without outside help. Current rates leave educational provision below the levels expected, but one difficulty is to persuade people that sacrifices are worthwhile and that education is a vital form of national investment. It is certainly not seen as such by everyone, and not all people, moreover, are prepared to accept as desirable that kind of education which should bring the most immediate economic returns.

Competing for resources with education as a social service, of course, are the health services, defence, communications, and other public facilities. Most of these can be regarded as making some contribution to economic growth. Usually some sort of balance has to be found between them, but it should be remembered that the advantages of some of these services to individual users are more obvious than is the case with others. Where the personal advantage is clear the market can operate more freely and national investment is less necessary. Education, however, has always attracted more resources than the operation of the market would normally provide. That is to say, the consumers never pay the full costs of the education they or their children receive. Consequently social needs, as determined by special groups, have been given as much emphasis as consumer preferences in the allocation of resources within education. Marked changes are now taking place, however, in the control of education, with the result that the allocation process has become more complicated in its operation.

In most democratic countries the clash is between those who regard education as a human right and those who give great importance to economic considerations. In low-income countries where the former view prevails high priority is given to the establishment of universal primary schools. Where education is considered rather in terms of its contribution to economic progress, emphasis is given to the extension of technical and higher education. Again in industrialised regions the demand for more technical education is related to the need for economic progress; the extension of general secondary education to all is based upon a belief that all children should have equal educational opportunities to develop themselves fully as individuals. Naturally few politicians make clear the decisive character of the choice before the public and may consequently pursue mutually incompatible aims, or propose one policy and carry out another.

Broadly speaking, however, a basic choice in allocating scarce resources is between policies designed to restrict the demand for goods and services by investment in basic industries and attempts to maximise production. Conditions in countries with liberal democratic forms of government make the former policy difficult to operate except in time of war. The voluntary restriction of consumption becomes more difficult when promises of a better life are made by the political parties competing for power. For example, a policy of restriction was recognised as imperative by several post-war reconstruction committees in Britain just before the end of hostilities. The Labour government, however, was attacked for maintaining rationing and controls, and the Conservative victory was based partly on its promises to free the economy from the shackles of socialist planning.

Communist policy, of course, has always emphasised limitation of consumption in order to accumulate capital for further investment. The Five Year Plan of Yugoslavia showed what heavy stress was laid on investment in basic industries rather than on consumption. Where the state owns the means of production this kind of policy is practical, and does not depend for its success as much as elsewhere on the willingness of the public voluntarily to forgo present gains in favour of long-term economic progress. In this respect Lippmann has contrasted the ruthless yet successful policies pursued by the Chinese government with those followed in India. Evidently the Indians are not prepared to sacrifice certain political ideals in the interests of more rapid economic progress.

The success of either policy in fact depends upon a complex of factors which should in comparative studies be sought in the three societal configurations mentioned. Among the most important are: *natural resources, capital, technological skills, organisation,* and *cultural attitudes* or *norms.* Education has a real contribution to make to each of these, with the exception of natural resources and capital, and even here the proper use of capital and the ability to exploit natural resources depend upon the other factors and thus indirectly on the quality of education.

The next stage of a comparative study is to identify the factors relevant to the problem and its solutions, and weight them. In this case it is against the pattern of theories of economic development that each factor has to be assessed. In other words, judged against one set of theories certain norms or institutions could inhibit development; judged against other theories the same norms and institutions could help to promote it. Here a broad distinction has been made between classical liberalism or laisser faire economic theory and socialistic or Marxist views.

It is equally evident that assessment of educational policies should be made against clearly defined assumptions. The specific context will help to determine whether institutions which work well in one country will meet with the same success in another. In general the educational choice lies between the extension of universal schooling and improvements in the quality of selective education. Realistic choices should be made on the basis of an analysis of the needs and resources of the country and in relation to other aspects of national policy.

Natural Resources and Capital

It is abundantly obvious, for example, that the mere presence or absence of natural resources will help to determine the rate of economic development. To be sure, economists disagree about the weight that should be given to the presence of such resources without taking account of their accessibility and ease of exploitation. The obvious and rather special cases of easily exploited resources are the oil-bearing regions, provided that a handful of skilled personnel is available. In contrast some natural resources are extremely difficult to exploit: in Nigeria, for example, the physical problems of clearing the bush in order to develop agriculture present almost insuperable difficulties. In a similar way communications often hinder development; thus their inaccessibility makes the utilisation of the potentially profitable hardwood forests of British Guiana uneconomic.

Certain demographic features are relevant also. The development of nineteenth-century America was in large measure due to the scale on which immigration was allowed to take place. In contrast the immigration policies of Australia and Canada have been much more conservative. Of course the Indian problem is one of overpopulation. Her resources cannot be easily exploited, whereas in the oil-bearing regions of the Near and Middle East extremely small populations (Kuwait has some 300,000 inhabitants) are able, with outside technical help, to build up very rapidly a profitable industry.

Related to the difficulties of developing natural resources is the problem of accumulating or attracting capital, either from within the country or from abroad. The prospect of quick returns is likely to attract foreign capital, but in all too many economically underdeveloped countries the need for capital is acute and the difficulties of building it up severe. Often their basic source of wealth is land. To accumulate capital, cash crops are needed, and in order to produce these other sectors of the economy usually have to be developed. The necessary mechanical equipment has either to be made by building up a home industry or else imported. Modern agricultural methods also need the support of a fertiliser industry. All these developments themselves call for capital. The vicious circle is extremely difficult to break.

Another possible approach is based on the assumption that what is needed is for an existing subsistence economy to be temporarily retained but very considerably improved. Community development projects aim at using local people to construct roads, build houses and hospitals, improve agricultural methods, and so on. This kind of solution is implicit in the fundamental education programmes which have been sponsored by UNESCO and other organisations since the war. It seems particularly suited to conditions where large-scale mechanisation and industrialisation seem out of the question for some time to come.

Examples of national campaigns to accumulate capital by the use of unskilled manpower are found in Communist countries. The Chinese government has used mobile labour forces to construct a network of roads and bridges and to improve communications generally. But fundamentally, successful dispersed economic development depends upon the production and distribution of electric power, and these tasks cannot be completed without skilled personnel. Since the training of highly skilled manpower takes time, it is often more appropriate to introduce cheaper technologies rather than up-to-the-minute industries. Another reason of course is that modern technologies are difficult and expensive to maintain. It is improbable that they can be introduced into agricultural countries without massive capital investment from abroad.

The difficulties associated with the introduction of foreign capital are both economic and political. The two main sources are private investment, and loans or grants from foreign governments or international agencies. Private capital is often limited, and investors are reluctant to invest in non-profit-making enterprises such as the social services and public facilities. They also wish to ensure that they will not lose their capital through political action. Security of this kind depends upon assurances from the governments receiving aid and the firmness with which they are prepared to abide by their contractual agreements. Bilateral arrangements between governments frequently have political implications, particularly in the context of the Soviet–United States confrontation. For the same

reason massive capital aid channelled through international
agencies may meet political difficulties, although at least some
of the problems of capital are being met by the technical agencies of the United Nations. As a general rule, however, a figure
of 5 per cent of the investment in education has been given as
the limit of capital involving foreign exchange.

Whatever policy is pursued there are major educational implications. In the first place the educational system helps to
develop norms which can accelerate or impede economic
change. Again, the system inculcates associated concepts of
leadership and skills. It also acts as a selective device, either by
design or not, by directing young people into certain kinds of
occupation. Finally it provides members of special groups with
the knowledge required to promote economic development and
to reduce the gap between supply and demand. Evidently
education is not the only factor in the success or failure of
attempts to solve the economic problem outlined, but its contribution in certain circumstances can be decisive. Doubtless for
this reason economists are again urging the governments of the
world to spent more on education as a form of investment. It
seems desirable, however, to see how some of the other factors
already mentioned as contributing to economic growth depend upon the kind and quality of education provided and how
they may, on the other hand, minimise the advantages gained
from education.

Honest Government

Today national governments whether overtly or not participate
actively in the allocation of resources. This and other aspects of
planning are in themselves not enough to ensure success; technical know-how and quality of government are important and
should be given great weight in assessing the possibilities of
planned development. At one level this means, for example,
that public officials should be able to resist the temptation to
use their position for the purposes of direct personal gain. At
another level there is need for a corps of technocrats and
administrators who will act energetically, knowledgeably, and
responsibly in the interests of their country. In Europe great
emphasis has been placed upon the inculcation through educa-

tion of this kind of official honesty. Rewards, not only in the form of cash but by the conferment of high public status, have helped to give reality to these concepts of integrity.

It would be foolish, however, to imagine that the highest ideals of western probity are universally accepted either in theory or in practice. At worst most governments recognise the need to maintain a level of law and order so that economic development can proceed, but government control of investment policies and the distribution of capital accumulated is not necessarily a guarantee of sound economic growth. The quality and integrity of management in a competitive free enterprise economy in which self-interest provides powerful motivation has to be weighed against a situation in which the planners are public officials. There can be no general conclusion about which is better, since in each country it will be necessary to discover how leaders are recruited and with what kind of attitudes and knowledge they are provided. Since few modern economies are either totally planned or entirely free, the distinctions between the company director and the government technocrat are becoming increasingly narrow. Resistance is still found, however, in some political circles to the concept of political planning.

Social Organisation

Within the institutional pattern, several other indigenous institutions may retard development. One of these is the extended or joint family. The system implies that nepotism is a social duty. It operates against western standards of probity and indeed tends to be a disincentive to hard work by the energetic, who must share their returns with the family, and as little incentive to the lazy, who are able to enjoy a similar standard of living to their harder-working brethren. In a similar way, caste systems operating as a selective device deny to many of the more ambitious and energetic members of the community access to positions of greater responsibility. Another social institution is land tenure, which constitutes a firmly established barrier to economic development. It appears in different forms. The simple accumulation by an aristocracy or wealthy élite of vast tracts of land may result in its unproductive use, and the remainder of the land may be so broken up into small areas that they also are economically unproductive. In parts of Africa land tenure has, however, deeper psychological and social roots. For example land, in the first place, is often not a negotiable asset in Africa; it is held jointly by the clan or tribe. Group mores and prohibitions regulate its use by a family or an individual. Any attempt by a clan member to extend his area of cultivation may be feared and resisted by the leaders as a threat to their own power. Moreover, if land cannot be sold, industrial development is necessarily restricted and the movement of more energetic or better farmers into fertile areas is prevented. Land tenure is frequently one of the first problems government planners tackle. Fundamental organisational changes are often necessary as well as basic modifications of attitude. It should not be assumed, however, that the only way to solve the problem is to remove the land from communal control and pass it over to individual ownership. Such proposals usually meet with fierce and organised resistance. Where industrialisation is not contemplated in development plans a more effective approach is by educating the community or clan (if this is of manageable size) to which the land belongs. Such restrictions on industrialisation inevitably place some limitations on the extent and rate of a country's economic development, but the fullest and most rapid growth is not always desired or desirable. The number and severity of major societal adjustments which have to be made increase in proportion to the speed and completeness of the economic process.

Other important institutional resistance factors have been examined by O. F. Raum,[12] who points out that in Africa initial hostility to economic development was closely linked with the contacts made in its initial stages between African and European. The establishment of European schools undermined the authority of the kinship group. Urbanisation drew men away from the rural reserves, left broken families behind, and signalled a breakdown in moral standards. Parental authority was soon disregarded by the emancipated young and the position of the chief was placed in jeopardy. Often tribal authority was destroyed by force of arms. Out of this kind of situation new sources of leadership emerged, one of which, with an economic bias, was trade unionism.

The power of organised labour is, of course, a fundamental feature of modern industrialised societies, and the industrial and political activities of trade unions should be distinguished. In Europe and the U.S.A. they achieved power gradually, but British unions tend to be more active politically than those in America. During the nineteenth century industrialisation went on as it did with inevitable hardships for the masses, slums, long hours of work, and so on, partly because the unions were neither very strong nor effectively organised. In contrast, in semi-industrialised countries today (e.g. South Africa) the evolution of trade union power has been rapid. The political activities of trade unions and their power to influence productivity, labour mobility, hours of work, restrictive practices, and the like, become an extremely important factor in the process of development. Generally speaking, the hard price paid by the nineteenth-century European and American workers for the benefits now enjoyed in those countries is not today acceptable to organised labour anywhere. And union organisation is now such that political action is often effective. Consequently, the attitudes towards production and technical know-how of labour leaders are extremely important.

To be sure, restrictive practices are adopted not by workers exclusively; management and owners more interested in profits than in production may wish to restrict it so as to maintain prices. Again their willingness to invest in long-term compared with short-term projects, in indirectly productive rather than immediately profitable enterprises, and in low interest long-term returns instead of high interest and short-term gains will affect development. At the same time wage increases based on improved productivity are in principle still rejected by many trade unionists. The need for an industrial education to meet the new circumstances is apparent.

Education and Ideology

Ideological factors too are necessarily involved in the promotion of economic development. Certainly André Siegfried has said that within the European traditions there 'is a peculiar concept of the nature of production which has grown out of the industrial revolution of the eighteenth century, but which found its full realisation in its American phase during the twentieth'.[13] No doubt this is meant by foreigners when they refer to Americans as materialists. Perhaps Napoleon was saying much the same thing when he referred to the British as a nation of shopkeepers.

Max Weber and R. H. Tawney have, of course, linked a particular Christian ethic with the rise of capitalism, and Perry Miller[14] has made a special study of the attitudes of mind in America which contributed to economic development. Adam Smith was prepared to argue that the individual's own self-interest as he competes with his fellow-men would keep the process going. But the ability to pursue distant goals rather than immediate gains, a sense of dedication to hard work, an attitude of thrift, a spirit of adventure, ruthlessness, and charity have all contributed to the growth of industry and commerce in European countries and the U.S.A. These are not exclusively Christian norms, and many of them have been successfully copied by non-Europeans; for example by the Japanese when they transformed their country from a medieval to a highly industrialised society through action initiated at the time of the Meiji restoration. Such habits as punctuality, persistence, accuracy, and cooperation have been built into the activities of individuals working in industrial societies. Many of these habits are sanctioned by norms, others have been enforced by the processes involved in industry.

In any case it should not be supposed that everyone within the Greco-Judaic-Christian tradition shares all these norms equally. Platonists reject change as necessarily bad. The Aristotelian dichotomy between manual labour and that which befits a gentleman remains very much a part of the European tradition. Moreover the emphasis on the happiness of all the people rather than on self-interest, preached in Europe by such people as Robert Owen, has become an integral part of the normative pattern of some European societies. Some socialists in Britain have strongly urged that the element of competition in society should be reduced. If this were done new incentives would have to be devised to encourage production. Under Communism competition in the interests of the state or society has replaced competitive self-interest. Now liberal democracies committed to social welfare may have to look for incentives different from those which were effective before the war.

The resistance set up to economic and industrial development by non-European attitudes is well known. Fatalism, anthropomorphism, ancestor worship, and so on, are usually associated with norms which contrast rather sharply with the Greco-Christian traditions of rationalism and individualism, and with the concept that man, through the application of reason, can control his environment. Deeply ingrained habits of thought are not easily changed and the creation of incentives to work harder is difficult. Food, money, and prestige may all operate as such incentives, but not always. Food taboos, for example, are extremely difficult to break. The nutritionist does not necessarily succeed in changing food habits which hinder production by pointing out the nutritional advantages of one food over another. Taste is a marked cultural peculiarity, maintained in many cases by taboos and religious beliefs. To an Andean community the propitiation of the gods is more important than the cultivation of the sunflower (an unlucky and accursed plant to them) as a source of food. The oriental concept of *karma* reconciles a person to his present fate—the inevitable outcome of his behaviour in a previous life.

In summary it may be useful to draw up a list of relevant factors or data which should be taken into account when considering the outcomes of any proposed policy of economic development.

SOCIETY AND INSTITUTIONS

(i) Authority: age, birth; position in family, tribe etc.; religion; democracy; family-run society.
(ii) Ownership: land; property; means of production; livestock; remote management; large-scale industry.
(iii) Status: material possessions; number of children; cattle; initiation ceremonies.
(iv) Contractual Arrangements: law of contract; equality before the law; bride price.
(v) Social Taboos: caste: food habits.
(vi) Role of women: marriage; divorce; remarriage; position of widow; education; industry.
(vii) System of exchange and incentives; barter economy; monetary incentives; status.

(viii) Work incentives: personal need and satisfaction; virtue of work; profit; consumer goods; geographical mobility; social mobility; punctuality; leisure.

(ix) Responsibility: nepotism; charity; social good; self-interest; functionalism.

INDIVIDUALITY

(i) Uniqueness of individual in his life-span: stages of fulfilment of personality; actualisation of potential; concept of women; transmigration.

(ii) Inheritance of ability: innate ability; status by inheritance; fundamental characteristics of innate ability and occupation; caste system.

(iii) Equality: Christian; before the law; family and tribal status; caste; ancestor worship.

(iv) Value of individual life: fatalism; saving life; population control.

THEORY OF KNOWLEDGE

(i) Nature of truth: absolutism; relativism; true values; instrumental values.

(ii) Source of Knowledge: God; scriptures; religious texts; essentialism-empiricism.

(iii) Methods of acquiring knowledge: analytical reasoning; contemplation; mysticism; action.

(iv) Value of knowledge: power; know-how; for its own sake; wisdom.

(v) Attitude to change: degeneration; progress; conformity.

(vi) The real world: manifestations of knowledge; unity; atomisation; specialisation.

Another way of saying that some or all of these factors, either as norms or institutions, will restrict economic growth is that if policies designed to initiate economic growth are to succeed many attitudes and institutions will have to change.

Over the years a good deal of evidence has accumulated about the difficulties of introducing, and maintaining at a vastly accelerated rate, processes of industrialisation which in Europe and North America took centuries to complete. From successful examples of rapid economic development, such as Japan and the U.S.S.R., lessons can also be learned, as will be seen in subsequent chapters when some of the less desirable consequences of rapid industrialisation are analysed. The crux of the comparative educationists' role is to make choice in educational policy less arbitrary and haphazard, and to show the dangers of pursuing mutually incompatible aims. In all this, more attention should be paid to the ambivalent attitudes of the public and the degree to which new institutions and skills can succeed only in a climate of opinion conducive to their reasonably smooth operation. Two educational tasks are to prepare management to work out policy and reveal its implications and the public to make realistic choices between alternatives.

Social Justice and Educational Expansion

In the event, until the sixties, post-war educational policies were based more on concepts of social justice than on realistic assessments of allocation problems. Minimum standards of desirable education were laid down by governments. In some instances these turned out to be statements of intention beyond the possibilities of fulfilment. In other cases they more or less gave statutory status to provisions already in existence.

One of the most important standards against which the adequate provision of education is measured is length of compulsory schooling. Already at the end of the war, between seven and ten years of schooling were compulsory in Europe, North America, and some British Dominions. Post-war policies in these countries included proposals to lengthen these periods. Debate turned on the precise increase in the number of years and the date of introduction. In many low-income countries, on the other hand, statutory compulsory education had to be set up *de novo*, but the more optimistic estimates of the immediate post-war era were modified at conferences held in Addis Ababa, Karachi, and Santiago in the early sixties.

Of course from a comparative viewpoint crude comparisons between lengths of compulsory schooling may be misleading, since the length of school years, and the number of hours of instruction per week, also vary. A very comprehensive survey of the time young people are *expected* to be in school throughout the world is given in UNESCO's comparative study *The Organization of the School Year*.[15]

143

Standards of equipment, textbooks, and accommodation can also be laid down fairly easily, and in the post-war reconstruction period lavish provisions of space and facilities were accepted by the Labour Government in Britain, and in some local authority areas school buildings were placed in the luxury class. Apart from basic classroom space specifications, criteria can also be established concerning such special academic facilities as gymnasia, science laboratories, libraries, and sports grounds. On the health side desirable hygienic facilities, and the inclusion of dental and medical inspection rooms, can easily be specified. Frequently in low-income countries expenditure on these aspects has been lavish.

Again it is relatively easy to state the maximum class size of, say, primary and secondary schools. Figures of forty for primary schools and thirty for secondary schools are not unusual as desired maxima. Related to these standards are those of pupil-teacher ratios, which, if considered separately from class size, give some indication of the number of lessons a teacher is expected to give each week. In France for example the standard for a *lycée agrégé* is 15, in the Soviet Union for teachers beyond the fourth grade 18. These and other formal conditions of teacher service give some idea of acceptable minimum standards. So too do formal recruitment, training, and certification requirements.

Less easy to state unequivocally are minimum content requirements, although in many countries, notably France and other continental European nations, curricula are prescribed and can be obtained from Ministry publications. These curricula obviously follow the school types and are closely related to school-leaving examinations and certificates. The latter, parenthetically, serve as a form of assessment not only of the use individual pupils have made of the school but of the system itself.

It is, of course, in these areas that measures of minimum standards are difficult to devise in a manner acceptable to everyone concerned. In other words consensus about minimum standards is likely to exist in very few sectors of the educational pattern, and even here the indices are crude. Evidently in periods of debate and reform the possibilities of reaching principles of allocation on this basis are remote in practice, if not in theory.

The total cost of providing these minimum services when once laid down can, however, be calculated if the apparatus necessary for collecting the required statistics is available. Accurate estimates of the total number of school-age children are difficult to obtain in some countries where census-taking techniques hardly measure up to the scope of the problem. Afghanistan reported, for example, that the census estimates on which her development plans were based had given a figure 20 per cent lower than the actual one. Even so, the determination with which the Japanese suddenly in 1947 increased the period of compulsory education from six to nine years has been matched in few, if any, countries. Nearly everywhere, for example, one index of the failure of governments to meet what are often statutory obligations in educational provision is the shortage of teachers measured against accepted standards of class size and pupil/teacher ratios. Other indications of progress falling far behind development plans will be referred to in later chapters. The reasons for the discrepancies are political and economic. Faced with other demands, governments frequently find that the neglect of education creates fewer difficulties than other kinds of neglect. It is also apparent that not all the aspects of investment were considered when some plans were drawn up. Manpower resources and needs are notoriously difficult to anticipate, and in England, for example, little attention was given until the early sixties to the problem of wastage among young women teachers. In some instances, as in the case of India's stated intention to provide universal primary education in a far shorter time than was possible, political ambitions were economically unrealistic. In short, even when plans are based upon what were considered to be minimum educational standards, it is still necessary for an order of priorities to be established if development plans are to proceed with reasonable satisfaction. Again the basic problem of allocation presents itself.

By the early sixties most of these points had been taken. Conferences organised or supported by UNESCO were held within a short space of time in Addis Ababa, Karachi, and Santiago. At each of them the human rights principle concerning access to education was proclaimed, but was ameliorated by a great awareness of the allocation problem. Certain targets were established in terms of the needs of the various countries within each region by breaking the requirements first into financial, material, and manpower needs, and then further specifying requirements in each of them. Estimates of cost led to two conclusions: first, that external aid would be needed, and second, that orders of priority would have to be drawn up. In general, however, the objectives were stated rather modestly. The Karachi plan envisaged that member nations would attain by 1980 free and compulsory education for at least seven years. Further assessment of resources persuaded some governments that even these aims could not be achieved, and Nepal reduced the 1980 goal to five years' schooling. In general, however, estimates of cost led to the same two conclusions at each of the conferences, namely that external aid would be needed, and that orders of priority would have to be drawn up.

The principle adopted was really the economic one. Education was explicitly regarded as a factor in economic growth. And in a variety of forms the conclusion emerged that in the interests of economic growth priority should be given not to the extension of primary schooling but to the provision of technical and vocational education at the secondary and higher levels, i.e. for the fifteen to twenty age group. The object of this decision was to make possible the rapid creation of higher level cadres of manpower. Nevertheless it was recognised that the maintenance of a balance of development between the different stages of education was necessary. Over-emphasis on primary schools would jeopardise economic growth; over-development of higher education would result in a group of educated unemployed.

Within the wide field of the educational sector, some general recommendations were reached. It was noted that in the United States and in the Soviet Union the distribution of expenditure on education between the three levels was: primary 60 per cent, secondary 25 per cent, and tertiary 15 per cent. In western Europe the respective figures were 70 per cent, 20 per cent, and 10 per cent. At Karachi it was hoped that there could be a movement towards this kind of distribution of expenditure in the member countries.

The second area of choice concerns the type of education to which the major portion of resources should be devoted. The big issue turns on the merits of investing in vocational education rather than general education. Policy decisions in this field lead either to reforms in the curricula of existing schools or in the establishment of new school types. At Addis Ababa the claims of science were strongly urged, and in each of the three conferences the importance of developing technical and vocational schools was appreciated, although in Karachi the main aim— the provision of universal primary education—was kept well in mind.

These decisions recall to mind the kind of debates which were being pursued with vigour during the nineteenth century. Then in Europe and America the allocation issue was argued, if perhaps not in present-day terms. More or less adequate public support was first made available for secondary rather than primary schools in many European countries. In these one curricular choice lay between the classical languages, modern languages, and the natural sciences. On the whole the battle to retain the classics—still being waged with some success even today—was won. The place of commercial and technical studies also provoked heated controversy. One policy implied that they were not suitable subjects for school instruction at all; another that if they were taught the abstracted principles should be presented in general education schools; a third position was that they were important and should be provided in as practical a manner as possible in schools recognised as vocational. The European answers were in general different from those finally accepted in the U.S.A. Typically a multi-school type organisation of post-primary schools was established in Europe, although the differences in detail between the English, French, and German prototypes were considerable. So also were the differences in curricula. In general importance was given to the academic schools. This fact is borne out by a review of investment policy in education in England and Wales. During the 1902–39 period far more money went into the development of academic grammar (then termed 'secondary') schools than into any other of the various types of post-primary schools.

Careful comparative studies (largely historical) of this kind would be very revealing. They would not, however, provide general conclusions about a correct order of priorities of investment within education based upon economic growth. Naturally the general order of investment is also important. Certainly the evidence from nineteenth-century Germany indicates that extensive investment in vocational schools at a number of levels beyond the primary stage including higher technological institutions is an important factor in rapid economic growth. Equally successful were similar policies introduced in the U.S.S.R. during the nineteen-thirties. But American educational expansion took place from 1870 on at the high school level, and far more general-curriculum schools than vocational high schools were established. It seems clear that in many low-income countries today investment in higher education would result in less wastage and higher short-term returns. In principle such a policy implies the acceptance of a selective system of education based no doubt on a slowly expanding system of primary schools.

Once a basic decision to relate educational investment to economic returns has been taken it is apparent that public educational policy can be directed to the achievement of specific economic goals. A good deal is known about the kind of skills modern industry needs. To be sure, on the management side a debate on the relative merits of the liberally educated person as compared with the specially trained administrator continues even in the U.S.A. Europeans have traditionally tended to leave top administrative and commercial functions to men trained in either law or the classical languages. How to train personnel for the technical branches of industry is not quite so debatable. Four groups of technically trained personnel can be distinguished. First, the technologists with the highest qualifications in pure and applied science are expected to make signal and creative advances in design, techniques, and fundamental processes. This, it is sometimes argued, is necessarily a small, highly selected group, invariably university trained. Great attention has been paid to the production of this group both in western Europe and in the U.S.S.R., through technological institutes and the universities.

Middle-range technologists and technicians are those people who are capable of limited research in design but whose main role is routine research and analysis in industrial processes. They are concerned with the immediate techniques of manufacture, production line operation, and so on. Usually they form a much larger group than the technologists, perhaps in the ratio 5 to 1. Frequently they have a university degree or its equivalent from a technical institute.

Craftsmen are the men with special skills not only in the traditional sense of producing articles individually but in the tasks they perform in industry. An example of a craftsman in a large industry would be the person who judges the timing of the various processes. While many of these skills were previously acquired by long experience in a particular industry, they are now being replaced by routine analysis carried out in special departments and laboratories and staffed by personnel in the middle technologist group. Operations in the plant are performed on the basis of the information provided by these special departments. Many of the technical and vocational schools in Germany and Holland continue to train craftsmen for this group. Clearly, as industrial processes become more automatic, the technical skills of this group will be in less demand, and training approaching that of the middle-range technologists will be necessary.

Finally the machine operators in industry perform mechanical routine tasks on the assembly line. The skills used by this group can usually be learned very quickly. Previously this group was the most numerous in any industrial operation of any size. Increasingly their tasks are becoming even simpler.

The situation in industrialising countries corresponds in many ways much more to nineteenth-century industrial developments. Skills can usually be taught and learned very quickly under expert instruction, but they are difficult to retain without constant supervision. Moreover, although operating skills can be learned, the ability to maintain and repair equipment (involving routine maintenance schedules) is less easily acquired. For instance, foremen in the west generally have many years of factory experience. The newly industrialising countries clearly have not had time to develop such a corps of veterans, so that personnel at this level of management are perhaps the most difficult of all to recruit. Another serious question concerns the actual skills taught. Those taken over from highly developed economies are often quite inappropriate for the type of industry in a less industrialised country. For example, the skills learned for assembly line production in a U.S. automobile factory are of

Socio-Economic Problems and Educational Policy

little use to the mechanic who virtually has to make the whole car. Automation, indeed, involves a shift from line operations and skilled craftsmen to personnel trained as middle and upper range technologists. The real resources required to train these men in the numbers in which they will be required in very modern industries are bound to be greater than where apprenticeship training was appropriate. Examples of the way in which industrial skills have been broken down and training programmes devised to meet the special requirements of an industry are given in the *Year Book of Education, 1954*, and in particular in the accounts of the training schemes of ARAMCO in Saudi Arabia and the SENAI organisation in Brazil.

The Consequences of Investment in Education

There is little doubt that selective investment in certain kinds of education is likely to lead to more immediate economic benefits in low-income countries. To ensure the success of such policies implies that some members of the public can be persuaded that in their own long-term interests it is better to forgo some apparent benefits in the immediate future. Of course if public demand for education is matched by public determination to ensure the success of policies proposed the solution of restraint would be less necessary.

But, as Mendes-France says, the processes through which demand and choice operate make the allocation of resources to education in terms of a single purpose, e.g. economic return, virtually impossible. The weight given to investment in education will depend almost entirely on its vote-catching appeal. Since relatively few members of the public benefit directly, appeals for increased funds are less effective than in the case of, say, health services. Again, the hierarchical position of a government minister or official in charge of education *vis-à-vis* his colleagues will help to determine the importance given to education. His ability to acquire a larger portion of the national investment cake will depend in part upon his own strength of character and political ability. The election campaigns in postwar Britain reflect the relatively low priority given to education compared with health, housing, and the nationalisation of industry. American national politics are such that unearmarked

150

federal aid to education has little chance of being accepted by either house of Congress.

As for the type of programme envisaged, it is evident that left-wing political parties are more inclined to press the human rights argument and advocate policies of investment which ignore the practical economic possibilities of implementation, and to pay little heed to the economic consequences except in very general terms. Right-wing politicians are generally more disposed to listen to and accept the economic argument; and certainly if industrial efficiency depends more upon technical skills and organisation and less on individual attitudes and industrial relations, the investment in technical education of a narrowly vocational kind would seem wise. Unfortunately for the supporters of this viewpoint, industrial relations in many countries in the second half of the twentieth century are as vital to economic progress as technical skills.

As for the public, individuals and groups have ambivalent attitudes concerning the value of education. The assessment of private gain even for parents and children is not easy to compute; in any case it is likely to be long-term rather than short-term. This is one reason why it is difficult to retain children in schools, particularly in the early periods of universal schooling. The choice between keeping their children at school and allowing them to work on the land or in factories presents itself to parents as one between immediate tangible advantage and distant, somewhat uncertain, benefits. Compulsory attendance laws in France and Britain, among other western nations, were until fairly recently enforced only with the help of school attendance officers.

In subsistence economies the time spent by a child in school represents a personal investment in education, since he could otherwise spend it profitably on the land. And naturally, the older the child the greater his economic value. Thus in many areas, and particularly in Asia, a high initial demand for education soon falls off, perhaps, in part, because some parents quickly see the futility of traditional forms of formal education. Literacy has little meaning or use in innumerable villages of the East. Much attention has been given to this problem in India. The basic school programme has tried to meet the difficulty by basing the primary school work on local crafts and industries.

Paradoxically, however, a long history of English-type education makes literacy an alluring goal at some stages. Just as before independence the vernacular schools failed to attract as many students as the English schools, there now remains the question whether the basic schools will become acceptable to the population in general. The paradox is not hard to explain; while some of the long-term benefits of an English-type education have become apparent, those that are likely to accrue from the newer-type schools have not. Here, as elsewhere, a conflict between national policy, as a reflection of social and national needs, and the wishes of parents arises. Can the demand for education, when it has been aroused, be directed into different avenues in a way which will satisfy parents and achieve national goals? In countries like India and in some parts of Africa straightforward personal preferences seem likely to determine the kind of education provided. Some western observers deplore the continued interest of African universities in classical languages on the ground that more science is now needed. But if qualifications in the classics still confer political power, many students understandably continue to study them in spite of the fact that the more immediate national need appears to be for technologists.

The scale of individual preferences in the light of norms differs so much that generalisations about them would be of little value. Each scale has to be assessed in terms of a particular culture or context. Many examples imply that in few areas of Africa or Asia are non-academic non-European studies acceptable at the higher levels. The prestige of European-type education is considerable and may remain so. The incentive is in many cases political rather than economic, so that students who have become technically qualified often prefer to return to politics rather than to a professional occupation. Evidently consumer demand operates against the economic interests of the country through its influence on allocation policy. To be sure, a powerful executive may be in a position to determine allocation policies against the general wishes of the people; and it is perhaps the success with which Communist governments have followed rigorous policies in the interests of national economic development which has impressed outside observers.

But, as will be analysed in a later chapter, excessive interest in economic development has led even in the Soviet Union to unwanted and very difficult problems of readjustment. It is important to reiterate that were the proportion of public money that it is desirable should be spent on education known; were the best techniques of allocation within education available; and were it possible to enforce these choices, it would still be an open question whether or not the economic criterion alone was sufficient to justify action being taken. The economic consequences of rapid development should be weighed against other possible non-economic consequences before vital decisions are taken. It is all very well to correlate in comparative studies per capita income and production costs with national expenditures on education, but the results do not give a complete picture either of the factors contributing to high incomes or of the other consequences of educational expenditure.

For example, serious political instability is easily recognised, but the constituents of desirable stability are much harder to define so as to become the goals of education. Traditionally the schools have achieved something in this field. But the dangers of political disintegration and warfare accompanying rapid economic development should be apparent from the history of the twentieth century. Even more difficult to evaluate are such criteria as social harmony and personal development. How can the optimum rate of social mobility be judged? What are the consequences of rapid social mobility and how can they be weighed against slower rates? Similarly, how can the effectiveness of personal adjustment to rapid societal changes be judged? Do present-day mental illness figures provide an index? Or do the increases in number merely reflect changes in diagnostic techniques?

Equally important then is the attempt made to assess the likely non-economic consequences of educational policy designed to improve the economy. Educationally this has resulted in continuous debate about the relative merits of specialised technical vocational education compared to general liberal education. What are likely to be the political consequences of introducing a highly differentiated secondary school system into an authoritarian-oriented society? This kind of system obviously gives rise to or consolidates certain class structures and might place political power in the hands of a small unrepresentative élite. A number of criteria may be adopted to assess the desirability or otherwise of the consequences of certain policies.

These may include, in addition to those already mentioned, social harmony and personal development. It is immediately obvious that the consequences fall into various categories. Some indices, such as economic viability, technical efficiency, and even political stability, are fairly easy to draw up. The others are vague but nevertheless important. Criteria may have to be devised to make them in some way measurable.

Certainly to be realistic the criteria should be related to the normative patterns and the proposed goals of any social order. The crux of the problem today is that, however vaguely defined, the economic expectations of millions of people throughout the world far outrun their ability to satisfy them. The deficiencies are to be found in all three patterns—in the availability of resources, in the institutions through which economic development takes place, and in the attitudes of the very people whose expectations are so high. It is to the educational implications of these manifold problems that some comparative educationists are turning their attention.

Chapter VII

ADMINISTRATIVE SYSTEMS AND DECISION MAKING IN EDUCATION

THE allocation problem is central to the success or failure of the planned development of education. But as Hayek's analysis suggests, it is not only a technical problem but has associated with it political issues with long histories. Broadly these concern the aims of education and the methods of achieving them. Clearly in periods of educational flux, as the post-war period has been, not everyone is agreed on either the ends or the means of education. To be sure in the new situation powerful new forces have entered into the conflicts to control education. Many current problems, however, retain in modified form the characteristics of those which originated for the most part in the nineteenth century.

Within the European-North-American context, for example, there were two, not necessarily unrelated, battles for the control of education. At one level there was a prolonged fight between the clerical and secular authorities, and at another between the central and local governments. Indeed during the nineteenth century the anxiety of some reformers to establish some form of lay control over education was matched only by the determination of the Church or churches to resist it. In many countries almost continuous battles between the Church as a political institution and non-sectarian and secularist groups occurred, the details of which naturally vary. If in France, for example, the power of the Church was checked by the Revolution, the conflict was soon resumed. Not until the 1880s was public education effectively laicised through legislation; since that time the Church-State controversy, which flared again after the second world war, has taken a somewhat different course, but the protagonists continue to be the churchmen and the anticlerics. In England the fight was between churchmen of different persuasions, and the denominational issue was one on which Kay Shuttleworth, widely regarded as the founder of that country's system of primary schools, was finally defeated. Even in the United States sectarian groups did not relinquish their authority without a struggle.

At the same time the second conflict persisted. Many reformers feared the consequences of the central government's gaining control over education. They appreciated that the State had some responsibility, but over what spheres of education it should exercise control was debatable. Liberal theory maintained that the best government was the one which interfered least with the self-interest of individuals and simply protected their rights. Yet educational provision, like defence, could not simply be left to private individuals. The organisation of a sound service necessitated the exercise of power by some individuals or groups of individuals. Politically one of the arguments advanced against the authority of monarchs and the aristocracy was that power rightly belonged to the people. In more specific terms this theory implied that as many individuals as possible should participate in the activities of government, or in other words, control should be at the local rather than at the central level.

A number of educational issues were also debated in the context of these major controversies during the nineteenth century. One was whether emphasis should be given to the education of future leaders or to that of the masses. In the event various answers were given and found expression in the policies which initiated the development of national systems of education.

The importance of leadership in a democratic society was recognised in most European countries. Educational policy was designed to ensure a steady and growing supply of educated leaders and administrators. The growth of secondary schools throughout Europe is a reflection of this awareness. In many continental countries this task was taken to be a responsibility of the central government. Napoleon's establishment in 1808 of high quality State secondary schools (*lycées*) is an example of a policy widely followed in Europe. Jefferson too had in mind a system of schools which would ensure that national leaders were selected from among the aristocracy of talent when he made his proposals for a State system in Virginia. England, to Matthew Arnold's dismay, was slow to follow this policy, even though the revitalised 'public' schools were in part meeting the social demand for more political, industrial, and commercial leaders and for administrators at home and abroad. Even in 1902 under the Morant Act the new, publicly financed, 'secondary' schools were to be administered by local education authorities. In the United States the policy of the federal government's taking a large measure of responsibility for the maintenance of secondary schools has virtually never been seriously considered except in the area of vocational education.

As for the education of the masses, policies in Europe showed another face. There was a widely accepted principle that primary education should be the responsibility of the local communities. Legislation in Prussia, France, and Sweden, for example, reflected this faith. In England, too, the elementary schools came under the local school boards in the 1870s. Faith in local control in the United States, although not unchallenged, was reflected in a proliferation of local school districts. In fact circumstances in many countries made it necessary for regional or central government agencies to intervene even at this level by providing a measure of financial support, by establishing systems of inspection, and by attempting to make attendance at school compulsory. In many instances the difficulties of raising sufficient money locally to provide for all children comparable facilities and similarly qualified teachers were instrumental in promoting various forms of central control.

One approach was through the establishment of a corps of educational administrators. Many of the nineteenth-century pioneers of comparative education were, as previously indicated, concerned with the administration of emerging national systems of education. Indeed, many of them were the first incumbents of secular administrative positions in education. Not infrequently they helped to establish the foundations of future national systems of administrative control. They were, of course, unable to perform this task on the basis of principle alone. Each system was created within a particular power structure and in the context of specific national norms. Yet each of the pioneers of comparative education faced rather similar problems as far as the control of education was concerned. Solutions to them have occupied the attention of reformers ever since.

Centralised and Decentralised Systems of Administration

On the whole, over the years, there has been a growth in the power of central authorities. One of the main reasons for this development has undoubtedly been the increased cost of providing educational facilities which measure up to national standards. Yet for political reasons local control is often still regarded as desirable even though much of the money for education comes from central agencies. The danger for comparative educationists is that in classifying national systems of education as either centralised or decentralised simple conclusions are drawn; for example, that the former are necessarily totalitarian and the latter democratic. Certainly one aspect of the liberal faith has been, and is, that there is a direct relationship between democracy and the decentralised control of education. It is, however, one thing to argue that the diffusion of power is a desirable aim of democratic policy, and another to maintain that establishing, under any circumstances, systems of local control (particularly of education) will necessarily promote political democracy. Certainly it is possible to hold as a fundamental principle that democratic systems ought to be decentralised, but, in practice, the successful operation of any system of administration depends on a complex of relationships between it and the societal configurations.

In fact, in any analysis of administrative systems it would be well to recognise that in all probability there will be some kind of formal organisation concerned with the control of education at each of several levels; namely *national, regional, local,* and inside individual *institutions*. The subtle interaction of these should form the basis of a thorough comparative study. Apparently these relationships differ according to individual aspects of education, often in accordance with legislation. No better example of this principle can, perhaps, be quoted than the provisions of the American Bill of Rights which, except where otherwise stated in the Constitution, leaves responsibility for education to individual states. Interpretations of the Constitution have made possible the provision of earmarked federal aid to education. Similarly, on the basis of the English 1944 Education Act, a distinction should be drawn between national salary negotiations between local government officials and teachers' organisations, and the payment by the local authorities of teachers' salaries.

An even closer look is required, however, at the policy-making processes within each formal system of administration. Indeed there is need for a conceptual framework for rigorous comparative studies of administrative systems. The analysis provided by Talcott Parsons in *Administrative Theory in Education*[1] provides an excellent starting-point. It presupposes that the mechanics of administration and control through decision-making processes are never simple, that inside any organisation there is constant interaction between groups of persons, and that any formal organisation of this kind is in constant and reciprocal interaction with other institutions within the social context and responds in some way to the demands of individuals or spokesmen of groups in society. A further assumption made here is that examples of Parsons' formal organisation are found at every level—central, regional, local, and within an institution—of the educational system. Only a careful analysis on the basis of function, level, and aspect of policy, and the interactions between a complex of institutions will enable a rigorous comparative study to be made.

Formal Organisations

Parsons maintains that in any formal organisation three levels should be distinguished, the technical, the managerial, and the public interest. Each level is identified by the functions its members perform. Thus in education the technical functions are performed by teachers, the managerial by administrators or executive officers, and the public interest by a variety of elected or appointed persons serving on committees, boards, or in institutions. As for relationships between the levels, in no case, according to Parsons, are the vertical relationships between personnel purely authoritarian. Orders issued by the top échelon are never simply passed down the line. In terms of policy formation, adoption, and implementation there are subtle inter-actions at the two points of articulation, first between the public interest level and the managerial, and then between this level and members of the technical group. Moreover certain relation-ships may, and in some cases do, exist between the technical and the public interest levels, which modify the other relation-ships. Indeed it may not always be possible sharply to define and place without reservations into one or other of the groups the functions of each person working within the formal organisa-tion. In general the English headmaster is less likely than the American school principal to be placed unequivocally in the managerial level. Indeed one object of a careful comparative study would be to reveal the extent to which overlaps of func-tion exist between certain members of the articulating groups.

Perhaps at this point it should be noted that nationally, re-gionally, locally, and in single institutions the formal organisa-tion will include members of some or all three levels. There may be elected, for each system, public interest groups concerned with education. In the same way at the managerial level there may exist national inspectors and education officers with re-gional and or local counterparts. Again some teachers may, as civil servants, for some purposes fall conveniently within the national formal organisation, while others as employees of the local authority should be considered members of another formal organisation. The precise functions of the personnel within these different organisations will vary, but it is obvious that relation-ships between each of them are likely to be close. This is not to say that contact between the national public interest level will necessarily be with the regional or local public interest group, or that contact between the respective managerial personnel will be closest. These relationships too should be the subject of comparative analysis.

Certain principles should facilitate the study both of these inter-organisation relationships and the vertical relationships within each of them. First, some relationships will be regulated by legislation. Teachers' certification may fall into this category. Similarly the appointment of local education officers may need, by law, the approval of the national agency. Many relationships are not, however, regulated by law, and so they should be studied by reference to the power structure and the mechanics of its operation. For example, members of one group often organise themselves to protect their own interests. Teachers' unions operate in this manner, either at the local or national levels. The effectiveness of these associations will vary greatly from one country to another just as within any educational system the extent of their power will depend upon the sphere of activity. One basis of power, for any group, will be the esoteric knowledge possessed by its members by virtue of which they are able to perform their special tasks.

In fact, statutory position, the institutionalised power of his position, and the role accorded to him by custom will combine to determine the manner in which each person performs his task. An inspector may be given certain specific tasks to perform *vis-à-vis* the schools, such as advising on methods of teaching, assessing teachers, and organising courses of study. The manner in which he is able to perform these duties will depend upon the institutionalised power of the headmaster or principal of the school and the role traditionally accorded to him. In this respect it is therefore necessary to study the norms associated with the fulfilment of roles. Using the model presented by Jacob W. Getzels in *Administrative Theory in Education* it should be possible to assess the relative importance given in selected countries to personality and institutionalised behaviour in the performance of tasks. Selection procedures will, of course, indicate in a practical manner this relative weighting. Thus, for example, personality traits (including intellectual ability) may count for more in the appointment of inspectors than the possession of formal paper qualifications. Again, glancing at differences of emphasis in England and the U.S.A., it is clear that the English teacher is expected in an intuitive way to know his students without carefully compiling record cards. American counselling schemes, particularly in large schools, reflect a more institutionalised approach to the problem. It should be remembered, of course, that community attitudes and sheer school size also help to determine the policies adopted and the roles assigned to personnel within the organisation.

Naturally the possession of esoteric knowledge by members of each of the groups helps to determine the vertical relationships. Recognition by the public interest group that members of the managerial and technical groups possess skills and information which they do not, restricts the spheres in which they are prepared unilaterally to formulate policy and attempt to have it adopted. Legislation or custom usually define rather precisely the area in which members of the public interest group elected on the basis of political party affiliations are expected to exert their influence. In general they may claim the right to decide major issues of policy without wishing to formulate the detailed regulating policies. Equally important in the examining of these relationships are the codes of ethics shared by the managerial and technical groups. For the managerial group loyalty to whichever political party is in power may be central to its professional code of behaviour. Similarly it may be an unwritten law that teachers do not normally strike to press wage claims.

At the other point of articulation between the managerial and technical levels the three principles can again be seen to operate. A sense of professional solidarity, and an appreciation, sometimes on the basis of special qualifications, of the esoteric knowledge possessed by members of the technical function group could give to members of the two groups a considerable sense of equality. Other forms of protection for the technical group are possible; thus while the French inspectors make a full written report on individual teachers, the latter are shown what has been written before it goes into their dossiers. The duty of Her Majesty's Inspectors in England and Wales is merely to advise and not to issue directives. Tradition makes this more than a polite fiction.

Indeed prior to the introduction of mass education the sense of professional community between members of the three levels within the educational establishment was very considerable. In medieval Europe close relationships existed between the schools and the universities; men educated in the communities of scholars entered all fields of public life. Even when State secondary schools were set up, as in France, this situation continued. Since administrators shared with teachers in the schools and university professors the same standards of academic learning, their prestige was high and their power considerable. Many elements of this professional solidarity between administrators and teachers remain as far as the secondary school systems of Europe are concerned.

The introduction of universal primary instruction resulted in the partial breakdown of the established order in education. Few countries could afford, or indeed wished, to have all the teachers trained in the universities. Moreover the autonomy of the latter was such that they could maintain that the training of primary school teachers was not their concern, being no doubt convinced that few of the intending teachers could benefit from university courses. The growth of a dual system of teacher training in Europe weakened professional solidarity in many ways. Through the power of their numbers the less qualified school teachers (i.e. non-graduates) in England have been able through their trade unions to win salary advantages at the expense of their university-trained colleagues. For a number of historical reasons, however, they do not have the prestige associated with persons to whom a university degree has been awarded, and the relationships between teachers and the managerial group, many of whom are still university graduates, often from Oxford or Cambridge, are consequently less close and more hierarchical. The reform of teacher training is in many countries the key to the re-establishment of a truly professional group of educationists.

Power was also dispersed in the two ways already mentioned. The churches, providing members for each of the three levels, began to lose their dominating control over educational policy, and the introduction of local financial autonomy in education in many countries, which were nevertheless attempting to create national policies, meant that a special corps of administrators operating at the managerial level had to be built up. These officials were in certain fields able to ensure a measure of national conformity in spite of the local control of policy in many fields.

Administrative Reforms

Administrative reforms have tended to place in the central agencies more and more responsibility for policy framing and adoption. This is particularly the case in those aspects of education which are considered vital to national security and economic development. This has been the case for more than a hundred years in the U.S.A., and it was written into the Indian system of educational control when the country became independent. Indeed in spite of a strong desire to retain local autonomy national legislation in many places tends to operate powerfully in certain areas of education if not yet in all. For example, although in England and Wales teachers are employed by local authorities, there is a national salary scale for teachers in publicly maintained schools, there are national entrance requirements to training colleges, and the status of qualified teacher is a national award. In France there are nationally devised curricula which are followed not only in the State and municipal schools but also in the private institutions. Again the Napoleonic concept of a national university and a national corps of administrators finds practical expression in the administrative arrangements in France. Obviously the extent to which the federal government is able to participate in the formulation, adoption, and implementation of policy in the United States is strictly limited, but there are nevertheless national agencies which operate in a way which enables a greater measure of uniformity to exist than would be supposed from the system of local autonomy.

It is doubtful whether or not the universities in any country should be regarded as falling within any of these formal organisations or not. In many cases they are national institutions and faculty members are often civil servants, but the autonomy they enjoy as institutions complicates any analysis of the mechanics of policy formulation *vis-à-vis* the public interest group. Certainly the universities have attempted to maintain their ancient privileges and in many respects continue to dominate some features of the entire educational system, particularly in the academic rather than the financial or administrative spheres.

In spite of the general tendency everywhere for the central government and semi-public national organisations to become more powerful in policy matters there are in most countries a number of built-in arrangements which prevent the formal organisation from becoming completely monolithic. Undoubtedly the universities represent an important safeguard because of their traditions and power. A more detailed analysis of the basis of this power has already been given. Protection against the usurpation of power has also to be sought in the codes of professional behaviour (either formalised or implicit) and the sense of social responsibility shared by members of each of the levels within the formal organisation. These codes together with the esoteric knowledge possessed by members offer internal protection, and give a professional solidarity to personnel. There is nevertheless danger, particularly as the quantity and complexity of the esoteric knowledge available to members of a formal organisation increase. Thus it is also necessary to study the relationships it has with other social institutions in what Parsons describes as lateral relationships.

Moral and Professional Authority

Before returning to describe some of the institutions through which these relationships operate in education, it would perhaps be well to analyse briefly the basis of professional authority in education. Critical dualism again throws light on the dilemma of responsibility for decision-making in education. It implies that a distinction can, and should, be made between the professional authority of the educationist and his moral obligation to listen, and perhaps respond, to certain kinds of requests or criticisms from the lay public. The assumption that there are sociological laws or predictive generalisations implies that the professional authority of the educationist rests upon his ability, based upon research in its broadest sense, to formulate these testable laws and apply them to the operation of educational institutions. On the other hand the broad cultural assumptions or norms of the society in which the educationist works should be known to him, but his authority to accept or reject them is certainly no greater than that of the lay critic or reformer. In other words it is not for the educationist *per se* to determine the norms in accordance with which the educational system is to operate. His professional task is to use his knowledge of sociological laws or predictive generalisations to achieve stated aims and objectives.

Unfortunately professional studies in education have developed rather slowly and the volume of tested material is limited. Psychology was the first social science to receive much attention. More recently there has been a growth of interest in the sociology and the economics of education and in comparative education. A growth in the study of the politics of education is to be expected. On the American side of the Atlantic progress has been fairly rapid and a corpus of esoteric knowledge is being built up in education. Certainly the strengthening of professional autonomy in education finally rests upon the greater availability of knowledge based upon the research findings of workers in these various fields. This information has to be synthesised and made available for use by educationists at whatever level of the formal organisation they perform. Its availability is a prerequisite to claims of professional autonomy.

As for the moral obligation of the formal organisation to respond to suggestions, advice, criticism from other social groups the answer is not so straightforward. Certainly to understand the processes a study of the lateral relationships within society is necessary. Naturally, existing political institutions help to determine what is possible. Free and periodic elections, a free press, freedom of individuals to organise as political parties or pressure groups are important elements in the maintenance of democratic forms of government. Nevertheless the efficiency of an educational system to achieve certain goals may depend on the delicate balance of power and authority between the agencies of the general public and the administrative organisation. The extent to which members of the public recognise that personnel within the formal organisation have a unique service to perform, and that they alone possess the knowledge and skills necessary to perform it, will, of course, profoundly affect the freedom of the professional group to pursue its course of action without constant interference from the public.

At the same time some of the theories held by members of the formal organisation will determine their willingness to respond even in the area of aims and purposes in education. If, for example, its personnel share the view that change is in any case undesirable they are likely to see their role as that of preservers of a worthy tradition, and proposals for change will be regarded with suspicion. Again if they hold an absolutist view of knowledge (including what education is), and how it can be acquired they may resist curriculum change and defend an educational policy designed to ensure that the accumulated wisdom and knowledge of a society selected by them be transmitted to the new generation. On the other hand, a different set of assumptions about change and knowledge held by members of the formal organisation would lead them to respond more readily to requests from members of the public to change aspects of school life.

An important characteristic of a democratic society is nevertheless that freedom is allowed to individuals to challenge its norms and normative laws, and to change them through democratic processes. Many norms are based on fundamental philosophical assumptions and the laws derived from them are somewhat arbitrary. Belief in the basic goodness of all men, and in their fundamental human rights; theories about the natural abilities of individuals and an aristocracy of talent have neither been conclusively confirmed nor refuted, although evidence has been adduced by proponents on both sides. The same could be said about educational and political aims. If these are taken as the ends towards which men in society are working, then the assumption of the open society is that they can be challenged, and new ones proposed, either by individuals or by the representatives of groups. Whatever the consequent difficulties, political democracy implies that this kind of freedom to challenge and reject should be allowed.

The professional responsibility of the administrator under these conditions is not to reject criticism but to point out the logical consequence of such choices, their institutional implications, and the possibilities within the framework of available resources of accomplishing them. This is the basis of their professional esoteric knowledge. True authority implies that a range of sociological laws is known to members of the managerial and technical groups which will enable them to predict the consequences of choice of aims and policy decisions based on them.

If this ideal is a vain hope at the moment it is certain that critics of education often fail to distinguish between normative and sociological laws (and in this respect some advocates of reform cannot be exonerated). Statements of aim and proposed innovations are frequently assumed to be related as a sort of normative law—democracy and decentralised control; equality of opportunity and the common or comprehensive school; higher productivity and more education. While these relationships are extremely important they are not simply logical. They are operational and need to be studied in context. This seems to be the task of the professional scholar and administrator whose specific roles in the joint operation need not be too carefully prescribed although both fundamental and operational research would be included.

National Politics[2]

In the light of these general principles some reflections may be made on how types of administration respond to 'consumer' or parental demand, through the lateral relationships held to operate in any society. Neither type of demand is easy to identify. Citizens including parents usually act through organised groups, but in the case of private fee-paying schools they have some degree of individual choice. Even this will be limited. Social demand is still more difficult to judge. Certain groups within any society identify their own expectations with those of society generally. The gauge of social demand is therefore particularly difficult to read—little more than estimates can be given of the agencies through which it operates.

Typically, in Europe, a member of the government is appointed as Minister of Education. Depending on the importance placed on education, he may or may not be a member of the cabinet. The protocol of his appointment also varies. In principle, however, he is the member of the elected government responsible for general educational policy. He is therefore, in an important sense, the representative of the national political party with a majority in the diet, house of assembly, or parliament. In coalitions, his appointment is a matter of agreement between the various parties. There may also be other ministers with some responsibility for education. The Minister of Agriculture may be in charge of agricultural schools; the Minister for War of certain military educational institutions, and so on. The prestige of the Minister of Education varies from government to government; in Britain it is not one of the senior Cabinet positions, ranking well below the Treasury, the Home Office, or the Foreign Office. The Minister's hierarchical position is important because it determines his ability to press for money for education and to have important reforms adopted. Nevertheless the Minister of Education is the highest officer in the administrative organisation; he has to answer directly to the national assembly, and through it to the national electorate.

Aspects of educational policy are formulated at this level, of course, and general legislation and finance debated. The ability of an elected public interest group to have general educational legislation adopted depends upon a number of factors. In the first place, if education is a topic over which political parties are divided rather sharply, at least in some respects, the ability of the party in power to push legislation through will depend upon its parliamentary strength. Such has been the composition of successive French governments since the war, at least until General de Gaulle assumed power in 1958, that general legislation has been virtually impossible, although a number of bills have been prepared for consideration by the Assembly. Some aspects of educational policy have always tended to be issues on which coalitions in France found agreement difficult. On the other hand, the 1944 English Education Act, which contained sweeping new legislation, was passed during World War II by a coalition government, although the differences between the Labour and Conservative parties on some educational questions are sharp. An illustration of a somewhat different approach to education comes from Sweden when, after long years of preparation and study, a major reform bill was passed in May, 1950, during a short period when the Social Democrats were able to form a Labour government without support from any of the other parties.

There is therefore more than a tendency for educational discussions in Europe to be channelled through national political parties. Usually fairly fundamental theoretical or ideological differences divide them. In the twenties, it was the socialists who, in France, were constantly attempting to introduce the *École Unique*. Similarly the post-war agitation for the radical reorganisation of secondary schools in England has come from the Labour party. The process means that debate is often about general principles rather than local issues. Naturally each and every party claims to represent in its policy not only the interests of its own members but of the nation as a whole. Parliamentary debates, the submission of proposed legislation to subcommittees, and the formulation, often prior to an election, of party policies on education are important ways of keeping the public informed and of allowing for the expression of diverse opinions. This does mean, however, that a positive parental or consumer demand operates rather indirectly and consequently somewhat slowly. Party policies are formed through the active participation of a number of interest groups representing various sections of the society. Parents can influence this process as members of local political parties. Doubtless their proposals are filtered through the various agencies and interest groups before coming to the attention of the party leadership. They may, of course, be active through the churches, the voluntary associations, and so on. Parental criticism can also be expressed through the press and by having questions asked in parliament. Nevertheless, a fairly accurate generalisation is that parental interest as such finds rather indirect positive expression at the public interest level of the administrative organisation. Even so, it exists, and were the public to seize the opportunity of making education a general election issue it could be very effective.

Informed Opinion

If the direct operation of parental wishes seems rather weak at this level, systematic attempts are made in most European countries to assess social and pupil needs through the appointment of councils, commissions, or committees to advise on policy. Characteristic of these are the permanent national and regional councils in France and the advisory councils in England and Wales. Another device is the appointment of special committees to report on specific aspects of education. Major advisory reports were produced in the United Kingdom before and during World War II by a consultative committee set up by the Board (now Department) of Education. The findings known as the Hadow, Spens, and Norwood reports were extremely significant precursors of the legislation, and its interpretations, enacted in 1944. Similar commissions in Sweden (1940 and 1946) laid the foundations for the 1950 reform Act. In France, throughout the twenties, a number of commissions reported upon the state of education, and the well known Langevin-Wallon committee sat after the war under the chairmanship of a man whose leadership in proposals for educational reform was widely accepted in the inter-war period. A major report on the reform of Indian education had Sir John Sargent as the English adviser. There can be little doubt that attempts are made to sound professional and qualified lay opinion in the compilation of these reports, but it would be difficult to say with what success.

Certainly care is often taken to include evidence presented to these commissions from representatives of the major social pressure or interest groups; industrial and trade union leaders, voluntary bodies, philanthropic foundations, the teachers, the universities, and churchmen are often consulted. This body of opinion tends to be representative of the national leadership groups rather than of the public generally or of parents. It cannot be stated categorically that these commissions necessarily reflect conservative opinion, although in Europe theories of knowledge as they apply to education are often in the Platonic tradition and reject change. The Hadow report of 1926 was regarded as very progressive by many educationists: the Norwood report of 1943 as equally reactionary. Both were influential in framing post-war policy. On the other hand, to many Frenchmen the proposals of the Langevin committee appeared too progressive, although they do not differ radically from those advanced in the nineteen-twenties. Understandably, it often seems safer to rely on tried methods than to rush into adventures whose outcome seems obscure, even when the pressure to reform education is great.

At the local level of administration somewhat similar agencies operate. Frequently local elections to the municipal council, by which committees in charge of education are appointed, are fought in terms of national politics, so that the composition of the local councils frequently reflects national trends. National policy, therefore, tends to be debated, though not exclusively, at the local level too. It still happens, of course, in England that the majority group in a local council may represent the opposition party in Parliament. Its freedom of action in educational matters is restricted by national legislation but also by the interpretation the national government places upon it; the power of the ministry to accept or reject development plans is a previously mentioned illustration. Obviously, although allowing for diversity of opinion among parents and interest groups, the public interest level of local administration is less vulnerable or receptive to parental demand or to pressure from powerful local groups than in the United States. It would be a mistake to assume that even where great faith is placed in local and parental control, national interest groups play no part in the formulation of federal policy, or that the role of the latter in local educational affairs is negligible. National agencies representing the various levels in the formal organisation are very active. Indeed the situation in the U.S.A. as exemplifying a decentralised system provides an interesting case study.

The Situation in the U.S.A.[3]

At least two activities at the federal level should be noted. The first concerns the role of the United States Supreme Court in its interpretations of the Constitution. Frequently its decisions have set precedents, at the normative level, for changes in local educational policy and practice. This is particularly so in the case of segregated schools. The ruling in 1954 of the Supreme Court that the refusal to admit Negro students to public schools was unconstitutional was the climax of a number of decisions bearing on this same point. The immediate success in practice of the policy thus advocated remains in the balance, but the importance of this federal agency's power to set the goals of local policy should not be underrated.

Another important role of the federal government has been more direct through the allocation of funds for specific educational purposes. There is a long history of federal aid for special purposes. Briefly the Morrill act of 1862 (followed by a number of similar acts) established land-grant colleges for the purpose of protecting the economic viability of the nation. Such acts have had far-reaching implications. Universities which included in their courses of study both the liberal arts and technological subjects grew out of these institutions. No doubt the initial investment of land in them attracted more money to higher education. But since the budgets of these institutions were partly controlled by the state legislatures, a certain loss of autonomy regarding entrance requirements was inevitable. These examples, which could be analysed in much greater detail, serve only to illustrate that the local administrative organisation is certainly not absolutely autonomous in the United

States in spite of the fact that a very small fraction of the total money spent on public education comes from federal sources.

In general, however, the system does represent local administration, and aims at meeting as much consumer demand as possible. Nevertheless, no nation can afford to allow its educational institutions to respond only to this kind of pressure. Certainly the American schools have been one of the agencies through which a measure of conformity and unity has been given to the United States. It is groups acting at the national level whose power to influence policy is greatest. National associations of people professionally concerned with education have been, and are, influential in the establishment of a national climate of opinion about education. Nor should the role of the professors of education throughout the country be forgotten. Indeed, it is against the growing monopoly (according to him) of educationists that A. E. Bestor protests. The areas in which control rests with educationists should be examined. Evidently the difficulties of re-establishing highly competitive entrance tests, either to state universities or to departments and colleges of education, suggest that consumer demand has strongly influenced policy regarding admission to colleges over the last fifty years or more. On the other hand, it is true that the national presidential commissions appointed to advise on educational policy, and the policy commissions of the national educational associations, have reflected professional opinion of educationists as much as, if not more than, those set up in Europe. The political battle to control the formulation of policy in education is often sharp and inconclusive.

Bureaucracies[4]

Although procedures for assessing social demand are not very different, one characteristic of the normative pattern in the United States introduces an important element into the approach. The wide acceptance among educationists of change, not only as inevitable but as desirable, runs powerfully through all échelons of American life. There is consequently less reluctance to propose and discuss changes, at least in certain aspects of education, than is often the case in Europe. And the influence of the professional educators in any national commission seems greater because the findings of research can be brought to bear on its deliberations. Yet because the feeling remains so strong that education should be in the hands of the people, there is perhaps more difficulty in the United States than in Europe in defining the area of executive or professional authority based on esoteric knowledge. In some senses administrators are placed more strategically than in Europe to effect change; in other ways their position in the power structure is much less secure.

In European countries, for example, the Minister of Education usually has a national secretariat or directorate under him whose concern is with the general implementation of policy. The executive powers of its members contrast sharply with those held by the United States Commissioner of Education, whose duty is limited to the collection and dissemination of information. This task is also performed by European secretariats, but in addition they exercise, at the staff level, considerable control over financial matters dealing with the hygienic facilities, the buildings, and the equipment of the schools. Moreover, there is the influence of this top échelon of the managerial group on general planning, teacher qualifications and recruitment, and general investment policy. This influence can be very considerable indeed where general legislation, because of the political scene, is difficult to pass. Then, as in France, many policy decisions are taken by decree. This is particularly the case as far as financial policy is concerned. In most parliamentary governments the budget is a powerful instrument of public interest control; but the allocation of the monies made available by Parliament may be the responsibility of the secretariat. When a large proportion of the total cost of education is raised through national taxation considerable power rests in the hands of the public interest group and with the top levels of the managerial group. Indeed, this kind of control, other than one aspect of inspection, is the major weapon in the hands of the central government in England and Wales under the 1944 act. In France financial arrangements mean that a certain amount of money can be spent only with the approval of the Assembly; another amount is freely at the disposal of the administration, which by its investment policies in technical education or teachers' salaries can influence in a very significant manner the direction educational evolution will take. There is, then, an area of close overlap between the national interest and managerial levels.

However, certain concepts lie behind practical financial arrangements. Although there is a high level of expenditure on education by national governments in Europe, the principle that he who pays the piper calls the tune is applied to some, but not all, aspects of policy. The British government provides from public funds through the University Grants Committee some 80 per cent of the revenue of the universities. The government's control over the way the grant is spent, either for scientific education or the arts, is weak, and university politics are very important. This extreme example of national support to education without national control applies to a considerable, if not to the same, extent in other European countries too. The freedom of the universities has important implications because of the control they exercise, in practice, on national systems of education through the examination systems. On the other hand, Ministry control of the teacher training colleges (usually municipal or Church) in England through the financial mechanism is fairly direct. Studies considered important in the national interest can be promoted by raising funds for salaries, equipment, and accommodation, for example, in face of a need for science teachers. Similar direct control operates over the policies of the national and municipal colleges of advanced technology. It is necessary, therefore, to compare, country by country, the actual fiscal arrangements for the allocation of resources to various aspects of education to see the influence they have over policy matters. Here is an important index of the actual influence of the managerial (both central and local) and public interest groups on the formulation and implementation of policy.

Managerial Group Members

When most of the money is raised locally the importance of the attitude towards education of the interest groups at the local level on whom the burden of taxation for schools will fall most heavily cannot be over-emphasised. It places tremendous power in the hands of a particular interest group, for example, industrialists with high real estate taxes to pay, or farmers with large tracts of agricultural land. It may be cheaper, for example, for the industrialist to move out of a district than to pay heavy property taxes to support education. Equally, farmers in a rural area often oppose tax increases on the ground that they benefit the children of those parents who commute daily to the nearby town. The difficulties frequently result in unequal educational provision. In many countries, including the United States at the state level, therefore, financial formulas often operate to equalise the per capita amount spent on education. These often, however, reflect attempts to prevent the minimum from falling to a level below which it is felt that adequate provision is impossible.

The mechanism used in most European countries to ensure that uniform minimum standards are maintained throughout the country is a corps of inspectors. Usually they are more directly concerned with academic affairs and are, of course, more closely in touch with the schools than members of the secretariat. At this level of the managerial organisation, very considerable differences exist from country to country in the detailed nature of the inspectorate's work. In principle, however, there are national and local inspectors, although, as in France, they may all be national civil servants. In England and Wales, in contrast, there is a national inspectorate and locally appointed Local Education Authority inspectors. Distinctions are also generally made between the various sections or *ordres* of education—so that there are staff inspectors for, say, the primary, secondary, and technical branches. France now has a staff inspector for sport and one for higher education. The latter post is not unusual where either the universities or the teacher training colleges are state institutions or come under some aspects of state legislation. In addition, the national inspectorate may include members in charge of special subjects, particularly at the secondary level. The secondary school general inspectors in France are split up into specialised groups dealing, for example, with mathematics, physical science, philosophy, history and geography, and boarding schools. There are, in most countries including France, regional inspectors. The relationships of these men, very often appointed nationally, with the local authority inspectors vary considerably. In Sweden and in England and Wales, the local inspectors are responsible to the local board or school authority; in France, through the national inspectorate and academies, to the Minister of Education.

The training and methods of recruitment of these officials give them considerable independence; they are not political appointees, but usually permanent officials recruited either on the basis of competitive examination or on the recommendations of selection commissions from among university graduates of some distinction. In continental Europe many of these men are trained as lawyers; in England in classics or arts at either Oxford or Cambridge. They have a high sense of social responsibility and a professional ethic which implies that they do their best loyally to implement the policies of whatever government happens to be in power. This is a strong check on the abuse of their undoubted authority, a danger which was recognised even when Condorcet proposed to establish a corps of national inspectors during the period of the Revolutionary Convention.

It is true that at this level the opportunities of the extra-educational agencies, including parents, to influence administrators are few. Public control depends upon the vertical pressures between the levels of administration rather than on the lateral relations. Deeply ingrained traditions and powerful institutions of political democracy in countries like Britain, France, and Sweden, among others, are the most effective defence against an unscrupulous administration. The position of the administrators is nevertheless secure; the method of their recruitment has several implications. They all share a somewhat similar ethic as the consequence of great homogeneity between one university and another. The prestige they are accorded, the honours which can be bestowed upon them as responsible servants of the nation, are important elements in the maintenance of professional integrity.

On the other hand, the character of the European universities has also to be taken into account. Where so-called rigorous standards of admission and attainment have been maintained the quality of the administrators may be assumed to be high. But university traditions may be such (and tend to be in Europe) that innovations are considered very carefully and new subjects introduced for study very reluctantly. The question then becomes whether or not the administrators are suitably prepared to fulfil their professional tasks. It has been argued, for example, that in England too little research has been done on the managerial problems associated with industrial relations. It may be that in recruiting new members administrators cling rather fiercely to the kind of training through which they themselves passed. There is, then, in some senses rather close administrative supervision of recruitment. The need to change the background of professional study is not always apparent, and the kind of pressures which operate in the medical or legal professions are not so immediate or challenging in education. The tests of adequate medical treatment are fairly obvious; so, too, is the success or failure of a lawyer. But the consequences of educational action are rather long-term, however judged. One result of highly competitive examinations may be that clever men are selected, but they are somewhat inadequate tests of the professional competence of personnel to assess socio-political consequences. In short, the pressure to keep up to date in professional study is not very great. There is danger that the administration becomes over-cautious, too conservative, unaware of the full range of consequences, simply because the corpus of knowledge possessed by its members does not include significant findings from the social sciences. If these are readily available through independent work in the universities the point would not arise, and if more research were available more men of the quality demanded by the administrative services would be encouraged to study in these fields. The inclusion of education as a subject for study in the faculty of philosophy, as happens in many continental universities, is no guarantee that a person has gained insight into the sociological aspects of education or into administrative theory.

Conversely, great emphasis on professional studies, conceived rather narrowly, could lead both to an inadequacy of preparation in subject-matter of germane fields of knowledge, such as history and philosophy, and to a narrowness of vision which is important in the formulation of policy and in the exercise of judgement. This does not imply that a return in this modern world to the traditional liberal arts with a sprinkling of professional work is a solution. It seems obvious that among the data of importance to the administrator, those drawn from the fundamental natural sciences, sociology, psychology, economics, and political science should rank high. Unfortunately, these subjects, ancillary to educational administration as the natural sciences are to medicine, are not, at the moment, with the exception of the natural sciences, well developed. The continued effectiveness of an administrative organisation may depend on radical changes in the educational system so that a corpus of knowledge is developed on the basis of which the modern administrator's professional authority rests. Unfortunately, not all the administrators themselves are aware of the modern need for training in the theory and practice of administration.

The Inspectorate and Teachers[5]

The actual duties of inspectorates vary considerably. They may be examined in the light of a number of criteria on the basis of which an educational system may be said to be centralised or decentralised.

Among these may be used (*a*) the number of students enrolled under one authority, (*b*) power to raise taxes and distribute money for education, (*c*) control of the curriculum, and (*d*) teacher promotions, appointments, transfers, and salaries. To these may be added (*e*) power to inspect plant, (*f*) the ability to control examinations, and (*g*) the responsibility for the administration of facilities of a specialised nature. The position regarding finance has been mentioned: executive officers rarely have power to raise money or decide on the amount that should be allocated to education (this is the job of the public interest level), but they often play an important part in the allocation and distribution of grants. The other criteria are useful from the viewpoint of analysis. In general the inspectors have no control over the curriculum in England and Wales; this is the responsibility of the headmaster, although he is bound rather closely by university entrance requirements and thus the examination system administered by the universities. European inspectors, on the contrary, are responsible for a greater measure of control over the curriculum. Thus it is possible to publish national curricula for the schools of Sweden and of France as well as for many other countries. Some curricular changes, it is true, have taken place only after considerable debate at the public interest level. For many years, in the twenties, the issue in France was whether or not Latin should be compulsory for all secondary school (*lycée*) students or not.

Each country has its own methods of qualifying and appointing teachers. In England the possession of a university degree is a licence to teach. Examinations taken by intending non-graduate teachers are administered by the universities. In France a complex system of State examinations operates to ensure that teachers in the various *ordres* or branches of education have both the appropriate secondary school and college certificates and the State qualifications. Each type of qualification is, however, closely supervised, and standards are set, by teachers and administrators closely associated with the universities. The insistence on examination qualifications for all teachers reflects the determination of the French authorities to maintain the level of academic training of all their teachers. The system is fiercely competitive, although in the post-war period considerable incentives have had to be given to attract more teachers to the profession. Promotions too in France are based on rigorous examinations and inspection. Disciplinary action against a teacher can be taken only by a committee representing the public interest level, and the teachers' union, affiliated with the general trade union movement, is able to exercise considerable power in support of its members. In England the principle is that inspectors should do no more than advise teachers and headmasters. On the other hand, they are charged under the 1944 Act to ensure that local authority and private schools reach national standards of efficiency as far as facilities are concerned. On the basis of detailed reports by the inspectors, private schools can be recognised as efficient by the Ministry. The power of inspection in the French private schools is restricted to ensuring that nothing is taught contrary to ethics, the law, and the constitution, that general facilities are adequate and that compulsory attendance is enforced. Rather closer control over textbooks is exercised in France than in England, where most individual teachers are free to use just what they please. Experiments in teaching methods and curricular changes are more closely supervised in France than in England. It should not be assumed, however, that the administrators in France can dictate teaching methods or curricular change; the opposition of the teachers of the classics to radical moves away from their subjects to the sciences and modern languages has been well organised and effective.

Reform and the Type of Administration

From the viewpoint of how reforms take place in a school system, F. S. Cillié's[6] enquiry carried through in the United States in 1941 is very illuminating. Briefly stated, in two areas Cillié tried to isolate from all other relevant socio-economic factors the type of administration. He then attempted to relate to the form of administration a number of adaptations that take place in a school. Some, it was presumed, prosper under decentralisation, others under centralisation, while some are independent of the type of administration. He approached his task recognising that in the United States a strong feeling exists that decentralised control promotes adaptability. He then sought two areas with matching features of geographical situation, educational finance, socio-economic conditions such as family income, and professional features which included the proportion of parochial schools, class size, teacher salaries. Within the limits of his resources he found two areas in and near New York City which met these requirements.

Two observations are immediately necessary on the method used. The analysis of centralisation and decentralisation does not correspond with that proposed by Parsons. Moreover, it should be noted that if numbers are regarded as the most important criterion of centralised control, then the big cities of the United States like New York, with a population which compares with that of the whole of Australia or the Netherlands, and is about half that of South Africa, could be compared with these countries. Such comparisons may be useful. Certainly Cillié's findings throw up useful hypotheses for comparative study. The second reservation on method is quite fundamental. According to the methodological principles outlined earlier, the contexts of specific initial conditions important in the operation of any system of administration would include the 'ideal' or 'actual' normative pattern, the rest of the institutional pattern, and the major environmental elements. No possibility exists of finding any precision in matching all these features.

The areas of adaptability studied included: flexibility of

organisation, individual pupil needs, provision for deviates, provision of health services, teacher conditions, the curriculum, school relations with the community, and the quality of professional administration. The elaborate methods of testing the adaptations in these various areas need not detain us, but some of the major conclusions should be summarised. Decentralisation favoured experimentation and more flexible schedules; there appeared to be more freedom for the children in the elementary grades, and more extracurricular activities with the greater use of individual instructional material. More provision was made in the decentralised system for the non-academic children with more participation of teachers in the selection of material classroom supplies. They also tended to experiment more. On the other hand, in a centralised system the teacher seemed to be tied more closely to the text, few teachers took advantage of the opportunities to modify the course partly because of the mechanics of the operation through the principal, the assistant superintendent, to the divisional officer and finally to the superintendent. The curriculum was also tied by the existence of 'city wide' tests which not only evaluated the student but also the teacher. In the centralised system any radical reorganisation of the whole curriculum tended to be pondered deeply and long before any action was taken. On the other hand, the quality of experimentation was better, innovations touched a greater number of children, facilities for handicapped children tended to be better, and the provision of special vocational schools more adequate.

One important area was that concerning the position of teachers. Curriculum construction in the centralised system was rarely the function of the individual teachers. Here it is desirable to distinguish between the organisation of the subjects taught and the syllabus of individual subjects. The centralised system encouraged professional studies by teachers, whose terms of tenure, salary schedules, leave provisions, and retirement arrangements were better.

A great many points of adaptability were found to be independent of the system of administration. Applying these findings to various systems one recognises the considerable degree to which they can be applied. The exceptions to the general rules are as important as the findings which appear valid. In both England and France the security of tenure of the teacher is very great indeed; the freedom of the secondary school teacher to experiment is perhaps greater in England than in France, and might be greater than in some parts of the United States. On the other hand, it is true that the examination system in both countries tends to change rather slowly, but the possibilities of changing it in France are certainly as great as in England. Comparisons of this kind should be made cautiously.

Parental Control

One final point should perhaps be made about the extent to which parents contribute to the processes of policy framing and implementation. Frequently they are in a position to make limited choices. The school system itself, for example, offers some opportunities. In many countries these are restricted in the publicly maintained system to a type of school—either academic, commercial, or technical—at the secondary level, and selection to the one most highly esteemed by parents is often very competitive. On the other hand, where private schools exist the wishes of the parents can be more readily met. Parochial schools are special examples, but a good many private experimental institutions are found in Europe. In these schools new methods, different curricula, and less traditional principles of discipline are frequently practised and have a slow but perceptible influence on the national school system. Similarly, certain changes may be made in private schools, rather more traditional in outlook, but with high prestige. Modifications in the English 'public' schools are likely to be followed by similar changes in the competing State schools. In the fifties, for instance, there was heavy investment by industrial concerns in the extension in the 'public' schools of science-teaching facilities. Thus as occupational needs arise consumer pressure is exerted on private institutions which, if they respond rather quickly, set new patterns for the general system to follow.

On the other hand, attempts to free the curriculum of 'new-type' schools does not always work, because of the prestige of traditional ones. The municipal *collèges* in France were set up with the intention of providing a somewhat less classical curriculum than the State *lycées*; they quickly fell into line with the latter, partly for prestige reasons and partly because the examination system of the *lycées* opened the path to lucrative jobs and further educational opportunities.

Apparently the mechanics of public control over education are subtle and complex. Any broad categorisation of a system as either centralised or decentralised is misleading. The administrative organisation will respond in accordance with the various possibilities that exist through the political or social systems to influence various aspects of education. The operation of the administration is such that certain things within education may be more open than others to influence by certain interest groups; this is particularly the case as far as parental influence is concerned. A review of the major issues debated by the national political parties in Europe indicates which aspects of education are regarded as important and in need of change. The degree to which these parties attempt to appeal to the electorate for the purposes of vote-catching indicates how seriously mass opinion about educational reform is regarded. Unfortunately laymen rarely appreciate more than a few implications of certain institutional innovations. Resistance to reform arises because certain consequences are seen and feared. On the other hand, certain policies are advocated because a direct relation between these and one consequence is assumed. This danger becomes rather acute in countries where there is a commitment to democracy but where the level of education is such that few of the possible implications of policy decision can be appreciated. Vote-catching tends to make it necessary to obscure many of them in the policy statements of competing parties. Frequently these are couched in utopian terms although the prospects of achieving all the aims are remote in terms of the foreseeable future.

On the other hand, the rather close control of an educational system by locally elected officers (at the public interest level) is likely to introduce local politics into educational policy-making. These may or may not be related to national politics. The possibility and danger of petty power politics operating in terms of Myrdal's lower valuations entering into the running of education always exists.

It is difficult to judge which of these political influences will have the most baneful effects on education. Generally speaking, where members of the administration, either at the technical or managerial levels, are appointed on the basis of qualifications other than political affiliations, the prospect of checking the influence of political manœuvre is greater. But it should be emphasised by repetition that the ethics by which elected officers and appointed officials operate are important in deciding how the schools are run. Totalitarian self-appointed governments may seize control of a national managerial administrative group. Conversely, authoritarians may well be able to manipulate local administrators with great success. The ability of either type of administration to resist certain kinds of pressure and respond to others is important in maintaining a balance between professional autonomy and democratic procedures.

PART THREE

NATIONAL CASE STUDIES

INTRODUCTION

IN these chapters the themes running through the first two parts of the book are related to selected parts of the educational pattern and, for the most part, to particular national systems. Thus, for the sake of clarity, but at the cost of some repetition, the suggested general sources of common problems and their main features are again outlined in specific contexts. In other words, these case studies are intended to make clear the special national features of widely shared difficulties of reform in education. Consequently there is no intention of presenting comprehensive descriptions of the educational systems of the U.S.A., England and Wales, the U.S.S.R., and Japan. The data and accounts of current debates are highly selective on the ground of their relevance to the issues under consideration.

The first of these concerns teacher training—a world-wide problem—which has important theoretical and organisational aspects. Attention has been concentrated on the United States, not because the problems there are typical but because the pattern of policies which have been adopted offers for many other countries guide lines for development.

The reorganisation of secondary education in the post-war period has not been restricted to European nations, but it has perhaps received more attention among them than elsewhere. One interesting feature of a common debate is that traditional policies can be compared with Communist solutions. The conflict of opinion turns on the relative merits of retaining a highly differentiated or multipartite post-primary school structure and of moving towards a common or comprehensive secondary school structure. The case of England and Wales is particularly instructive because the aspirations heightened by the war found expression in major legislation even before its end. The very framing of the 1944 Education Act, however, left a great deal of room for political manœuvre, but post-war economic conditions reduced the possibilities of achieving stated objectives.

The content of education is another area in which the need for reform has been hotly debated. The need for scientists and technologists has been widely recognised, but less attention has been paid to the need for scientifically literate populations. Perhaps because structural reorganisation took place in the Soviet Union several decades ago more attention has been paid there than in most countries to the problem of curriculum reform. Polytechnicalisation, the solution proposed, is really a principle of education designed to permeate the whole system. It involves much more than the introduction of more vocational training and its theoretical basis, dissociated from its party political ideology, offers possibilities of solving problems common to all industrialised nations.

Japan has been selected for the fourth case study because attempts were made after the war to reorganise the whole educational system and particularly its methods of administration and control. It provides an example of enforced cultural borrowing and illustrates extremely well that policies that work well in one country may have quite different outcomes in another environment. Against this background of radical reform and gradual readjustment a problem which touches all individuals has been examined. Its special features in Japan are of central interest to many educators there, but they also reveal, in more extreme form, a universal moral problem.

Chapter VIII

TEACHER TRAINING AND THE
PROFESSION OF EDUCATION
(THE U.S.A.)

THE success of policies of educational expansion, whether to promote economic development as a human right, or in the interests of maintaining peace and democracy, obviously depends in part upon the possibilities of recruiting enough teachers to staff the schools. After the war the explosion of population accentuated the difficulties of an already formidable task. High birth-rates and low death-rates resulted in rapid increases in population, and soon the school-age proportion of the population was considerably higher than previously. At the same time the low birth-rates in the thirties meant that the age-group from which potential teachers could be drawn in the fifties was relatively small. It has been difficult to find enough teachers. Almost everywhere emergency measures have had to be taken to meet the situation. These have tended to be based on the view that any kind of teacher is better than none. But unfortunately the tasks of the teacher in a rapidly changing world have become much more complicated. The simple literacy of the nineteenth century—the three Rs—is no longer sufficient for the mass of people if they are to meet the challenge of the new scientific age. Thus as important as the problem of finding enough teachers are those of approving their quality by reforms in the methods of recruitment, education, and professional training and by considering new methods of teaching and the possible application of new methods in the classroom.

Of course the precise nature of these world-wide problems varies. In many economically underdeveloped, newly independent nations the greatest need is often felt to be for teachers to man the schools set up in attempts to establish, sometimes for the first time, a system of universal primary education. At another level, in Europe there has been strong pressure to extend opportunities for secondary education and to make them less dependent than previously on the accident of birth or wealth. Again, and notably in the United States of America, higher education has been expanded very considerably since the war. Each stage of education has competed for potential teachers, and everywhere the greatest shortages have been in mathematics and science, because in these fields the competition with industry has been more acute.

These obvious differences of detail are important, but they should not prevent further analysis of general issues relating to the reform of teacher education. A distinction based on critical dualism seems again useful. For instance it is necessary to reconsider some basic assumptions about the role the teacher should play, the kind of person he should be, and the kind of knowledge he should possess. The other area in which problems of reform are found is the organisation of teacher training. Naturally, proposed changes in theory and practice should be closely related, but it seems desirable for the purposes of analysis to distinguish between changing concepts of the 'ideal' teacher and proposals to reorganise the practical methods of training.

The 'Ideal' Teacher[1]

Certainly concepts of what qualities should be possessed by the 'ideal' teacher have changed over the centuries. They are again in a period of considerable debate and transition. One major issue concerns the nature of his basic function. Should he be the conserver of tradition, the mediator between one generation and the next? Or should he be the chosen agent of social change—a dynamic element in a changing society? Traditions in most countries accord to him the former of these roles. On the other hand in the United States some educationists have thought that the teacher should be an instrument of change—a viewpoint which may well be accepted where the idea that social change is good is widely held. Evidently the degree to which education is seen as an instrument of progress will help to determine views on the nature of the teacher's role. And it is doubtful whether in the rapidly changing world of the twentieth century the older tradition is any longer appropriate.

Another issue concerns the kind of knowledge the 'ideal' teacher should possess. On the one hand faith in knowledge of subject matter drawn from the established disciplines stands against a belief in the need for the teacher to know the psychological needs of his children and the sociology of the background from which they come. In other words the debate turns on the relative merits of subject matter or professional subjects in the training of teachers. In practical terms this has meant a constant battle between professors in the faculties of arts and sciences and the professors of education.

In either case the possession of esoteric knowledge has always been regarded as important and has given to the teacher both status and power. It has enabled him to perform a public service. The flow of events has, however, raised new questions about what knowledge is of most worth for the teacher.

Again there have always been arguments about the desirable personal qualities of the ideal teacher. Should he be righteous, wise, honest, and paternal? Should he be kind, patient, understanding, and sympathetic? Or in the interests of learning the reverse—somebody who would drive the student on, by cane and whip, to commit his lesson to memory? Moreover, should the possession of these qualities be regarded as more or less important than the possession of knowledge and wisdom? Rarely has the choice been clear-cut; in most concepts of the ideal teacher personal qualities and scholarship have been regarded as important. The balance in terms of emphasis has changed.

Undoubtedly among the prototypes the *priest-teacher* is important. His duty was to know about life and death; about the stars and their behaviour, about social affairs and modes of individual behaviour, and about down-to-earth phenomena such as rain, fire, the seasons, and agriculture. In a sense the whole universe was his province. Frequently too this kind of teacher was held to be divinely inspired—in touch with a supernatural being or beings capable of transmitting to specially chosen persons knowledge of a unique kind, i.e. virtually infallible. Such persons, the great prophets, should be able to transmit to others the knowledge thus acquired, a process ensuring the maintenance of esoteric knowledge. Under these circumstances the ideal teacher is clearly one who has either direct access to the supernatural authority or indirect, but nevertheless reliable, contact with him or them (because often the supernatural authority has been personified). One example of the process by which the *priest-teacher* may acquire knowledge is through revelation.

Another and less exclusive view is that, whilst the source of all knowledge is certainly a supernatural being, direct revelation is no longer possible, and therefore reliance should be placed on the writings or sayings of the few persons who were originally privileged to acquire knowledge through direct communication and either passed it down through the oral tradition of learning or committed it to writing and thus preserved it. The sacred texts then become the important or even essential basis of learning. Who can doubt that the Vedas of India, the sayings of Buddha, the Qur'an and the Bible embody many ideas that have entered profoundly into the content of education?

In ancient India, for example, it was the supreme duty of the *guru* to pass on to his students all he knew of the sacred texts. But the ultimate aim of education—knowledge of Brahman or the Absolute—could not be achieved simply from literature. A teacher was necessary whose relationship with his pupil, as a member of the household, was in the highest degree spiritual. This relationship of paternal love was established over a long period of studentship spent in the *guru's* house—a form of apprenticeship during the course of which the student performed many menial tasks for his teacher, learned humility and how himself to become a *guru* possessed of the necessary powers of introspection, dedication, and contemplation.

Moslem thinkers, too, stressed that a vision of ultimate truth could be acquired only after a long period of preparation. Truth was essentially mystical. Knowledge was acquired either through revelation or by the application of experience and reason. For traditionalists the source of all knowledge was the inspired revelations of the Qur'an. Other thinkers stressed the role of reason. Since the teacher was indispensable in the process of learning, his status was high. Wisdom was closely associated with learning, which could best be acquired if the scholar cut himself off from men in order to contemplate God. The teacher's role was paternal—his pupils should be treated as his children, humanely and with compassion.

Somewhat conflicting concepts of the ideal teacher have prevailed from time to time in the Christian tradition. After the Reformation, for example, a sharper distinction was drawn between the authority of revealed knowledge and the word of the sacred book, the Bible. Subsequently it was possible to visualise the growth of a well-trained lay teaching profession. Another example of the different emphasis given to knowledge in the selection and training of teachers is found in the rivalry of the Jesuits and the Jansenists. The former built their educational edifice on the foundation of knowledge. Priest teachers were prepared over a long period and before taking their final vows taught the 'lower studies' for a time. To teach well they were expected to be thoroughly skilled in what they were to teach and were required to conform to the pattern set up for the whole Order. Even so they were to lead pupils rather than drive them and were to know the character and ability of each one of them. Saint-Cyran, a Jansenist, was prepared to take great pains to find the teacher he wanted. Piety rather than knowledge was the object of the little schools of Port Royal, and consequently goodness and intelligence rather than long and rigorous, and by implication pedantic, training were the qualities required of the teacher. These contrasting views in fact represent one of the debating points in western education. In both knowledge of God and of the child was important, but in the final analysis the choice was between a knowledgeable (or learned) man and a good man. The two are not incompatible, but the differences in emphasis in selecting and training teachers are important even today.

The secular tradition should not be regarded as entirely distinct from the religious. Hindu and Moslem texts, for example, contained a great deal of information which was concerned with the practical day-to-day organisation of society. The secular schools and teachers often served rather specific functions. In Athens the *rhetoric-teacher's* command of the techniques of style and diction enabled him to prepare his students to make their case in the democratic institutions of the city. The Confucian tradition of ancient China is of the *examplar-teacher* who should above all set an example of morality or of a particular way of life. His special knowledge was of the laws and ceremonial in accordance with which society was organised. As for his own virtues he was expected to be benevolent and humble, to show filial piety, and to accept his obligations and responsibilities. Gentleness towards students and great respect for teachers were virtues necessarily associated with this kind of paternalism.

Through the secular tradition runs the thread of absolutism, namely belief in the possibilities of getting past the ceaseless flow of experiences to the reality and permanence behind them. It has two branches; one in which knowledge of ideas gives certainty, the other in which knowledge of the material stuff of the universe gives certainty. Marxists, who believe in the absolute nature of scientific truths, can be placed in the second group. The Sophists represent another tradition. They were attacked by both Plato and Isocrates principally on the ground that they were professionals. The objections ran deeper. For Protagoras the basis of authority was man himself. Again the Sophists consciously catered for the interests of their students and responded openly to their demands for skills of a certain kind. In accepting the changes going on around them they were far from being mere conservers and defenders of the established order. They provided a rationale for the democratic tendencies of their time. Later democratic movements in education were linked with Bacon's general epistemology and Comenius's theories of education. The vision of Comenius included Christian and secular traditions. Pansophism implied that there was a realm of universal knowledge which could be investigated by all—a view which justifies the extension of education and makes it possible to regard the ideal teacher as being as much, if not more, the product of careful education and training as the result of rigorous selection from a small élite.

Many persisting concepts of the ideal teacher are found in the university tradition of academic freedom, which contains a number of norms. It implies that a university should have the right to decide several things. First, it should be able to decide who shall teach within its walls. Secondly, it alone should have the right to say what should be taught. Thirdly, it should retain the right to admit or reject students who seek admission. Finally the tradition maintains that choice of methods of teaching should fall entirely within the jurisdiction of the university. Within this framework of institutional autonomy there exists, of course, the academic freedom of the individual teacher or professor. He too should rightly assume responsibility for what is taught, for the way it is taught, and to whom. To be sure, in medieval Europe, the master gathered students round him, and since his livelihood was based upon fees, what was taught and by whom depended a great deal on the wishes of students. Capricious choice was to some extent controlled by the practical value of what was offered.

There was, moreover, some consensus of opinion about what should be taught. The knowledge worthy of attention included virtually all that was known in the ancient world, and the basis for this was to be found in the trivium and quadrivium. Syllogistic reasoning provided a method for acquiring rational knowledge of reality. Whatever professional training the universities in fact provided, there was nevertheless a strongly held view that knowledge should be sought not for the power, status, or occupational opportunities it bestowed but for its own sake. Consequently scholarship and research—the promotion of which has been a primary aim of the universities since early times—tended to take on specific characteristics. It implied that the scholar should be familiar with all the precedents, know all the literature, have studied all past criticism, and have located all published and unpublished documents germane to his sphere of interest. The opinion that the possible applications of research should have very little relevance to the work itself accords well with the belief that the scholar *per se* should not become involved in politics or other practical affairs. The intellectual interests of such a community of scholars should, however, know no bounds. Their search was for universal knowledge even if, when the universities were founded, this had clearly defined limits. The international composition of the communities was regarded as desirable. Recognition of *studium generale* gave legal sanction to and encouraged the belief that through the interchange of scholars universal knowledge could and should be disseminated. A licence to teach in one institution empowered a master to carry on his vocation at any similar centre in Europe. This ideal of the internationalisation of knowledge, that truth knows no frontiers of race or nationality or culture, remains fundamental to the university tradition.

Against this brief outline of some of the norms associated with the teacher's role and authority it may be possible to see present debates against a common framework. Evidently the degree to which traditional norms have been challenged, rejected or modified will depend upon a variety of factors, and national differences must now be expected.

The Institutional Framework

Control of teacher education is also a controversial issue today. The protagonists in many countries include the Church, the secular government, the universities, and the professional educationists. In Europe since they were established the universities have profoundly influenced the whole pattern of education including teacher education. Since the European university has served as a model throughout the world somewhat similar conditions apply in many countries. The reasons for the dominance of the universities are in general fairly obvious. From the start they trained the clergy, the lawyers, the physicians, and the teachers. Each professional group was in its own way near to the centres of political power. As political advisers some academies suffered the consequences of engaging in political life, but those who chose to remain within the confines of academic or professional life benefited. As individuals they enjoyed considerable freedom which was protected by the collective strength of the group. Against town, established Church, or State the universities were, as communities of scholars in considerable public demand, able to establish and maintain a *de facto* independence and autonomy which belies much of the relevant legislation.

Gradually the dominance of the Church declined, and as nationalism grew so did the differences between the national universities and the methods of control over them. Thus the French universities are State institutions and the professors civil servants. The English universities are established by royal charter; a large proportion of their financial resources come from the national government, but faculty members are not civil servants. Many major American universities were created by Federal funds as state institutions and are controlled by trustees responsible finally to the elected state government.

This variety in methods of control affects a number of aspects of policy. In particular the close links which exist everywhere between the academic secondary schools and the universities are regulated. Frequently the final school-leaving examination from these schools serves as a basic admission requirement. The French *baccalauréat* is in fact regarded as an award of the university, and like the German *Abitur*, the Scandinavian *Studentexam*, and the Italian and Austrian *Matura*, gives access to the universities. In the United States graduation from an accredited high school often confers upon a student the right to enter a state university within the state. In England for the purposes of student grants entrance requirements are based upon results in the O level and A level examinations of the General Certificate of Education.

If *de jure* admission regulations differ widely, *de facto* admission procedures still depend very much on the whim of individual universities, departments within the universities, and the professors themselves. Obviously the way in which teaching is organised profoundly affects the mechanics of admission. In federal universities such as Oxford, Cambridge, or London admission rests largely on the college and then on the subject department. Most unitary universities are organised for the purposes of teaching into subject departments each exercising a considerable measure of autonomy. The continental pattern is for individual professors to admit students to their own courses.

The success of such policies depends mainly on the size of the operation. In selective systems a relatively small proportion of an age cohort attends academic secondary schools and the fall-out, either throughout the course or, as in England, at special points in it, is considerable. Under such conditions the preparation of students for university entrance and the selection from among them of the potential research workers and teachers may be relatively simple. So in the past, since teachers belonged to one of the four professional groups and the possession of a degree gave them entry into the teaching guild, little attention was given to professional training. Problems began to arise when educational opportunities expanded. At first, since the expansion of elementary or primary education was independent of the established secondary school system the pressure on the universities to train teachers was not great. Two virtually independent systems were established in most countries. There was an elementary school system in which pupils obtained a rudimentary general education, completed it either in special training colleges or as student teachers, and then returned to teach in the kind of schools in which they were educated. The academic secondary school pupil went to the university, obtained a degree, and returned to teach in the kind of school he knew as a boy. The points of contact between these two systems were at first almost non-existent. One consequence was that the normal schools had to complete the general education of the pupils coming from elementary schools.

Since the elementary schools were regarded in most countries as the responsibility either of the local authority or the Church it followed that control of teacher training tended to fall into the hands of one or other of these two agencies. A frequently copied pattern was the one established in Prussia. Henry Barnard,[2] for example, gave in detail the regulations about teacher training in the Ordinance of Frederick II in 1763. In this the principles of control were clearly stated. With the help of superintendents and inspectors the clergy were to control teachers by seeing that reckless, wicked, incompetent, or otherwise unsuitable persons were not employed. Subsequently intending teachers should be trained in a teachers' seminary. Before appointment their qualifications should be assessed by actual examination and certified by inspectors. Nobody should be allowed to teach unless he had obtained a licence to do so. Even in the absence of fully qualified candidates for the profession those aspiring to teach were to take an examination and give trial lessons under supervision.

Victor Cousin visited Prussia on behalf of the French government and reported very favourably on the normal schools, both the small private institution and the large ones maintained either by the provincial authorities or the municipalities. He based his proposals for the reform of French teacher education on the legislation he had consulted and the visits he had made.

Horace Mann, who had been instrumental in the establishment of a normal school in Massachusetts, was equally impressed by what he saw of Prussian 'Seminaries for Teachers'. His admiration for Prussian teachers stemmed from his observations of their lively teaching methods and their humaneness in handling pupils. The basis of his own efforts to reform education in Massachusetts was the vital need for well-trained teachers.

By the middle of the nineteenth century the principle of training elementary school teachers was widely accepted in the major European countries and in North America. Undoubtedly the personal qualities of intending teachers were regarded as very important, and everywhere, in spite of reductions in the formal control exercised by the churches, the concepts of desirable personal qualities were consciously Christian. Students were, however, still recruited from the elementary schools, in effect distinguishing them sharply from prospective entrants to the university. The training institutions provided an alternative form of further education, frequently completed their general education, and prepared people for a desirable occupation, but one which could hardly be accorded at that time the status of a profession. One indication of this situation was the battles for control of teacher training, principally between the churches and the secular authorities either at the national or local levels. Another was the fact that teachers in elementary schools began to organise themselves into effective trade unions, e.g. the National Union of Teachers in the United Kingdom and the *Syndicat National des Instituteurs et Institutrices* in France. Control over entry into teaching, over courses of instruction, and over certification was not acquired by such unions.

Today, in fact, ultimate responsibility for teacher training frequently rests with a government agency. In Germany the training of teachers for all kinds of school comes under the general supervision of the several *Länder*. Both in Canada and in the United States of America the certification of teachers is a provincial or state responsibility. In Australia too there are no national agencies of teacher education. Elsewhere the system of control is more national than local or regional. France epitomises a pattern which is not uncommon. National legislation during the first half of the nineteenth century made it obligatory for each *département* to maintain a teacher training college for elementary school teachers. Later, each *département* was expected to maintain two such institutions—one for men, the other for women. Generally speaking, however, then as now, the ability of the central or local governments to control elementary education and the training of teachers for it was greater than their corresponding power over secondary school teacher training. Whatever the *de jure* administrative control government agencies have over the training of academic secondary school teachers, in academic matters much of the control in most countries in the world is exercised by the universities.

Most of the problems of organisation in teacher education arise from dualities in education. Everywhere elements of the distinction between 'elementary' schools and their teachers and secondary schools and their masters remain to separate members of what should be one profession. Methods of recruiting students to each of the two systems of teacher education may vary; formal entry requirements differ. Certification procedures at the end of training courses may differ too, so that members of the teaching staff in the two types of compulsory school may have quite different qualifications from each other.

The staffing of the training institutions tends in general to accentuate the differences. The staff in the normal schools were and are frequently experienced teachers recruited from the elementary schools. The professors in the institutions preparing academic secondary school teachers were, as now, as often as not appointed on the grounds of scholarship rather than long teaching experience. Often the two systems recruited students and staff from different socio-economic groups; each had its own pattern of attitudes and theories about education; and each had its own place in the hierarchy of social institutions.

Even if this picture is too sharply drawn the separation between the forms of teacher education constitutes a major problem. It is intensified by the sharp divisions within the educational pattern as a whole and the fact that each system of teacher education has its own complicated set of relationships to institutions both within the educational sector and to institutions in other areas of the social pattern. Any reform of

teacher training involves changing a whole network of relationships. In principle the problem of unification of the profession
may not be insuperable. In practice the task is difficult because
vested interests find good reasons to maintain many aspects of
the *status quo*. Nevertheless tendencies are towards removing
some of the differences by bringing together both types of
teacher education.

Professional Control

In general today the universities tend to dominate the academic
affairs of the training of academic secondary school teachers;
the secular authorities the finances of the teacher training
institutions concerned with the education of the less- or non-
academic sector of education. Few teacher training institutions
enjoy the traditional autonomy of the universities. At one level
there is a struggle for power between the university men and
the teachers of teachers. At another level there is a struggle for
control of many aspects of teacher education by the authorities
who finally finance the school system and therefore pay the
teachers.

These two aspects of a power struggle can perhaps be most
usefully viewed against a common framework of what constitutes a profession, and the criteria used by Myron Lieberman
in *Education as a Profession*[3] seem particularly appropriate. The
first of these is that a profession should have a unique and
essential public service to perform and that this should be
recognised by the public at large. Secondly members of a
profession should have a code of ethics in which public service
is placed before private gain. Finally in order to perform these
unique services each member of a profession should possess
esoteric knowledge—i.e. an understanding of special intellectual
operations and the possession of special skills and techniques.
The possession of these characteristics would justify two
elements of control and responsibility. The organisation within
which members of the profession work should be comprehensive
and self-governing. Thus recruitment, training, and certification of practitioners should, in the final analysis, be in the
hands of the membership or its appointed officers. Moreover
the organisation itself should draw up standards of professional

conduct, insist upon the acceptance of them by members, and be in a position to deal with any violations of them.

Thus one question is, who should determine the code of ethics by which teachers live and work? Who should determine the public service they are expected to perform? What should the esoteric knowledge on which these services are performed be based? And who should determine admission, training, and certification requirements? Obviously the older traditions of academic freedom gave to members of the universities the right to establish these standards and conditions of service. Their power was such that under most circumstances against Church or State the universities were able to withstand attempts to infringe their autonomy. Because of the division within the ranks of teachers, because of the uncertainties about the role they should play, because of the expanded demand for their services and because of the explosion of knowledge in recent years few of the questions can now be answered unequivocally in any country. Even in the United States of America where the process of evolution from the traditional European patterns has perhaps moved further than anywhere else, debates about the organisation of teacher education and the struggle for control over it are intense. A useful distinction suggests that if the aims of education are the responsibility of organised society the technical means of achieving them should be controlled by the teaching profession.

Teacher Education in the U.S.A.

One issue concerns the content of courses for intending teachers. In the U.S.A. the protagonists are on the one side the members of the faculties of arts and sciences—the liberal arts men— and on the other, the professors of education. In the sometimes vicious struggle parents, legislators, public figures outside education, and the trustees of institutions of higher learning have become involved. Well-known public figures like Admiral Rickover have not hesitated to blame education for the apparent failure of his country to lead the U.S.S.R. in space travel. The charges made by liberal arts professors, of whom A. E. Bestor[4] was for many years one of the most voracious critics of education, have been specially directed to the worthlessness of the courses given by professors of education and to the low quality of the degrees granted to students who have devoted much of their time to these courses.

A second complaint is that as a result of a conspiracy between professors of education, educational administrators, classroom teachers, and representatives of national educational associations, a monopoly has been acquired over teacher certification procedures and requirements which has effectively placed control of entry into teaching in the hands of one group dominated as far as the content of teacher education is concerned by the professors of education. All this has occurred in spite of the fact that there is no national system of certification. Naturally the attitude of these critics is that the older university tradition of the university as a medieval guild granting degrees in the liberal arts and conferring teaching rights on graduates is better. More specifically, of course, the argument is that for intending teachers courses provided in the faculties of arts and sciences would form a better basis than those in education. Undoubtedly the critics imply that professional studies occupy too large a part of the intending teachers' course or programme of study and too small a part is concerned with the acquisition of subject matter. Teachers may consequently know a great deal about Johnny but practically nothing about what Johnny needs to know.

Another argument is that teachers have usurped their authority by assuming that they have widely ranging social functions to perform. At one level this criticism turns on the introduction of new subjects or data into school curricula at the expense of the so-called established disciplines. At another important level the belief of such men as Harold Rugg that the teacher of teachers should be the dynamic agent of social reconstruction working finally through the schools has been vigorously challenged.

The sputnik, at least for a time, certainly strengthened the hands of the critics of American education and teacher education. Their most virulent attacks were directed at the professors of education, their methods and survey courses, and foundation studies in education. The extent to which these criticisms were justified is hard to say, but certainly some explanation of the situation is to be found in the extent to which in the last hundred years educational opportunities at all levels have expanded enormously. The decisive battle for 'common' elementary schools was fought and won during the 1840s by Horace Mann and others. The next step was to expand secondary schooling. Since 1870 the growth has been extremely great. Then there were some 80,000 pupils throughout America in public secondary schools. In 1950 there were 5¾ million, and in 1960 over 11 million high school pupils. Already during the 1890s decisions were being taken which meant that the high schools were to become 'common' schools preparing young people not only for college but for many other occupations. Special courses were provided in these schools for intending teachers rather in the tradition of the eighteenth-century academies. The forces making for expansion in secondary education also began to operate to increase enrolments in institutions of higher learning so that the percentage rise has far exceeded the normal growth in population. In 1939 of the 18–21 age group some 14 per cent were degree credit students in institutions of higher learning. In 1960 the figure for a numerically smaller group had risen to 37 per cent. Between 1944 and 1960 the population of the United States increased by 28 per cent, the college age group by 66 per cent. In the early years of the sixties there were some 24,000,000 pupils in primary and junior high schools (grades 1 to 8 inclusive), about 11 million in grades 9 to 12 inclusive. About half the high school graduates continued their studies in one of some 2,000 institutions of higher learning, about 500 of which were two-year Junior Colleges. Thus there were some three and a half million students in institutions of higher learning.

To keep this vast operation going there was a total of 1,366,884 teachers, 61 per cent of whom taught in primary schools and 38 per cent in secondary, suggesting that teacher/student ratios are smaller in the latter than in the former. In 1959 the figures were 21 pupils per high school teacher against 28 per primary school teacher. The problems of drawing them together into a unified profession with a common basis of esoteric knowledge are obviously very great. They are complicated by the fact that over 1,200 of the institutions of higher learning are concerned in some way or other with teacher education. There are many types of institution, ranging from the Junior College, in which the first two years of a four-year degree course may be provided, through the liberal arts (offering a variety of vocational programmes as well as the general course) and teachers' colleges, to a few universities in which only post-graduate courses in education are provided.

Some features of this complex situation are relevant. In the early sixties between 10 and 20 per cent of teachers were prepared in colleges which could be clearly designated 'teachers'' colleges. Within the previous forty years or so the single-purpose normal schools evolved into multi-purpose colleges, so that in 1964 of all the institutions which dealt with teacher education less than 100 were concerned exclusively with it. In fact the evolution has gone further; after 1920 many of the normal schools became first teachers' colleges, then state multi-purpose colleges, and finally state universities—which in American terms is taken to mean places where post-graduate studies either at the Master's level or beyond are provided. In short, most of the institutions of higher learning in the United States, including teacher-training institutions, have become multi-purpose degree-granting institutions—except the Junior Colleges. Perhaps in consequence it was possible in 1962 to claim that all high school teachers and 75 per cent of elementary school teachers are graduates. Soon all school teachers will either have or be expected to acquire degrees in order to enter the profession.

Perhaps inevitably in the face of this kind of expansion control of so-called academic standards has been difficult to maintain and there are enormous differences between institutions. Certainly few Americans would hold that all degree-awarding institutions are equally good—however measured. Expansion has presented educators with hard choices. The amazing growth of the secondary schools made it possible for all intending teachers to be recruited from these schools rather than, as previously, from elementary schools. The normal schools were soon able to concentrate on professional studies rather than, as before, on completing the general education of students entering them from elementary schools. But the vast increase in the proportion of youngsters completing high school forced curriculum changes both in the schools and the colleges. Soon, for a variety of reasons no doubt, the colleges were again undertaking the task of providing in the first two years of the four-year course, at least, a measure of general education. Because they admit, without retaining for the full four years more than about a third of those who enter, about half the vast number of graduates from high schools whose sole purpose is no longer to prepare youngsters for college, some characteristics of higher education have changed. Research and scholarly teaching are by no means the only objectives of a college education. Moreover the measured attainment of students has changed. In 1963 an I.Q. of 111 and above corresponded roughly to the upper 30 per cent of the high school graduating class over the country as a whole: a far cry from the theory and practice of higher education in even the most generous European country, and particularly in England, where the majority of students entering universities, colleges of advanced technology, and training colleges are from grammar schools and consequently are likely to have a measured I.Q. of about 115 or higher. Teachers in the U.S.A. have to be trained to cope with a radically different situation from that which exists in countries where on the foundations of mass education a highly selective secondary and university system of education is maintained. Today in America the principles on which practice is based are in dispute, but in spite of diversity certain patterns can be discerned.

The Content of Teacher Education—U.S.A.

In general intending American teachers are expected to cover three areas of knowledge. There seems little argument that these should be (*a*) general education, (*b*) specialised study in a given field or fields, and (*c*) professional studies. The balance of these three ingredients and the content of each are matters of considerable debate. Practice differs widely too, but in general there tends to be a different emphasis in courses prescribed for intending elementary school teachers from those for potential high school teachers. As for balance in one state university in Ohio the 1962 catalogue indicated that between a third and a half of the intending teachers' programme should be devoted to general education; a further 40 per cent should be given over to the acquisition of mastery over the subject or subjects he will be expected to teach; and professional preparation, including teaching practice, should occupy about one-fifth of the time. In his book the *Education of American Teachers*[5] J. B. Conant recommends that for secondary school teachers half the time should be spent on general education, more than a third of the time in the area of concentration and related subjects, and about an eighth of the time including teaching practice on profession subjects and special methods courses. Future elementary school teachers should spend half their course of study on general education, a quarter on the field of concentration and the remainder (a quarter) on professional studies.

Of course, concepts of what constitutes the subject matter of a sound general education for teachers vary considerably. Theory leads one to suppose, however, that in many institutions it will be drawn from the three recognised areas of the social sciences, the natural sciences, and the language arts. Thus through this general education an intending teacher's understanding of society and crucial social issues will be improved; his awareness of the impact on American and other societies of applied science will be increased through acquaintance with the behavioural and social sciences. His knowledge of world and American literature will be strengthened, as will his insight into ways of thinking and modes of expression. As for the professional courses they should be based on the psychological and sociological foundations and on special methods courses and practice teaching. All these practices have the general backing of theories propounded and elaborated by progressive educators, it is true, but few opponents of the professors of education and the so-called Establishment deviate greatly from belief in this kind of pattern for a degree course for intending teachers. Some would like to postpone professional studies until the fifth year and reduce the proportion of time spent on them. But by and large the three ingredients are accepted.

Certification Procedures

The crux of the matter is who should mix the ingredients and control the balance. Over the years the professors of education have certainly gained an enviable measure of control. This has been achieved through certification procedures which are based upon the responsibility of each state under the Constitution for education. Usually there is one state agency responsible for the certification of all teachers working within the state. But the differences between the states are very considerable. Moreover state certification patterns are complex. A review of the types and classes of certificates awarded in Ohio may serve to illustrate the principles involved. *Temporary* certificates are designed to meet an emergency and are issued on these grounds for one year only. *Provisional* certificates are valid for four years and can be awarded on the basis of a minimum two-year course of study. They may be renewed and converted into *Professional* certificates valid for eight years and requiring twenty-four months successful teaching plus additional training. These certificates too can be converted into *Permanent* certificates if the teacher has forty months of service and a Bachelor's degree if in an elementary school and an M.A. if in a high school. In fact in 1961 some 41 states and the District of Columbia required a Bachelor's degree as a minimum qualification for elementary school teachers. All states required a four-year degree course at least for secondary school teachers, and some insisted upon a fifth year of probationary service under supervision.

Certificates are closely related to the level or type of school in which a teacher will work. In Ohio for example there are six classes. The *Elementary* certificate qualifies a person to teach in (*a*) an elementary school, (*b*) deaf children, (*c*) slow learners, (*d*) gifted children, and (*e*) dual programme at this level. A *Kindergarten-primary* certificate is for early childhood education. The *General High School* certificate is awarded in a number of stated fields—the usual academic subjects plus science comprehensive and social studies comprehensive. *Special* certificates are issued for art education, health and physical education, industrial arts, music, speech, trade and industrial education. *Special Education* certificates are intended for work with exceptional children such as the deaf, the gifted, the slow learner, and those in need of speech and hearing therapy. Finally the *Dual* certificate is intended for persons wishing to prepare themselves for junior high school teaching.

Evidently formal certification is operated by an agency or

agencies of the state Board of Education. Since they work very closely in co-operation with the state universities it is certainly correct to say that the content of the intending teacher's course is very considerably influenced by the state Boards. The combined power of the professors of education and the state educational officials is certainly resented by many liberal arts professors. Certification procedures have, however, also tended to keep elementary school and high school teachers apart. In many colleges of education there are two distinct departments, one for elementary and the other for high school teachers. Often each department provides a full range of courses, and in the case of the elementary teacher courses emphasis in the subject fields is on material appropriate to classroom teaching. The distinction is a reminder of the traditional European dichotomy between elementary and academic secondary school teachers both as far as content is concerned and the way in which it is treated. There is evidence that in many institutions the two traditions are merging. Common courses for elementary and high school teachers are now provided for example at the University of Illinois in the social and psychological foundations.

The divisive consequences for the profession of an already complicated system of teacher certification are further increased by the fact that each state has its own pattern. Thus geographical mobility is reduced because state requirements to teach vary so widely. The absence of national certificates to teach is deplored by a few outspoken critics of the system because it results in great variations in standards of teacher education. Attempts to meet this problem are made through accrediting procedures. The quality of institutions preparing teachers is assessed in terms of buildings, library and other facilities, faculty teaching loads, salary scales, and programmes of study. The six regional associations are in a sense checked by national bodies. In 1950 for example the National Commission on Accrediting was established, drawing its constituent members from a number of national associations concerned with higher education. One of them is the American Association of Colleges for Teacher Education. This association is represented on the National Council for Accredition of Teacher Education, a body of 21 members drawn from colleges and universities, state departments of education, teachers and administrators appointed by the National Educational Association, and school board members from the National Association of School Board Members. Thus national standards are to some extent in the hands of representatives of all the groups interested in public education, both professional and lay.

Progressive Education and its Critics

In practice, of course, the professors of education are well organised and exert a considerable influence on the content of teacher education. They come together particularly in the National Education Association which through its various departments brings into close alliance professional administrators, professors of education, and teachers. Undoubtedly over the past hundred years the overall influence of this organisation has been to help professionalise American education by providing a forum for the discussion of the aims of education and a code of ethics, by examining the basis of special knowledge needed by American teachers, and by strengthening the hand of its members in terms of controlling entry to the profession and establishing certification requirements. The influence has been indirect but nevertheless profound, although over the country as a whole it is perhaps true to say that the National Education Association has not succeeded in establishing any uniformity of policy regarding salary schedules and tenure arrangements for teachers.

Undoubtedly one of the major spokesmen for American education was John Dewey. Rarely in the early days of the NEA's life was he absent from its conferences or failed to speak. His influence was also widely felt through his association with Teachers College, Columbia University. Under the leadership of the Russells this institution obviously helped to shape the destiny of teacher education in America. One important decision in the early twenties was that Teachers College was prepared to undertake the education and training of as many teachers as possible; an acceptance of a policy of expansion which inevitably had in teacher education, as in other spheres, profound consequences. If the country wanted more and more teachers for the expanding high schools, then, said Dean Russell, Teachers College would see that it had them. This policy may be contrasted with the one pursued by Chicago University which has always tried to maintain educational studies within the wider framework of the university as a constituent and co-operating department and has always placed great emphasis on research and small doctoral seminars.

Doubtless other divisions can easily be discerned in the evolving pattern of American teacher education. The child-centred movement supported largely by psychologists can be contrasted with social reconstructionism urged by men like Harold Rugg, Goodwin Watson, and others at Teachers College in the thirties. Faculty members at Ohio State University under the leadership of Boyd H. Bode were perhaps a little more conservative. Yet for the most part the leading educationists belonged to the Progressive Education Association and paid allegiance to the leadership of John Dewey. This represented, in spite of differences in interpretation, the professional tradition in education. Stress was laid on the whole child and his development in a social environment. The learning process was interpreted to mean far more than academic subjects, and a bookish approach. Elementary school teachers were certainly not expected to be primarily scholars. They were to know the child, how he was likely to develop, and the social environment in which he would grow up and into which he would move when he left school. Consequently professional studies for intending teachers have been stressed, but not necessarily at the cost of general education. Indeed for school children progressive educators have tried to provide in the curriculum both for subjects which will serve to develop the interests and capacities of individuals and for a common core. Perhaps one point made by Dewey has received less attention than it deserved. He felt that vocational studies should and could be made the heart of a sound liberal education which for him and his followers would prepare young people to participate actively and intelligently in a democracy constantly in process of change under the forces of industrialisation, commercialism, and urbanisation. His more radical followers wished to see the schools do more than this—they were consciously to help remould society.

The opponents of the professional educationists have been and are more traditional in their approach. Critics like A. E.

Bestor and R. M. Hutchins[6] have wished to place restrictions on the role of the school so as to exclude vocational studies and deliberately socialising activities. Hence for such critics the curriculum should be restricted to those subjects which over the years have acquired the prestige of being known as intellectual disciplines. Through them the aim of formal education —the cultivation of the ability to think—can be achieved. Naturally the critics of progressivism tend to hold somewhat different assumptions about the constituents of thinking. In practice defenders of the liberal arts tradition have attempted to persuade a number of state legislatures to rewrite teacher certification rules. Such attempts have been defeated, but nevertheless certification reform in the early sixties in no case involved proposals to increase the number of education requirements in a four-year college course.

On the other hand the critics have succeeded in persuading many more educationists to take seriously the problem of the gifted child. These movements have their counterpart in teacher education, and several experiments have for the most part been financed by the Ford Fund for the Advancement of Education. Basically the fund supports projects in liberal education and stresses that the total education of intending teachers should consist of four interrelated parts; (*a*) liberal education, (*b*) an extended knowledge of the subject area taught, (*c*) professional knowledge as distinguished from professional skills, and (*d*) skills in managing a classroom, working with children, and supervising the learning process. These aims, it is thought, could be more effectively achieved if the schools themselves were to play a greater part in the preparation of teachers. One proposal, for example, is that there should be a fifth year of professional training consisting of an internship— a scheme tried at the University of Arkansas. In the Temple University project the liberal arts graduate course gave three years on-the-job training and was based upon the belief that teachers cannot be trained adequately in one professional year.

The Master of Arts in Teaching courses are designed to test the view that undergraduate and graduate education for teachers can be planned as a single unit and should include a fifth year of study for intending secondary school teachers. Two plans should be mentioned. One involves the graduate

214

taking full-time study during the first semester of the graduate year together with observation of teaching. During the second semester the candidate serves as an apprentice in a local school. Under the second plan the student is an intern with a salary equal to half the full salary; two students are employed as a team instead of a teacher, one for the first half of the year, the other for the second. Students also have to attend a summer school.

Basically these proposals seem to involve three principles. First they extend courses for teachers from four to five years, secondly they postpone professional courses and practice teaching until the final year, and finally they emphasise internship rather than supervised teaching practice.

Another type of experiment reverses this emphasis by the appointment of teaching assistants whose task is to relieve teachers of many of the non-professional aspects of their work. The Yale-Fairfield study of elementary teaching was designed to identify the student from the outset with school practice and professional study without losing sight of the need for liberal education. Here too students help qualified teachers with the chores. Undoubtedly a very considerable period of a teacher's time is now spent on activities other than teaching and the need to recruit assistants with clearly defined and different functions is apparent. Whether or not these tendencies presage a return in modified form to some kind of apprenticeship training for teachers is hard to say. The fact remains that two tensions are to be observed in the American scene. On the one hand there is the pull by the liberal arts professors on secondary school teachers in training towards the subject matter courses provided by liberal arts professors. On the other there is the willingness to accept that elementary school teachers can be trained on the job and need little professional education.

The Future

In spite of these disruptive forces the unity and strength of the educational profession in America is growing. Its members stand as a group (as few teachers anywhere else do) in a position to consolidate considerable gains. If they cannot yet serve as dynamic agents of change they have nevertheless helped to unify a nation of immigrants of whom the vast majority when they arrived were illiterate by the simplest of tests. In the process hard choices have constantly been made, most of them on the grounds that the schools are socialising agencies first and storehouses of knowledge next. The vast majority of teachers have degrees, having followed a balanced programme including general, special, and professional education. Certification procedures are in large measure controlled by members of the profession. In-service training in many states is obligatory and salary increases often depend upon the successful completion of advanced courses of study.

In England and Wales intending teachers are not required to undertake professional courses, a university degree which includes no educational studies is a licence to teach and the status of 'qualified' teacher is conferred by the Department of Education and Science (formerly the Ministry of Education) on degree holders who wish to teach. Many graduates, in fact, complete a year of professional training in one of the university departments of education. Non-graduate teachers are trained in teacher training colleges whose courses are three years in duration. Courses of study and examinations are under the control of individual colleges and committees of Institutes of Education. Certificates to teach are awarded on the basis of the recommendations of Institute boards. The sharp distinction between university departments of education and the training colleges has been breaking down for some time. Under the McNair proposals links between them were forged in the Institutes of Education. In 1963, however, the Robbins report on Higher Education recommended that schools of education should be established which would integrate all teacher training and educational studies more closely into the university. The debates will be protracted, but there seems little doubt that a pattern will emerge in which it will be possible for more training college students than at present to obtain university degrees and in which there will be a further breakdown of the nineteenth-century dichotomies in teacher education.

In France where much administrative control over teacher education is exercised by central government agencies the *écoles normales* have a proud tradition. The division between the system of training for future elementary school teachers and that for persons intending to teach in the academic *lycées* has always been marked, bridged to some extent by the fact that after the war the *baccalauréat* became not only an award admitting students to the university but is taken by students in *écoles normales* after two years of study, and in an emergency is regarded as a qualification to teach in primary schools even for students who have not passed through an *école normale*. In similar vein students at the colleges for persons intending to teach in the *écoles normales* (at Fontenay and Saint-Cloud) can now proceed to the *agrégation*, an extremely high award previously reserved for scholars hoping to teach in the *lycées*. Yet another indication of the movement towards integration occurred in 1957, when within each faculty of arts or science was created an institute for the training of secondary teachers (*Institut de préparation a l'enseignement du second degré*). To be admitted to the course students must have passed a preparatory certificate examination taken after the first year at a university. Once admitted students receive a salary as student-teachers and stay at the institute for three years preparing for a teaching diploma. They have to do a year's practice in preparation for the practical examinations, and this is carried out in the regional pedagogical centres (*Centres pédagogiques régionaux*) located in each of the university towns. Every attempt is made to bring students up to a standard from which they can proceed either to the certificate of aptitude for secondary teaching (*Certificat d'aptitude a l'enseignement secondaire* or *C.A.P.E.S.*) or for the *agrégation*. One consequence of introducing this course has been that of the students at the regional centres some 25 per cent go on to take the *agrégation*. In general the measures taken in France have resulted in a steady rise in the number of people entering the teaching profession in possession of the *baccalauréat* —a move towards a common university entrance requirement for all teachers.

Frequent attempts have been made in Germany to change the normal schools for elementary school teachers into academic institutions. Since 1945 in the German Federal Republic the training of teachers for all kinds of school has been the responsibility and has come under the supervision of the state. Indeed with one exception all teacher training establishments are state institutions. Unification of entrance requirements has been achieved by making the leaving certificate of the academic secondary school (*Abitur*) necessary in order to gain admission to any course of study. There are exceptions to this in some *Länder* for intending women primary school teachers. Even so there are to be found special institutions for the training of teachers for different types of school—the elementary schools, the middle schools, the vocational and commercial schools and the academic secondary schools. The teacher in the last completes his studies at the university and takes a state examination to qualify to teach and may go on to a doctorate. Except in one or two cases there are no special institutions where middle school teachers are trained; they are either elementary school teachers or persons with three years of university study who are admitted to special examinations. Elementary school teachers may be trained in one of three types of institution—an *Akademie*, a *Hochschule*, or an *Institut*. Previously the status of each was different, but now they are all accepted as academic colleges with professors and assistants under the direction of a rector elected by his peers. The pattern, of course, varies from Land to Land, but in general the trend is to provide a common base for teacher education in institutions enjoying greater equality of prestige.

In the U.S.S.R. three teacher training institutions exist. The pedagogical technicums prepare teachers for the first four grades of the common school. Teachers in the higher grades are trained either in the five year pedagogical institutes or in the universities. Indeed all university students undergo a course designed to prepare them to teach their special subject. As in most countries the university tends to place more emphasis on subject matter than perhaps is the case in the pedagogical institutes. Assessments of the two forms of training indicate that standards of academic scholarship may not be as high in the institutes as in the universities, and certainly there is a certain amount of rivalry between the two. Needless to say, however, in both types of training establishment great attention is paid to subject matter and to the acquisition of it by intending teachers.

In many low-income countries the problems of integration with the universities hardly arise; the demand is for training establishments which will turn out in vast numbers teachers able to man the growing number of primary schools. Frequently these institutions are little more than secondary schools and perform much the same kind of role. India has a well-developed system of universities and training colleges. The latter, preparing teachers for elementary schools, are controlled by state departments of education. The attainments of candidates vary very considerably. Recently the tendency has been to combine in teacher training institutions other tasks such as the preparation of young women for home making. Since basic education continues to be accepted as the desirable form of primary education special basic education training colleges have been established. However the divorce between the training of elementary school teachers and the secondary school teachers reveals the old European tradition. Secondary school teachers are to have one year of professional training after completing a three-year degree course. This is, of course, the English pattern. Experiments are going on with concurrent liberal and professional education in degree courses, and with less academic syllabuses for intending teachers. Many of the new proposals for reform are based upon American theories and practices. The struggle to break away from European patterns of teacher education will, however, be difficult in countries which have fairly recently gained their independence from colonial powers.

This brief review of some of the policies now being debated is intended to show that in most countries of the world teacher education is being subjected to and is responding in some way to similar forces. The demand for education is growing and is bound to increase. The maintenance of highly selective systems of secondary and higher education is now being more vigorously challenged. The need in democratic societies to reduce the differences between social classes and economic groups is apparent. Economic development based upon the application of science and technology requires personnel not only with new industrial and commercial skills but workers and managers with new attitudes and social skills. Undoubtedly the schools have some part to play, and a new type of teacher is needed: one who perhaps will regard his role in more exciting terms, that is, not as a mere conserver of tradition but as the moulder of another kind of society. To perform this task the teacher will need to be imaginative and creative. His skills and knowledge should be based on experimental and tested research, his pre-occupation not only with the classroom but with the organisation of his profession and the policies it is to pursue. The university traditions of academic freedom and a certain academic detachment may not be wholly adequate if the challenge is to be met successfully, nor on the other hand is the apprenticeship teacher training tradition of the nineteenth century. The need for a closer integration of university studies and teacher education is widely felt. The expansion of education at all levels has profoundly affected the nature of the teaching problem. It is for example impossible to contemplate an integration between subject matter and professional courses based upon the old dichotomy between liberal education and vocational training. Furthermore it is no longer possible to consider any person educated whose scientific knowledge is negligible. Some balance, in short, needs to be found in teacher education between courses designed to provide an extended general education, those intended to provide the teacher with a sound knowledge of the subject he will teach, and those which will deepen and enlarge his understanding of children, the society in which they live, and the role of the school which they attend and in which he teaches.

Evidently the American solutions to these problems are not universally accepted even in the United States. They are viewed with suspicion elsewhere. Certainly the policies generally pursued should not be regarded as a panacea. Nevertheless it is difficult, on the basis of an analysis of the problems associated with teacher education, to escape from the belief that they represent patterns of theory and practice which will provide acceptable solutions in many nations throughout the world at a comparable stage of economic development. For this reason they deserve detailed and critical study.

Chapter IX

SECONDARY EDUCATION FOR ALL
(ENGLAND AND WALES)

THE war had multiple effects on Europe. All the major powers suffered economically. Political changes were no less drastic. Germany was occupied and virtually divided into two nations. Governments, like that of Petain in France, which had collaborated with a defeated enemy were swept out of office. In some instances, in a bid to replace them, groups in favour of a Soviet form of government came into conflict with groups favouring western democratic forms of government. In Britain a wartime coalition government was replaced, with an overwhelming majority, by a Labour administration.

These changes were dramatic. Others, no less real, were in some ways less apparent. In the victorious countries, particularly, there was a heightening of aspirations and expectations, the overriding principles of which were egalitarian. In western Europe the demand was for peace, improved housing, better health services, bulkier pay-packets, and greater and less expensive access to education. From one point of view, therefore, one source of post-war problems in, for example, France and Britain, can be regarded as arising from the imbalance between heightened expectations and the availability of economic resources. Or again, the problems can be seen as a conflict between new aspirations on the one hand and old attitudes, reinforced by powerful institutional inertia, on the other. In the event, it was perhaps less easy to change the schools and the attitudes of those who ran them than it was to rebuild the material basis of devastated economies. In spite of the fact that the demand for education grew under the impetus of both arguments—education as a human right, and education as a form of investment for economic growth—major reforms were not readily accepted in many European countries. To be sure the 1944 Education Act for England and Wales represented a coalition government's contribution to one aspect of post-war planning. But in other western European countries major legislation was not enacted until the late fifties. A list of reforms is given by Jean Thomas and Joseph Majault in the Council of Europe's *Primary and Secondary Education*.[1] Only in 1959 were laws passed in France reforming many aspects of the educational system. In Italy primary education was modified by legislation in 1957, and some aspects of secondary and higher education in 1961. Three Scandinavian governments managed to have major educational legislation accepted; Denmark in 1958, Norway in 1959, and Sweden in 1962. In 1963 several projects of reform were still being considered by several governments. In those countries with Communist governments legislative reform was apparently somewhat less difficult to achieve. Yet only after years of discussion was a major law passed in the Soviet Union in 1958 intended to bring the schools nearer to life. Thus major reforms were almost everywhere preceded by lengthy debate. Even when the principles of reform had been accepted difficulties of precise interpretation and implementation arose.

One reason for this was that the demand for more education based upon egalitarian principles gave rise to somewhat different policies from those arising from calls for educational expansion on economic grounds. Attention was concentrated, however, in these widespread movements in western Europe on post-primary education. The socio-political reformers demanded 'secondary education for all'. Progressive educationists agreed that secondary education as a human right should be made freely available and stressed the interests of each individual child in their desire to introduce more active methods of teaching and learning. In general, however, the aim was to change the structure or organisation of post-primary education. The economic argument, when divorced from the demand for education *per se*, tended to lead to proposals further to differentiate post-primary schooling. More of the kind of education that prevailed in pre-war Europe may be a crude summary of the direction in which some of these arguments led.

In face of a general demand for education many proposals

were made simply to extend it by raising the compulsory attendance age. More significantly, however, attempts to reform the structure of post-primary education were countered by policies designed to increase the amount of technical education at this stage. The reason is obvious. The attack of the socio-political and educational reformers was directed, in effect, at the powerfully entrenched academic secondary schools and the attitudes and beliefs in accordance with which they were run. On the whole the theories of man, society, and knowledge which justified pre-war European systems of education were Platonic. The institutions which had grown up over the years reflected these views. It was thought that a few persons of superior intellect should be given the kind of education which would prepare them to discharge the tasks of social and political leadership, and prepare them for the traditional professions of law, the Church, medicine, and certain levels of teaching. In practice scholarship systems enabled poor but able boys to benefit from the highly selective education. In emphasis at least concepts of what constituted a sound liberal education gave the highest prestige to the type of education provided by a study of classical languages. With few exceptions, for those students who were not able, or wealthy enough, to attend academic secondary schools there were terminal elementary schools and various kinds of vocational schools. Thus vocational education was introduced in many European systems for children between the ages of 12 and 14, in many countries. In England and Wales it was thought undesirable to include it within the period of compulsory attendance.

The age at which pupils began to attend school varied, but in general, by 1939 transition from primary to some form of post-primary education occurred at about the age of 10 or 11. Academic secondary education continued until about 18, and post-primary schooling either in elementary or vocational schools until the age of 14 (or until children had completed 8 years of attendance). There were growing up, in several countries, schools which placed less emphasis on the classics and more on modern languages. In intention, however, these 'modern' schools prepared pupils for some, but not necessarily all, of the faculties of the universities. The relations between the universities and the academic secondary schools were indeed extremely close and criteria of success were closely geared to university requirements. Under these circumstances selection both for the academic secondary schools and the universities was rigorous.

The divorce between the academic secondary schools and the elementary schools was reflected in systems of teacher training and recruitment. By 1939 therefore, as a general rule, the two systems of education were separate and directed pupils into vastly different channels. The elementary schools were for the masses; the academic schools for a small élite whose members for the most part intended to go on to university and then enter politics, the administrative side of government, management or the professions. By this time too, differentiation was largely at the post-primary level since, with notable exceptions, universal primary education was available for all children for at least four (and often eight) years and a large proportion of children attended publicly maintained primary schools. A certain unification of primary schools had therefore taken place, although for the most part they were administered by those in charge of elementary education. In most countries this administrative division existed. Frequently, as in France and Denmark, some academic secondary schools were State institutions financed and largely controlled from the centre. The elementary schools were to a greater extent the responsibility of local communities, even though national governments subsidised them. This form of dual control only served to emphasise the differences between the elementary school and the academic secondary schools systems.

Another feature of pre-war European education was the continuing influence of the Church or churches. The situation varied widely from one country to another. Wherever the Roman Catholics predominated their influence on the publicly maintained schools system was very considerable. Where, as in France, sharp divisions existed between persons committed to the Roman Catholic church and those who were either anti-clerical or non-Catholic, considerable difficulties of policy formulation and acceptance arose. In other countries like Sweden the Church had virtual monopoly but attitudes had been powerfully influenced by non-sectarian views. In yet other countries, like the Netherlands (and in England and

Wales after 1944) relatively generous policies of support for parochial schools were in operation. Nevertheless wherever several churches existed each with a significantly large following tensions over educational policy—and in particular finance —were apparent.

Naturally the details of policy differed, but a general sociological pattern was clearly discernible. Because the academic secondary schools conferred so much power—economic, political, and social—on their alumni they were themselves extremely powerful institutions. At the same time the Platonic view of change, added to the fact that schools in any case perform the task of passing on from one generation to the next the accumulated knowledge of the society in which they exist, meant that the academic secondary schools were slow to change. Moreover since knowledge for its own sake, rather than knowledge for practical use, dominated the thinking of many academies, an appeal could always be made to the sanctity of academic standards when changes threatened.

In brief, a complex of forces, ideological and institutional, in post-war western Europe were ready, or quickly recovered their strength, after the war, to meet the challenge of the reformers. Initially, post-war economic circumstances made radical reform and expansion, in spite of aspirations, difficult. Already a deviant from the continental European pattern, the educational system of England and Wales soon experienced major legislative reforms. The nature of the proposals enacted in the 1944 Education Act and the problems of implementing them in the first decade after the war offer an illuminating case study revealing many features common to western Europe as well as uniquely English characteristics.

At the level of policy-formulation a number of proposals had been made by pre-war committees, but there were more radical policies for consideration. As for acceptance, wartime circumstances favoured general agreement being reached, not without debate of course, on a number of long controversial issues. In some areas the legislation was so phrased as to make almost any interpretation possible. In other respects it conferred quite specific powers on each of a number of interested groups. In the event problems of implementation were considerable. Normative adjustments were necessary, and

225

institutional reform in many spheres of life long overdue. It is with some of these problems of change that this chapter is principally concerned.

Heightened Expectations

The reasons for the explosion of aspirations in Britain during the war and processes by which they were heightened will not be analysed in any detail here. Suffice it to say that powerful unifying forces operated to draw all classes of people nearer together to create a climate of opinion in which the Welfare State could be conceived. Even during a fight for existence policy discussions took place and influential committees made proposals like those contained in the Beveridge Report which gave high priority to full employment, social security, and more adequate health services. Among the documents of this period the 1944 Education Act has been named the greatest piece of legislation in educational history. Superficially, at least, the Act implied the most radical changes in every sphere of English education. Yet because of the circumstances under which it was formulated and accepted it is hardly surprising that its provisions, while solving or ameliorating some long-standing problems, were based on educational theories and policies which had been formulated to meet the problems of education between the wars. Of these the conclusions and recommendations reached in the Hadow (1926), the Spens (1938) and the Norwood (1943) reports related most directly to post-primary education. In the post-war world they were essentially conservative and help to explain some of the difficulties associated with the reform of educational institutions.

The 1944 Education Act nevertheless represents a statement of intentions, the basic principles of which need be mentioned but briefly. The three stages of education—primary, secondary, and further—were at last to be brought together into a coherent pattern. A ministry of education was to have general responsibility for education (Section 1(1)) but local authorities were held responsible for the provision of facilities in their areas and had to submit to the Minister for approval their development plans (Section 11(1)). The aim of this national system of education locally administered was emphatically child-centred.

Education was to be provided according to the age, aptitude, and ability of each individual child of secondary school age (Section 8(1)(b)), and as far as economically feasible, in accordance with the wishes of parents (Section 76). The school-leaving age was to be raised (Section 35) and part-time education beyond the age of compulsory full-time attendance was to be provided in county colleges for young people (Section 43). In principle the policies, if implemented, represented a very costly programme of development.

Economic Changes

In the first place, however, the changed economic conditions of post-war Britain were not auspicious. Crucial to the whole situation was the destruction caused by war, the loss of foreign investments, and the shortage of materials and trained manpower. These major deficiencies in real resources affected education no less, and because of its place in the hierarchy of priorities rather more, than other services.

For example, by the end of March, 1945, over a million houses in London and South-East England, and throughout the country over five thousand schools, had been destroyed or badly damaged. A labour force in the building trade of 337,000 compared with some 1,000,000 before the war together with shortages of cement, steel, and timber slowed down the process of replacing out-of-date school buildings and putting up new ones. The problem of accommodation (to say nothing of teachers) was soon to be complicated by the rapid rise in the number of children of school age.

The loss of foreign investments posed quite basic issues. The United Kingdom had always imported raw materials of one kind or another, but after the second world war it was recognised that more than ever before imports would have to be paid for by the export of goods and services. The greater part of the foreign investments which had been built up over the years, and had made the country a leading creditor, had been sacrificed. It was also appreciated that the goods for export would have to be of high quality. Some previously profitable exports—like coal—had become negligible. A vicious circle had to be broken. There was an acute shortage both of exportable

materials and of those basic commodities—timber, steel, concrete, coal, etc.—on which a successful export trade of high
quality goods could be built.

There was also an acute shortage of labour. The birth-rate
during the thirties had been consistently low, and service in
the armed forces and losses during the war had not improved
the position so that the demand for labour was far greater than
the supply. Under such circumstances the distribution of
available labour was important. But although certain wartime
measures continued to operate to restrict occupational mobility,
the direction of workers into essential jobs was not continued
in peace, so that workers could choose their occupations rather
freely. Thus, for example, the mines were desperately short of
manpower. During the war the labour force dropped by nearly
100,000. Afterwards, despite a fourfold increase in the average
weekly wage of miners, many recruiting drives, additional
incentives, and benefits, the pre-war figure of men on the
colliery books was never reached. Against this fact it should be
recorded that the percentage of coal cut mechanically rose
from about 60 in 1939 to 83 in 1953. But it was difficult to
attract men into the mines. The main reason was that there
was a very high demand for manpower in less arduous employment. In general, none of the extractive industries, many of
which had suffered from inadequate development for years,
could cope with a simultaneous rapid fall in manpower and a
rapidly increasing demand for its products.

Other types of industry were short too, and continued to lack
trained personnel. Figures show that even eleven years after
the war's end, in mid-1955, there were in the engineering,
shipbuilding, and vehicle-making industries three to four
vacancies for every person unemployed. Shortly afterwards the
situation changed considerably when in the vehicle industry
alone there was a sharp rise in unemployment from over 4,000
in 1955 to more than 16,000 in 1956. Even so, in this most
sensitive industry, in 1960 the number of registered unemployed
was more than balanced by the registered number of vacancies.
The inference is that, under conditions of full employment,
there was still a dearth of trained men.

In the light of these demands educational policy was scrutin-
ised. Many of the skilled technicians for industry were, and are,

recruited through apprenticeships. Two types can be distinguished: 'student apprenticeships' whose products are 'professional technologists' and the craft and trade technicians. Industrialists were concerned about the number and quality of the recruits for these schemes. Not enough people were being trained at any of the three levels. Again the question was: Is there enough talent available in the population of boys and girls to meet the demands of industry? Opinion was not unanimous.

The complexities of the situation were admitted by the Carr[2] Committee set up in 1957 to investigate the recruitment and training of young workers for industry. Among the difficulties it encountered in its attempt to formulate realistic policy was the absence of data on the practices prevailing and statistics of the number of people involved. What is clear is that a great many young people seek to qualify themselves through attendance at evening classes and prepare for National Certificates and other awards. The wastage for a variety of reasons is very considerable.

In the mid-fifties claims were made that the needs of industry could best be met by a large expansion of technical college work; one industrialist compared the number of Higher National Certificates awarded in the United Kingdom with the annual number of students in U.S.A. who received a first degree (about 400,000 in 1950, of whom some 150,000 were available to industry). The two awards may be taken to be roughly equivalent qualifications. While the equivalence of awards made in different countries needs careful evaluation, the figures of trained technologists and technicians turned out each year in the U.S.S.R. are certainly impressive.

At the same time graduate scientists and engineers were in great demand and short supply. The post-war economy depended for its stability and growth as much as anything on the quantity and quality of these people. 'Never before', according to the Barlow Committee Report, 'has the importance of science been more widely recognised or so many hopes of future progress and welfare founded upon the scientist.'[3] This committee, appointed in December 1945, concerned itself with the recruitment of qualified scientists—either those with a degree or members of recognised professional institutions. As at other levels of the economy the twofold problem was to train enough scientists and guide them into occupations according to the needs of reconstruction and thereafter. The committee considered that by 1955 there would be a total demand for some ninety thousand scientists compared with the forty-five thousand registered scientists in 1945. The demand for them exceeded expectations. In spite of the fact that the output of scientists had been doubled by 1950, in 1954 there was still a grave shortage which by 1962, when the Technical and Scientific Register was closed and the data merged with those of the Professional and Executive Register, had by no means been reduced overall.

A similar shortage of personnel continued to exist in engineering. In 1955 it was reported that the total number of graduates recruited was 'some 25% below the number required, the reason generally being that insufficient applicants were available'. Projections are always more difficult to make than assessment of present shortages. For example, the Zuckerman Committee reported in 1961 that by 1965 'taking all disciplines together' the stock would 'be broadly in balance with demand'.[4] The balance, it was assumed, would be achieved by the shortage of technologists being offset by a surplus of scientists. Projections of supply were easier to make than predictions of demand. Perhaps for this reason the Robbins Committee on Higher Education in 1963 made little attempt to base the claim for an expansion of higher education on future manpower needs. What is clear, however, is that conservative estimates have tended to be falsified by events, as even the rather startling (at the time) Barlow Committee estimates show.

University and higher education expansion has been urged fairly consistently since then. The extent and form it should take has been debated. The Barlow Committee had argued that an expansion in the quality of science graduates should not be sacrificed to increased numbers, but had also pointed out that only one in five of those who could benefit from university education in fact received it. Consequently the committee was able to maintain that the increased demand for science students should not be met at the expense of the humanities. Industrialists were certainly not unanimously in agreement with this view. Several of them made plain their opinion that the expansion of science and engineering departments in universities could only be achieved by diverting some of the very able men from other faculties. 'It is unlikely that men of this calibre (University men with academic prowess, personality, and powers of leadership) are being missed by the university selection machinery, and it is probable that the numbers can only be increased by diverting the very able men from other faculties such as Arts and Classics . . .'[5]

Again some industrialists thought that the effect of university expansion had been to cream off from apprenticeship schemes too many of the brighter boys. University expansion was necessary, but not at the expense of apprenticeships, and only if the universities became, at the post-graduate level, more conscious of the needs of industry. The Advisory Council on Scientific Policy concluded that there was a need to expand university departments, and that there would be an ever-increasing demand by industry for scientists and technologists trained to the graduate level. It felt that the talent available in the population was sufficient to meet the needs both of the universities (in all faculties) and of technical apprenticeships. It hoped that more children than were staying on could be persuaded to stay on in the sixth form beyond the school-leaving age of 15, and within the courses provided for them a 'balanced attitude towards the different ways of training to become an engineer' should be maintained. By 1963 far more sixth formers than ever before had reached the minimum university entrance requirements, yet the aspirations of candidates were such that the engineering faculties and departments reported difficulty—in a period of very high demand for places generally—in attracting sufficient candidates of high quality.

Certainly the crude ratio of university students to total population in industrialised countries indicated that the United Kingdom was not fully utilising her human resources; the 1·5 students per thousand of population came very low on the list. Nevertheless the close balance of arts students to science and engineering students had been maintained. Evidence suggested, too, that in an attempt to maintain academic standards some institutions were not making full use of their available facilities. Both policies—the maintenance of a balance between arts and science-engineering students and restrictive entry—are possible only through the attitudes of university faculties and the position of autonomy the universities as such enjoy. It is a measure of their social irresponsibility that the balance has not been tipped in favour of a much greater proportion of urgently needed scientists and technologists. Meanwhile the social consequences of establishing separate Colleges of Advanced Technology were hardly considered until the Robbins Committee proposed they should become universities and award their own degrees.

Measured in manpower terms, then, the position after the war and for some twenty years thereafter may be perhaps accurately summarised by quoting from the Percy Report: 'the position of Great Britain as a leading industrial nation (was) . . . being endangered by failure to secure the fullest possible application of science to industry, and this failure is partly due to deficiencies in education'.[6] These deficiencies were not solely due to too little attention being paid to the expansion of education on the grounds of manpower needs. Post-war Britain required a system of schools which would help to ameliorate economic and political problems by fostering new attitudes as well as skills among its young people. Of these the norms appropriate to a Welfare State are among the most important.

A brief glance at the policies which were outlined just before the end of the war suggest the extent to which heightened expectations were incapable of immediate fulfilment. A Command paper of May 1944 suggested that the production of non-essentials should not interfere with essentials and that home consumption should be cut down. Rationing and price controls were to remain after the war was over; costs were to be stabilised; saving was to be encouraged; and the use of capital controlled. Nevertheless successive Chancellors, whether Labour or Conservative, urged the imperative need to step up industrial production for export if the economy was to be stabilised. The success of these policies depended on a variety of factors. Among them the attitudes of management and labour were extremely important. Then again investment policies had a significant part to play. Education could not be a panacea, but had a decisive role to play in the amelioration of Britain's economic position. There was need, in short, for the release of industrial intelligence.

Production Norms

Under conditions of shortage, in order to meet the heightened aspirations of the population at large, changes in attitude both by trade unionists and management were needed. Parenthetically, the former, lending powerful support to a Labour government with an absolute and adequate majority, were in a much stronger position than ever before. Unfortunately in the event, some industrial principles which had been accepted (and fought for) under entirely different circumstances were still held. Trade unionists opposed the recruitment of trainees, especially foreigners. The same Command paper noted that 'If any re-training schemes are to be a success, there must be the fullest co-operation between employers and Trade Unions. Difficulties have arisen in the past because some sections of industry have been reluctant to admit trainees . . . (to) safeguard employment of existing workers and their wage standards, and to maintain a proper standard of skill. In some cases the difficulty has been increased by competition between Unions.'[7] Under Labour governments the trade union leaders set their faces against official strikes, but many unofficial ones took place. With a Conservative government in power official strikes were more frequent, suggesting that industrial unrest was due as much to political as to industrial causes. One of its most serious aspects was the apparent inability of one side to communicate with the other.

There were signs, perhaps, of a growing awareness that under conditions of full employment and inflationary pressure, a nation's industrial efficiency and productivity could not be maintained at the highest level without some change in the kind of relations which had existed between labour and management in the days of unemployment. Evidently nationalisation of basic industries did not of itself solve the problem. Greater co-operation between management and men was needed for the new organisation to work. This was a matter of human approach. Yet in 1954, the Joint Committee on Human Relations in Industry reported[8] that increased awareness of the importance of the human factor had not been matched by extensive research in the field.

Generally speaking, the problem has been one of determining under what social, traditional, economic, and cultural conditions incentive payment schemes in industry would lead to maximum productivity. The issue was more than incentive payments in a narrow sense, and a Manchester University project concerned itself with production norms determined largely by the attitudes of workers and management. The investigators cited studies carried out in the U.S.A. which showed that the conventional norms of production existed in many industries and were important in affecting the level of output and the operation of incentive schemes. Several aspects of the problem were mentioned. Effective communication of information within the management and between it and others within the organisation was one. Certain human problems were recognised as slowing down or as preventing the effective and rapid introduction of new scientific techniques. The question of selecting, training and utilising talent to the fullest extent was also appreciated.

Many of the basic issues in political and economic affairs have been complicated by an educational system which tended to maintain traditional social class values. Labour was suspicious, management often unimaginative, yet the country's need for greater productivity demanded a far greater measure of co-operation than occurred. The situation has been particularly unfortunate in view of the acceptance by the government, even before the war ended, of a policy of full employment. Rarely have unemployment figures exceeded half a million. The changes in attitude necessary to make such a policy work smoothly have not been easily brought about on either side.

Wartime experience in Britain had had a considerable impact on certain of the norms without touching some of the others. Perhaps one important contributory factor in raising aspirations for a more equitable society was the evacuation of children from the industrial centres to the smaller towns and villages. During the war millions of children had been moved from their homes. Some of the effects of these mass migrations have been recorded by Richard Titmuss[9] and by other social workers. Perhaps for the first time the middle-class hosts were brought into close contact with the lower-class evacuees. The shock experienced in these meetings was traumatic, as though

Secondary Education for All

two different worlds had collided. The conscience of the middle classes was undoubtedly aroused. Here were children with standards of behaviour entirely different from many of those of their temporary foster-parents, who were shocked to discover that the children had no knowledge of the material refinements of middle-class living. It would be unwise to assume that such experiences were the most important factor in the return of the Labour party in the first post-war election, but they certainly made some contribution to this victory. The concept of the Welfare State was hardly the result merely of doctrinaire political thinking, it was in a very real sense the outcome of an awakening among the British people to the inequalities and hardships within their own society.

Popular demand placed health and housing high on the list of priorities. Under the Labour governments (1945–51) an extended and expensive socialised health service was established. The demand for improved living conditions grew apace and found expression in the theme of the 1951 election when better housing became the issue on which the result (a victory for the Conservative party) turned. The realisation of these aspirations within a viable economy necessitated more radical changes in political and economic norms than occurred among some of the leaders, and among the rank and file of the organised groups which wielded political and industrial power.

Resources were not adequate to meet all the aspirations. There was simply not enough capital, for example, to meet all the demands of the Welfare State. Some indication of the order of priorities can be gleaned from the investment policies. Relatively few resources were made available for education. A major portion of them went into the health services, housing, defence, and economic reconstruction. Up to 1955 the order of priorities in Britain's capital investment showed that except for agriculture the public social services came lowest in the list which included public utilities, transport and communications, manufacturing and distribution, and housing. Although by 1948 the temporary housing programme had been virtually completed, in that year slightly less than one per cent of the total government authorised building and civil work was for hospitals and schools.

Thus, translated into practical policies it is apparent that

235

education received a slender proportion of national resources. Consequently the problem of allocation within education itself became acute. Obviously education as a human right and educational expenditure as a form of investment were, and are, not always compatible. To consider only the economic returns of educational policy is folly, to be sure, but to ignore them is equally shortsighted. The pros and cons of this argument were presented at some length in the first post-war decade. Broadly speaking the Labour Party pursued policies which emphasised education as a human right (and a social equaliser), and the Conservative Party followed policies based on the country's manpower requirements. As for parents, perhaps the fact that only an interested (but articulate) minority placed educational opportunity almost as high as health, and higher than housing, on the list of priorities, accounts for the failure of educational policy to become a major electioneering topic. In fact many parents have found themselves since 1944 on the horns of a difficult dilemma.

Parental Norms, Socio-political Theory, and Institutional Change

The educational aspirations of parents were in many respects difficult to fulfil. The pre-war traditional 'structure' of the school system had created a strong demand for 'secondary' as opposed to 'elementary' education. After the 1944 Act when all schools at the second stage of education were dubbed 'secondary' the multipartite organisation maintained by most local authorities unquestionably determined the specific characteristics of parental or consumer demand for education after the war. A brief account of the growth of 'secondary' education in England since the turn of the century and the major reform proposals made during that time will serve as the basis of analysis of parental demand for education and the economic and social reasons for it.

Concepts of 'secondary education for all' have been a feature of the evolution of the school system in England and Wales. They have found most radical expression in the policies of such organisations as the trade unions, the Labour Party, and the Fabian Society. There has been, of course, in general, a demand for an extension of education opportunities for all and for a prolongation of compulsory schooling. In particular, however, the representatives of the so-called working classes have wanted either secondary technical schools providing first-rate vocational instruction, or common schools into which all children from a particular geographical area could go irrespective of ability or parental income. When, from the turn of the nineteenth century, non-vocational, somewhat literary biased selective 'secondary' schools developed, labour leaders sensibly made sure these were extended for the children of their supporters. Nevertheless, the desirability of establishing a comprehensive secondary school runs through the reform proposals of labourites and socialists. They were not against technical and vocational bias but against cheap alternatives. Many of the arguments and suggestions made in 1923 by R. H. Tawney in *Secondary Education for All* on behalf of an advisory committee of the Labour Party are still very germane to mid-century educational discussion in Great Britain. The case rests on egalitarian principles. Much of Tawney's argument was directed against industrialists who opposed 'secondary education for all' on economic grounds. His demand was not for 'identity of educational provision' for all children but within an 'elastic framework' for a co-ordinated system of primary and secondary schooling which would ensure the full development of all children up to the age of sixteen. The proposals were seen as benefiting society as well as individuals. 'What society requires for the sake both of economic efficiency and social amenity, is educated intelligence.'[10]

Educational development between 1902 and 1939 did not run altogether contrary to these proposals, at least in practice. Institutionally, three main trends may be distinguished: first, there was a substantial increase in the number of 'secondary' schools and in the number of pupils attending them. Secondly, there was a considerable rise in the proportion of pupils entering them from public elementary schools; by 1938 this was as high as 81 per cent, of whom more than half, i.e. 57·4 per cent, paid no fees. The third trend was that the proportion of free places or special places rose steadily, so that of the total admissions to grant-aided 'secondary' schools nearly 70 per cent had free or special places. Of these, nearly 80 per cent paid no fees, about 10 per cent received no exemption, and the rest paid partial fees. In 1938, some 470,000 pupils were in 'secondary' schools or about 19 per cent of the 11–17 and above age-group of children in publicly maintained schools. The opportunities for 'secondary' education for clever children from the elementary schools had steadily increased. Transfer to these schools took place on the basis of scholarship examinations taken by children at the age of 11 or slightly older.

Just less than half the pupils (about 47 per cent) paid fees. They were quite modest, ranging from about 5 guineas a year in a few local authority schools to over 30 guineas in some older foundation schools. For the most part, fees were between six and twelve guineas a year. These schools catered for, and in turn sustained and enlarged, the growing middle class. And because 'secondary' education conferred advantages upon its recipients (compared with pupils who went to elementary schools until the age of 14) parents were prepared to pay for it, if necessary at some sacrifice. The return on their investment in terms of occupational advantage, social advancement, and ultimately greater economic security for their children can be appreciated by a brief catalogue of occupations open virtually only to pupils from 'secondary' and 'public' (private, independent, fee-paying) schools. All the professions requiring university training—medicine, law, university and 'secondary' school teaching, scientific research, and so on—were virtually closed to pupils from elementary schools. Increasingly, teacher training colleges were recruiting students from among those with a 'secondary' education. Banking, accountancy, and other occupations associated with professional bodies demanded similar educational qualifications on entry. 'Secondary' education was also a considerable advantage for those pupils who aspired to commercial work, either as representatives or as clerical workers in industry. In short, practically all white-collar jobs were filled by 'secondary' school pupils.

It need hardly be mentioned that these occupations were particularly attractive in England during the 1930s. During unemployment, economic depression, and deflation, those who had fixed, pensionable, salaried positions were very favoured. Understandably 'secondary' education was in great demand. It did not matter that the curriculum was rather formal, that teaching was stereotyped, and that the amount of science taught was woefully small. A greater dose of education as such gave a person a greater chance of security, possibly a pension, better conditions of work, and generally a higher standard of living.

Evidently, the 'secondary' schools were middle-class schools; socially desirable as well as economically advantageous. They were in demand by the workers. The historical development of education in England had created a popular demand for schools which could compete with older, more famous 'public' schools—exclusive institutions for a socially or economically privileged élite. Neither the 'public' schools nor the 'secondary' schools were geared to the post-war need for more and more scientists, although unquestionably both types of school had made their unique contribution to the war effort through the adaptable leadership of their ex-students.

A Rationale for the 1944 Act

The provision of post-primary education under the 1944 Act was, in fact, based on a series of reports dating from 1926. Very little *new* educational theory emerged from them, and they contained hardly any sociological analysis of the role of education. The programme suggested was one of expansion in terms of the needs of the pupils. But these needs were so narrowly conceived as to disregard almost completely the vocational aspirations of other than the white collar workers. Nevertheless, at the time the practical proposals were doubtless regarded by many people in England as very radical.

The first of these reports, the Hadow Report, was very influential and virtually proposed the establishment of 'child-centred schools'. These should not, however, be confused with similarly named American schools, where the structure and curriculum of the common school made practice very different. Post-primary education in England, the committee reported, 'should be envisaged as far as possible as a single whole, within which will be a variety of types of education supplied, but which will be marked by a common characteristic that its aim is to provide for the needs of children who are entering and passing through the stage of adolescence'.[11] Child-centred education in England has meant that more attention should be paid to the development of a child's character (and, strangely, this has involved an ability to pass examinations) than with him as a potential adult worker. Consequently the Hadow Report went no further than to suggest the provision of a liberal, humane education for the majority of school children through a curriculum providing opportunities for practical work related to children's interests. Only the last two years, however, should be given a practical bias, and even this should not aim at giving a technical or vocational education but should be an instrument of general education.

The second important report, the Spens Report,[12] advocated a more strictly tripartite scheme of grammar, technical, and modern schools. The committee debated the desirability of establishing multilateral schools, large institutions with the three types of school brought together on the same site or campus, but rejected them as running contrary to the English tradition of small schools. The report's principles of curriculum development gave first priority to the training of the individual, but then included his training as a democratic citizen and as a future worker.

The third report, known as the Norwood Report, justified the tripartite system of secondary schooling by a frank return to Platonic principles of the innate abilities of 'particular groups of pupils'. Those children who were interested in learning for its own sake should go to the grammar school; those 'whose interests and abilities lie markedly in the field of applied science and applied art' should attend technical schools; finally, a pupil who 'deals more easily with concrete things than with ideas . . .', whose horizon 'is near' and whose movement 'within a limited area . . . is generally slow, though it may be surprisingly rapid in seizing a particular point or in taking up a special line'[13] should attend, with his fellows, a modern school. This, for better or for worse, was the system in wide operation immediately after the passing of the 1944 Act when all post-primary schools were designated secondary schools and classified as grammar, secondary technical, comprehensive, and secondary modern schools.

The views expressed in the Norwood Report were based on an archaic though reputable philosophy, albeit ameliorated by a somewhat warmer regard for children as growing organisms.

Secondary Education for All

The report ignored almost completely the economic and social implications of the proposals made. Criticism of the traditional, liberal education was countered by pointing out how adaptable 'secondary' school pupils had shown themselves during the war. It was a large step—but one that seemed implied—to assume that consequently the pre-war 'secondary' schools had met the requirements that 'the curriculum must fit the child, and not the child the curriculum'. In the thirties it was perhaps understandable that many people felt that the economic stability of Britain and the Empire had been built up largely on the commercial and industrial enterprise of leaders trained in a liberal tradition. The pre-war reports on which the 1944 Act was based could hardly be expected to anticipate the post-war economic situation of Britain. The framers of the 1944 Act might, however, have been expected to do so. On the basis of pre-war reports it was not surprising that the Act made it the duty of local authorities to provide enough schools in their area to 'afford for all pupils opportunities for education offering such varieties of instruction and training as may be desirable in view of their different ages, abilities and aptitudes . . .' The economic basis was modified. No fees were to be charged at publicly maintained schools, and the principle of consumer choice was to be established. Parents had the right to select the kind of education they desired for their children. Clause 76 stated: 'So far as is compatible with the provision of efficient instruction and training and the avoidance of un- reasonable public expenditure, pupils are to be educated in accordance with the wishes of their parents.' The direct parti- cipation of parents in the formal process of state-financed education is negligible in England. Joint effort by parent and teacher in the organisation of the curriculum, in methods of teaching, and in the content of lessons (except religion where there is a conscience clause) has never been part of the tradi- tion. The desires of the parents can be expressed within the public sector only through the horizontal structure of the schools and in their ability to contract out if they can afford to, by sending their children to non-State schools or by educa- ting them privately. In theory, parents were able in most areas to select one of three types of school for their children. In practice they were compelled to accept the decision of local

241

authorities as to which one of the three types of school their children should attend.

The choice of parents was seriously limited. After the war, as before, the demand has been for grammar school places. Apart from the traditional advantages, this climate of opinion was not difficult to understand. Between the wars the majority of educational investment had been in 'secondary' schools. Relatively little had been spent on selective post-primary schools (central and technical), and even less on the old elementary schools, many of which had been built during the elementary school expansion during the late nineteenth century. The facilities provided in these schools were much inferior to those provided in the newer 'secondary' schools. In general, in the non-secondary type schools only a watered-down 'secondary' curriculum containing very little, if any, science was possible. A halt was called in 1938 to 'secondary' school building, so that more of the other types of post-primary schools could be built. The accommodation position after the war was, of course, far worse than before because of the destruction of over 5,000 schools. An additional burden was thrown on school buildings when in 1947 the school-leaving age was raised from 14 to 15, and when the rapid increase in births after the war began to show in primary school enrolments. Since the war investment has been heavy in new secondary modern schools and then in extending science teaching facilities. By 1960 over 5,000 new primary and secondary schools had been built.

Educational Lag

In terms of tradition, building equipment and staffing the new secondary modern schools had little prestige. After 1944 attempts were made to create a demand for this kind of school. A high proportion of capital expenditure went into creating lavish buildings. Policy statements attempted to accord parity of esteem to all types of secondary education. This object can be achieved only at the verbal level. In practice, esteem is a measure of public demand; parity of esteem can be enjoyed by the secondary modern school only when there are as many parents who want their children to attend it as there are parents who want their children to go to a grammar school. This has patently not been the case. Few parents who had won places to pre-war 'secondary' schools wanted their children to have an 'inferior' education which might reduce their occupational opportunities and lower their social status. Many of these parents were aware of the economic advantages that their traditional humane education gave them. They still hoped, rightly or wrongly, that a grammar school education would safeguard the economic and social future of their children. In the post-war era they might have been mistaken, but they were right in thinking that secondary modern schools had nothing better to offer. They could not while their aims, methods and curricular offerings were pale copies of the grammar and 'public' schools. With less favourable conditions how could the secondary modern schools compete with these other schools in preparing pupils for the universities and white collar jobs?

It is apparent that the technical schools offered a somewhat better alternative to the grammar school than did the secondary modern. After the war white-collar jobs were not as desirable economically as they were, although they still retained considerable social prestige. Inflationary pressures lowered the relative position of salaried workers. The greatest shortages were in the engineering and associated industries. Unemployment figures until 1955 were negligible; in 1955 for instance there were 500,000 unfilled industrial vacancies and only 150,000 persons were registered as unemployed. For most of the period between 1945 and 1955 potential school-leavers were, like other workers, in great demand, and not, as in the thirties, competing for too few jobs. Adolescents leaving school had no difficulty in finding employment. Of social concern was the distribution of young workers, since immediate economic returns tempted many of them into unskilled work, dissuaded them from taking further courses of instruction, and discouraged them from taking trade or student apprenticeships.

A serious situation was created by the decrease in differentials between the skilled engineer and the unskilled worker. In 1900 the wage of the skilled worker in engineering was 172 per cent of the wage of an unskilled worker; by 1946 it had fallen to 119 and in 1954 to 116. Not everyone was convinced that changes in industry were such as to justify the argument that less formal training in industrial trades and crafts was now necessary. Certainly technological change has already made some hand skills obsolete, but it has also extended the range of skills required by modern industry. Many of these demand longer training, and often greater theoretical content, than formerly. But in the post-war world the wages of skilled men were not high enough to attract a sufficient number of men to acquire them during periods of full employment. In fact, the post-war baby bulge grew into adolescence and as unemployment rose so did the number of apprenticeships.

As their contribution to the resolution of this problem it could be argued that the schools should give far more pupils the technical and equally important social skills needed by modern industry. The indifference to what is offered in secondary modern schools could be changed if the skills needed to gain promotion in industry were taught. These are now a combination of technical competence in the operation and maintenance of machinery, applied intelligence in the handling of men, and a social knowledge of how to get on with fellow workers and superiors so that a group can function harmoniously.

The post-war economic situation also affected the grammar schools. Opportunities of employment being what they were, pupils who found the work either difficult or apparently unrelated to any of the problems they were likely to face dropped out, to take up employment before completing the grammar school course. The serious implications for industry have already been mentioned. The wastage involved was revealed by figures of pupils throughout England who left grammar schools before completing the course. Since the time of the *Early Leaving* report the schools have been able to hold pupils longer. This fact was pointed to with pride in the government's white paper on secondary education: *Secondary Education for all —A New Drive*.[14] By 1958 more pupils were staying on both in the sixth forms of grammar schools and beyond the compulsory attendance age of 15. Whether in the mid-sixties the number so attending schools beyond this age was adequate in terms of the country's economic position is still doubtful. Clearly the growth in sixth forms and the consequent increase in the number of pupils with *de jure* qualifications for university entrance shifted the problems of selection to the higher education stage.

In spite of improvements since the *Early Leaving* report the economic needs of the country were, according to many commentators, not being adequately served by the education system. There was, even in 1964, a shortage, compared with the United States, of a large educational middle class of men and women with an education which, while not scholarly and academic, extended far beyond the elementary level. The quality and shorter duration of education in England have contributed to the creation of a woefully small educational middle class which is for the most part highly specialised. Members of this class lack many of the social and technical skills needed in modern industry and commerce. At the same time an even greater number of young people, whose period of compulsory education in formal institutions will only in 1970 be raised from ten to eleven years, are ill prepared either for industry or for the social and familial tasks they must soon undertake. Many arguments against the wider extension of grammar and university education have been largely based on the theory that standards—whatever they are—must be maintained and can only be so by the rigorous selection of pupils both for the grammar schools and the universities. Equally important to the maintenance of standards is the continued acceptance of specialised curricula at both levels. About these questions there is undoubtedly much debate, but attention has been distracted from it by the concern the two political parties have shown over the organisation or structure of secondary schools.

Political Theories and Educational Policy—The Labour Party

On taking office after the war the Labour Party were, generally speaking, committed to policies outlined in the pamphlet prepared in 1923 under the editorship of R. H. Tawney. This meant, broadly, that Labour Party policy emphasised a radical reorganisation of the educational system so that the articulation between the parts should be better. In practice, the distinction between elementary education (administered under one code) and secondary education (administered under another code) should be broken down. A second practical, institutional, change which was advocated was that adolescents in one area should not be selected for different types of post-primary schools but should all attend the same common or comprehensive secondary school. The grounds for advancing these institutional changes were couched in terms of social justice and equality of educational opportunity. Not only was social policy directed towards the discovery and development of the talents of all children whatever the position of their parents, but it was also directed against the social distinctions created or maintained by the school system. Unfortunately there has been relatively little move on the part of socialist theoreticians away from the theory of innate psychological differences. This view is, of course, quite consistent with that of men like Condorcet and Jefferson, who held that within any society there was an aristocracy of talent, which should be the source of national leadership. But the criterion of ability, like birth and wealth, is one which makes possible the perpetuation of a power élite.

With the abolition of all fees to publicly maintained schools in the post-war period the criteria of selection to high-prestige schools were changed. In terms of the 1944 Act selection had to be based upon the 'age, aptitude, and ability' of individual children. Albeit general and vague enough to defy precise definition, these terms imply the presence in human beings of rather specific, innate, and measurable qualities. The validity of these assumptions has been increasingly challenged by articulate members of the population, particularly by those whose children failed to be selected for a grammar-school place. The specialised demand for secondary education is reflected in public criticism of intelligence tests as satisfactory instruments of selection at 11 plus. The movements of population to areas where grammar school facilities are good is another indication of parental preferences. In the early sixties several local authorities formally abolished the 11 plus, but other methods of selection will almost certainly have to be used.

Labour Party policy has, of course, strongly condemned the 11 plus selection tests as being socially unjust, and consequently has argued that comprehensive schools should be established. But in 1962 less than 4 per cent of all secondary school pupils were enrolled in such schools. Few socialist theoreticians have, moreover, touched the basic theoretical question concerning the determinants of 'intelligence'. Of those who have, few have been bold enough to state, and maintain, the view that intelligence levels are, for the most part, more closely related to environmental factors than to innate qualities and inherited ability. Conservative opinion, as illustrated so well by the assumptions made in the Norwood report on the curriculum of secondary schools, reiterates with slight modification the Platonic view that there are three types of child: the grammar school type, the technical school type, and the secondary modern type.

Here in a vital field of theory, political theorists of the left tend to be inconsistent because they find it difficult to decide between liberal or laisser faire theories of equality and more radical socialist or communist theories which deny the presence and measurability of basic, innate (and to some extent therefore inherited) personal, intellectual qualities. A rather easy way out of the dilemma is to argue that whilst these differences exist they cannot be determined with accuracy at 11 plus but only at a later age—a viewpoint widely advocated by reformers in continental Europe.

The lack of clarity in Labour Party policy is very clearly revealed in its attitude towards the 'public' schools. The more radical wing of socialist opinion has no hesitation in demanding that the schools for a privileged élite through which the perpetuation of privilege might be bought rather than earned should be abolished. Official policy is more cautious. This reflects a certain dilemma. In the first place it is a strong tradition in English education that children should, as far as possible, be educated in accordance with 'the wishes of their parents'. It is also the case that several members of the leadership group in the Labour Party themselves attended 'public' schools. Understandably, like parents who went to grammar schools, they are reluctant to deny their own children and those of their fellow 'public' school parents, the benefits of an education that served them so well. Thus, while articulate members of the middle classes demand the retention of the grammar schools, Labour Party leaders seem reluctant to abolish the privileged 'public' schools, but have little hesitation in advocating the argument that the 'tripartite' system of publicly maintained education is socially unjust. The choice is between social justice and parental ambition. Faced with this situation there is little doubt that many anxious parents who would be happy to pay the modest fees charged by the pre-war grammar schools now strive to meet the high fees of 'public' or expensive private schools for their children.

The Second Decade—Conservative Party Policies

Awareness of the persisting problems in English education prompted successive Conservative governments to invite a number of committees to examine various aspects of the system. The Crowther report, *15 to 18*,[15] dealt with a phase of schooling which for economic reasons had not received the attention promised in the 1944 Act. Recognising that hard choices had to be made in educational policy, the committee recommended that the school-leaving age should be raised to 16 as a matter of priority and before an attempt was made to establish part-time compulsory education from 15 to 18. As for the rest, the committee proposed, virtually, that sixth forms should remain more or less as before, providing highly specialised courses to highly selected grammar school pupils. The others should go either to technical or commercial schools. The recommendations in crude terms were for an extension of the tripartite system up to the age of 18. No doubt they were based rather significantly on economic arguments and were intended to increase the pool of talent by gearing the schools rather closely to occupational needs. Perhaps too little attention was paid to the industrial relations and social consequences of extending even further the traditional multipartite system of education.

In 1963 the Newsom Committee reported its findings. In *Half our Future*[16] the Committee made recommendations for the improvement of the education of those children who had not been admitted to the grammar schools, namely secondary modern school pupils. The committee studiously avoided any discussion of a desirable structure of secondary education in the second half of the twentieth century and made a few platitudinous remarks about curriculum, examinations, and teaching methods, without really making clear the social implications of many of the data that had been collected. Meanwhile the post-war birth-rate bulge was beginning to find acute expression at the point of entry to institutions of higher education. Free secondary education, and the prospect of generous awards by local education authorities to students with a certain number of passes at advanced and ordinary level of the General Certificate of Education, helped to swell the size of sixth forms and increase the number of students with *de jure* qualifications for university entry. Methods of applying and techniques of admission to the universities resulted in a considerable excess of applications over vacancies, and probably a somewhat less excess of candidates over vacancies. To bring some kind of order out of the chaos, clearing houses for the teacher training colleges and, reluctantly, for the universities, were established. The Prime Minister also appointed a committee under Lord Robbins to advise on *Higher Education*.[17] Its report published in 1963 advised considerable university expansion based upon the belief that the universities should remain in character, broadly speaking, as before. Colleges of Advanced Technology were to become universities and closer links between teacher training colleges, some of which were to award degrees in which educational studies would find a place, were to be established between them and the universities. Viewed against the pattern of higher education in the United States or even in the Soviet Union the report made few proposals of a radical nature. Indeed a new rationale, sadly needed, for the universities of England was not provided.

Thus, although education received much attention during the second decade of post-war development few basic, institutional reforms were recommended by official committees. Those made tended to be based on simple economic and comparative arguments which reinforced policies designed to make the schools instruments of occupational selection and preparation, and the institutions of higher learning places of privilege, still concerned more with the provision of an élitist type of specialised education or geared to industrial development than acting as institutions in which the large majority of young people continue their general education in an increasingly complex world, in which, in spite of new media of communication, an extension of formal education would appear to be a necessity if democratic forms of government are to survive successfully.

The Comprehensive Schools

If less has been said of Conservative Party policy than of its political opponents it is because Conservative governments have adhered, on the whole, fairly consistently to traditional norms about education and have tended to discourage the establishment of new institutions which threatened older ones. What expansion occurred between 1951 and 1964 was largely of institutions which had their pre-war counterpart. This generalisation, together with the hypothesis that the Conservative argument for expansion has been basically the economic one and the Labour Party's case largely based on the social opportunity theme, help to place the consuming debate of the immediate post-war period in perspective. In institutional terms this has turned on the establishment of so-called 'comprehensive' schools and the retention of the 'public' schools.

The debate, to be sure, has been couched largely in terms of principle rather than of the consequences which would arise from institutional changes, except that grammar school supporters have argued that the most important and most disastrous consequences of the introduction of comprehensive type secondary education would be an inevitable lowering of 'academic' standards and the retardation of the 'gifted' (i.e. grammar school type) children. One of the organisations which has been most active in its opposition to any change from the tripartite to the comprehensive type secondary structure has been the Association of Assistant Masters, drawing most of its members from the teachers in boys' grammar schools throughout the country.

The question of academic standards is important, but it is certainly not the only area within the societal patterns which is likely to be affected by the introduction of a new institution—the comprehensive school. If policy decisions are to be taken on the possible effects of the comprehensive school then all the consequences—social and educational—should, as far as possible, be considered. Debate, having moved more and more into the realm of party politics, tended to degenerate at worst into campaigns in which protagonists fight with slogans. At best the issue has been debated on the basis of social belief. Many studies have been undertaken to show how educational opportunity was still related to social class, and the same group of workers have analysed the distributive effects of the tripartite system as far as occupational choice is concerned.

The educational consequences of retaining the tripartite system are fairly obvious. The opportunities for 'late developers' to benefit from grammar school education are more apparent than real. Transfers from modern schools to grammar schools at about thirteen are fairly rare, and subsequent success largely dependent upon the attitude of the receiving school. The academic background of the transferees, particularly in mathematics, science, and French, is almost certain to compare unfavourably with that of the students who entered the grammar school at the age of eleven. Moreover, transfers at this age generally take place only in one direction; few students leave the grammar school (on academic grounds) to enter secondary modern schools. The latter remain, therefore, schools of least prestige, and the psychological effects on individual children, who, after all fees were abolished, could no longer claim that their parents could not afford to send them to the grammar school but only that they were not clever enough to go, are incalculable. The shock of rejection may well turn to apathy, and then to hostility, if the futility of what is being taught strikes home. Any resentment may turn into a bitterness tinged with scorn. These attitudes are likely to be carried over into adult life.

For this reason the possible social and political consequences of retaining a tripartite system seem fraught with danger. The pattern of political power in England was and is certainly very different from that of the pre-war period. Organised labour, closely associated with the Labour Party, is powerful both politically and industrially. It is able to veto policy. Some observers would argue that on the other hand it has failed to demonstrate on several occasions its ability to propose realistic alternatives. Its economic and political policies have lacked consistency. Under these circumstances the danger of Lippmann's hypothesis being confirmed is considerable. Any policy which increased the possibility of this situation hardening so that neither party in office can pursue consistent policies through the veto power of the other seems undesirable. It is apparent that except for important marginal groups the Labour Party and the Conservative Party will continue to recruit the bulk of their members from young adults with different educational backgrounds. The possibility of conducting national debates, either political or economic, realistically is reduced to the extent to which members of both sides take up positions determined by factors other than those which are relevant. The danger that resentments born of felt social injustice will militate against realistic debate is obvious. No suggestion is made here that the tripartite system is the only or indeed the most important determinant of the position described by Lippmann, nevertheless the possible consequences of its continuance when the children who passed through the secondary schools after the war become politically active and industrially important should not be ignored.

The more specific economic consequences of the tripartite system as it developed after the war were that too few students were directed into nationally important occupations and too few students were prepared to extend the period of education to qualify themselves for skilled and technical occupations. In the secondary schools very little initial training of specialists and technical workers was done, so that most of it had to be carried out after school before they could be fully absorbed into industry. The consequence has been that the training provided in industry has tended to be of a highly specialised nature. Another has been that technicians so trained have, after many years of experience, found themselves at a disadvantage in the promotion struggle compared with newly graduated university men. The policy of the Conservative government after the publication of its White Paper on Technical Education early in 1956 has shown itself to be aware of this need. The government paper prepared late in 1958 emphasised the fact that more children than ever before were being retained in the secondary schools of England beyond the age of compulsory attendance. By implication policy was that the tripartite system would be retained and extended to include young people between 15 and 18. These and other policies represented a fairly recent overt emphasis on education as economic investment.

Several historical examples show how the shortage of skilled personnel for industry and commerce was removed by the establishment of special technical secondary schools and colleges. Yet it is worth considering whether or not a tripartite system in post-war England provides the social education necessary to make industry and the economy 'tick', whilst at the same time safeguarding democratic institutions. It is apparent that in the new post-war configurations of political power in post-war England it is more than ever necessary to pay attention (in as unprejudiced an atmosphere as possible) to the training of students in the ability to make and take democratic decisions in the light of their national, as well as individual and group consequences. It is also necessary that students should be encouraged and trained to understand the wider implications of science and technology, and to understand, as far as possible, the basic principles of the nation's economy and the dependence upon it of the nation's political position in the world. To achieve these purposes necessitates some reorganisation both of the secondary school structure and the curricula of the various schools. Within a comprehensive school system opportunities of achieving a greater degree of social education seem possible. An institutional change which is implied by any such proposal seems to be that all the teachers within such a system should have similar academic qualifications, namely university degrees and professional training. It further implies that changes may have to be made in the examination system, in the methods of gaining entrance to the universities, and in the kind of emphasis given in the presentation of subject-matter in a number of important areas.

This kind of institutional proposal does not mean that comprehensive schools should necessarily be as large, for example, as those established by the London County Council, whose main argument, other than shortage of space, seemed to be that without some 2,000 unselected students in a school, adequate sixth forms could not be developed. The view that the comprehensive school should be large is often based upon the belief that the widest possible range of subjects should be offered, that some of the students should reach the same academic standards at 15 as the brightest grammar school students, and that academic standards in the sixth form should not be lower than in other selective schools. In placing such emphasis on the academic consequences of comprehensive school education, the possibilities of achieving important social objectives may, in fact, be denied. The obvious fact is that a new institution sets up a sequence of changes which constantly present organisational problems. Crucial choices have to be made. These will be taken in the light of normative patterns within which are included important educational theories. Few protagonists in the comprehensive school tripartite system debate have been prepared to acknowledge that in order to achieve certain objectives some sacrifices may have to be made. There is a tendency for supporters of the comprehensive school to maintain that all the benefits of the grammar school plus some additional ones will flow from the establishment of these schools. Opponents maintain that the basic social benefits flowing from grammar school education will be lost and they imply that the gain will not be worth this cost.

Clearly, to have a large unselective school in which the emphasis is on those aspects of learning which have been traditionally carried out in smaller selective grammar schools would be inefficient. American experience suggests that the schools doing the best job of preparing students to enter the universities are the smaller suburban schools, not the large comprehensive city high schools. In the former, the homogeneity of the student population, parental background and support, and the economic environment all play important parts in the success of the teaching. From the viewpoint of educational consequences proposals which envisage unselective schools serving students of compulsory attendance age within a geographical region seem to be soundly based. These schools providing a common core of learning experiences emphasising social and economic living need not be large. The curriculum may be one based on Herbert Spencer's views; that is, one which helps to prepare children to face the problems which arise in their personal life, those which are likely to arise in their future occupation, those which are concerned with the aesthetic aspects of life, and those which are concerned with their leisure-time activities.

Specialist studies after the school-leaving age could take place in separate institutions of the type proposed for the

Borough of Croydon. The kind of junior college suggested had much to recommend it. Selection would, if the feeding schools were non-selective, be delayed until an age when children are no longer compelled by law to attend school. The basis of selection would consequently be different. Greater emphasis would be placed on occupational intentions, the desires of students and parents, as well as upon academic achievements. Moreover these institutions would make better use of resources. Highly qualified staff, specialist accommodation, and so on could be used more efficiently than at present. In many school systems the number of students in the sixth forms is woefully small, and well qualified teachers devote a large part of their time to a handful (even one or two) of students. In many cases the classes are too small to provide intellectual stimulus, and the work is duplicated many times throughout a geographical area. The quality of the teaching varies considerably. Failure in some schools to provide certain science courses through lack of qualified teachers makes the process very inefficient. Furthermore, few people would argue that every graduate is capable of teaching the most able sixth-formers to the level achieved in the best 'public' schools, many of whose highly qualified masters devote the whole of their attention to sixth form work. In few publicly maintained grammar schools is it possible for adequately qualified persons to do this; a great deal of their energy is often dissipated on work in the lower school, leaving them little time to maintain and enhance their own scholarship. The tasks of preparing future specialists could undoubtedly be undertaken with much less waste in institutions similar to the proposed junior colleges. Equally interesting is the Leicestershire Plan of common middle schools followed by academic high schools, entrance to which at 14 is at the request of parents.

Of course, critics of any type of comprehensive school system maintain that this reorganisation would destroy the ethos of the grammar schools, that it would deprive them of leadership, and so on. Are the secondary modern schools to be deprived of this kind of leadership in order to benefit the grammar schools? Would there be no opportunities for exercising leadership in common secondary schools enrolling children from 11 to 15? And would there be no such opportunities in multilateral junior colleges? The dangers of losing the qualities of leadership that in the past have played a major role in the conduct of British affairs are apparent. Nevertheless, perhaps in the post-war world both the qualities of leadership and the conditions under which they can most successfully be developed should be re-examined. There are grounds for urging that the leadership group should be recruited from a wider section of the population than heretofore and that future leaders should remain in closer contact with a more representative cross-section of young people than was possible in a highly selective tripartite system of education.

The Prestige of the 'Public' Schools

One extremely significant feature of the institutional pattern that should be taken into account in any proposals to reform the English system is the presence of the private and 'public' independent schools. The 1944 Act made it possible, under certain conditions, for privately owned and run schools to remain open and continue to charge fees. It gave to that section of the community which could afford to pay the very high fees charged by the best of these schools an opportunity denied to the rest of English society. No doubt, many people regard the payment of high fees as an investment. Nicholas Hans has shown what positions of power, importance and wealth are occupied by products of the famous 'public' schools. More recent studies have confirmed this impression in spite of the fact that the social composition both of 'public' schools and Oxford and Cambridge is changing considerably. Parents who pay these fees may complain that, in addition, they help to support an educational system from which they derive no benefit. Yet since the war an increasing number of parents seem to have thought that this heavy investment in education, even though involving considerable sacrifice on their part, was worthwhile. There probably remain many parents who would be prepared to make a direct investment in education by paying the kind of moderate fee (adjusted to present-day money values) which were common in the pre-war fee-paying grammar or 'secondary' schools.

The difficulty remains that if the tripartite system were discarded, common or comprehensive schools would be in direct competition with the 'public' schools and would be at some disadvantage. Many of the latter are, of course, large, but their student populations are fairly homogeneous socially, in outlook, in ambition and aspiration, and so on. This would not be the case in the comprehensive school. Moreover, criteria of prestige in the 'public' school are not only academic. To belong to one of them is already a sign of some distinction. The publicly maintained system has for long been in competition with the 'public' schools and consequently the grammar schools were modelled on them. Over the years the grammar schools developed to a position from which they could successfully challenge the 'public' schools in the academic preparation of their students, but they were socially less esteemed, and their products were at some disadvantage in the commercial, industrial, and political fields. The comprehensive schools will suffer from all the disadvantages of the grammar schools and, in addition, it will be very difficult to achieve standards of academic achievement comparable with those of the 'public' schools without denying in the process many of the specific objectives advanced as their *raison d'être*.

The quality of the staff or faculty in 'public' schools depends upon the willingness and ability of the consumers to pay the price of high teacher salaries, adequate specialist accommodation, and a low student-teacher ratio. The latter is generally better than may be expected in a publicly maintained school. Conditions in the 'public' schools make it possible to select able boys for special attention from a very early age. The general prestige of the school means that the psychological effects upon unselected boys are less harmful (in one sense at least) than elsewhere. The ethos of the school makes it possible for less able boys to progress academically at their own rate without undue feelings of failure. Attendance at a 'public' school often confers a status considerably higher than great academic success in a publicly maintained institution. Opportunities are provided for the kind of education, general, vocational, and specialist, that parents demand and for which they are willing to pay. The change in composition of the 'public' school sixth forms has been quite radical. Perhaps few of them now have smaller science than classical sides. Even by 1955 there was a balance between the science and the arts sixth forms in independent and direct-grant schools. No doubt many very able boys are still encouraged to take up classical studies by the large number of scholarships open to them at Oxford and Cambridge in these subjects, and by the opportunities in the higher ranks of the Civil Service for classical scholars. Nevertheless, the growing number of boys who are pursuing scientific courses reflects both parental and social demand. Even so, many more potential scientists could be absorbed by industry were the universities willing and able radically to expand the facilities for science.

There is little doubt that the 'public' schools offer their pupils experience in making democratic decisions through a variety of activities and institutions. The high quality of education has to be paid for. It is difficult to estimate the per capita expenditure on education in 'public' schools because many of them are well endowed, receive many bequests, and so on; tuition fees may well reflect only a part of it. But in 1962-3 *fees* for day boys in independent schools ranged from about £167 per annum to £225. Typical in London schools were fees of £180. Preparatory school fees also showed wide variations, but they were of the same order as in the 'public' schools. Local Education Authority secondary schools for pupils under 15 *cost* £104 per pupil to run (£181 over 15), and LEA primary schools *cost* £65 per pupil in the same year. It is impossible to imagine new comprehensive schools providing as good an 'education' as the established 'public' schools unless per capita expenditures were at least as high. National investment would indeed have to be increased in order to achieve general equality at the secondary level between LEA and 'public' schools.

There was, and continues to be, a danger of the large comprehensive schools with children from 11 to 18 feeling obliged to compete academically with the 'public' schools. At the moment they can do this less successfully than the present grammar schools, unless they are organised to select for special attention the pupils who would obviously have gained admission to a grammar school (had one been available). Furthermore, an unconscionable amount of time would have to be spent on academic learning. The sense of failure which is implicit in much of what the secondary modern school does would be carried over to the common school. There is a danger that in attempting to compete, comprehensive schools would defeat their purpose of providing social education and equality of opportunity. Any proposed reorganisation of the publicly maintained schools should take the position of the 'public' schools into account.

The Case of France

In the same way the powerful position of the *lycées* in France helps to explain why educational reform in that country has been so difficult to achieve. In many respects the reform movements were motivated by objectives similar to those expressed in England and Wales. The barriers to effective change have been similar too. Immediately after the end of a disastrous war the impetus for reform was strong, but economic conditions alone were sufficient to prevent major changes in the traditional educational system. By the time economic recovery had advanced far enough to make wholesale reform a practical possibility, vested interests were in a position to obstruct it. For example, strong opposition to policies which would affect the *lycées* came from the *Société des Agrégés*. In addition, however, in contrast to the situation in England and Wales the political situation in France made it impossible for any government to pass major legislation until General de Gaulle returned to power. Political instability, the highly controversial question of financial support for Catholic schools, and divisions within the teaching community itself combined to prevent the acceptance of any of the reform projects prepared for presentation to the assembly. Deputies were subjected to pressure from a number of organisations, among which were those formed by members of the Catholic Church, school teachers, civil servants, and the trade unions. Not always, perhaps, were the issues debated the real ones, but in any case it was impossible until 1959 to get a bill passed as comprehensive in its proposals as was the English 1944 Act.

The proposals which were made shortly before the end of the war should be seen, however, as the culmination of a tradition in French education well exemplified, perhaps by the views of Paul Langevin. In 1918 he and his associates of the *Compagnons de l'Université nouvelle* planned a school, the *Ecole unique* or common school for all. Little was achieved between the wars, although in 1937 Jean Zay tabled a bill designed to introduce orientation class at the beginning of secondary education. This proposal, intended, in effect, to delay selection and sharp differentiation, has become central to the plans to reform education in many Western European countries. Towards the end of the second world war Langevin, in association with several radical educational thinkers including Henri Wallon, was responsible for far-reaching proposals to reform French education in a document generally known as the Langevin Plan. Like the English 1944 Education Act, changes were suggested for virtually every aspect of education. The school-leaving age was to be raised to 18, schooling was to be divided into three cycles or stages—primary to the age of 11, orientation (4 years duration) and a third cycle of selected education. Education was to be free and the orientation period was to ensure that children from various social backgrounds and of widely differing intelligence quotients came together in the same school. These views formed the basis of subsequent reform proposals, and the obstacles preventing acceptance of them have been well analysed by W. R. Fraser in *Education and Society in Modern France*.[18]

On the technical side the establishment of a comprehensive system after the eighteenth century revolutionaries suppressed the craftsmen's corporations, included institutions designed to train personnel at all levels and in a vast range of industrial activities. Regional coverage was sound, and the Loi Astier placed on industrialists an obligation to support technical education. Thus, even without major legislation, after the war a rational expansion of technical institutions at various levels was possible. Finally it should be remembered that France's post-war economic recovery from appalling beginnings has been achieved in part through an imaginative series of national plans. That it has been achieved in spite of the failure radically to modify the structure and administration of the school system makes a realistic comparison of the role of education in economic growth in the two countries extremely fascinating. Clearly, not only the gross or proportional investment of real resources in education is significant. A complex of attitudes, domestic institutional arrangements (political, economic and educational), and the availability of material resources should be analysed and weighted. Included among these important aspects of social life in the two countries for consideration should be foreign policies and those concerned with the dissolution of empire.

The French proposals regarding the reorganisation of the post-primary stage of education are interesting from another viewpoint. The basic intention of postponing selection by introducing a period of guidance and orientation lasting two years after the conclusion of primary schooling finds expression in one form or another in reform proposals in various European countries, for example, in Denmark, the Netherlands, and in the Rahmen and Bremen plans in Western Germany. In many respects the organisation of French post-primary education can be regarded as a prototype continental pattern which shows a greater degree of differentiation of school types and more emphasis on the classics in the academic secondary schools than is the case in England. For these reasons the French system and the difficulties associated with its reform provide a useful case study. The differences between France and England are as significant from a comparative viewpoint as the similarities. Within the European normative framework there are, for example, profound differences between French and English theories of knowledge. The rationalism of Descartes can, with advantage, be compared with the empiricism of Locke. Again the different institutional forms democratic aspirations take in the two countries are worthy of close comparative study. Among these the systems of administrative control and the theories behind each of them are of particular interest. Even institutions, e.g. the French *lycée* and the English grammar school, which are in terms of function comparable, show marked differences in ethos and organisation. Finally it should be remembered that the general environmental circumstances of the two nations show differences as well as similarities. All these affect the ways in which policies are formulated, accepted, and implemented. The object of this brief reference to France is simply to show how the kind of analysis Fraser makes of education in modern France can be used in more detailed comparative studies.

In summary then, post-war Western European nations faced

somewhat similar problems of reconstruction. Heightened aspirations were difficult to satisfy because of the heavy demands on economies seriously impoverished by losses in material resources and manpower. Among the expectations of parents, the demand for secondary education was considerable. In addition to the low priority given to education in general among the competing demands for resources, traditional forces made it difficult in most governments to give legislative expression to the proposals for reform. In general, these included suggestions about the reorganisation of secondary education and the extension of compulsory education. The crucial issue turned on the age at which selection for post-primary education should take place, and the processes through which it should be done. In the event the reforms which have been accepted, except in England and Wales, have simply tended to delay in some way or other the age at which selection occurs. The processes have been modified to encourage continuous assessment rather than selection by competitive examination. The demand for education has been increased everywhere by an explosion of population. By the nineteen-sixties this bulge in population consisted of young people of the age when they are ready for higher education. Thus, whilst the problems before this decade turned on access to secondary education, the issues in the sixties and seventies are bound to be concerned with higher education, and in particular with university expansion. These problems will be no less difficult of solution than those experienced at the secondary level in terms of institutional inertia. One big difference is that Europe has recovered her economic strength and the policies pursued will be against the background, in western European countries at least, of general affluence. If the will to extend and improve education exists, the possibilities of doing so are considerable. What is needed is a clear recognition on the part of more people that education is a worthwhile investment —it benefits individuals and contributes to the social wellbeing. At the same time, educational statesmen need to consider very carefully the changes which may be necessary in the organisation and content of education if it is to help promote the widely shared aspirations of Europeans to maintain and improve standards of living, remove the threat of war, and bring European nations more closely together. Indeed the explosion of knowledge which was, in part, a direct consequence of the immense investment of time and energy in scientific research has created both problems and opportunities. Yet the reform of the content of education is fraught with as many difficulties as the reorganisation of the structure of post-primary education. The next chapter deals with some features of this problem particularly as they are found in the Soviet Union.

Chapter X

LIBERAL EDUCATION AND VOCATIONAL TRAINING (THE U.S.S.R.)

CLOSELY linked with the major question of structural reform is the issue of curriculum change. Naturally the retention of several distinct types of school, particularly at the secondary level, makes the need to revise the content of education in each of the school types seem less pressing. Alter the organisation of secondary schooling by the provision of common or comprehensive middle schools, and the difficulties of retaining a traditional curriculum immediately become apparent. In the United States curriculum theory has already changed considerably since the middle of last century. Now Soviet educationists having established a common school are facing problems associated with the reorganisation of the content of education. In Sweden too, the establishment of comprehensive schools has been quickly followed by researches into the kinds of curricular change which will be necessary.

If the problems are more urgently felt in countries which have moved towards a more comprehensive type of secondary education, they are also beginning to be felt everywhere. One reason is that there has been a phenomenal explosion of knowledge in the twentieth century. It has been estimated, for example, that the fund of new knowledge doubled between 1900 and 1950 and that it doubled again between 1950 and 1960. Much of it has been in science and technology, and although the advances in knowledge have been inextricably linked with North America and Europe, the ramifications have been worldwide. During and since the second world war, fundamental discoveries in the pure sciences have increasingly been applied by men to the control of their environment.

Basic laboratory research in nuclear physics, the chemistry of molecular structures, and microbiology has resulted in enormous technological progress. Perhaps it is necessary only to mention the advances in medicine, the supply of power, transport and the communication arts to make the point. At one level man's ability to control his environment has become greater than ever before. At the same time his very success has endangered his chances of survival because the explosion in scientific knowledge has not been matched either by appropriately radical changes in attitudes, or by the establishment of new institutions through which the consequent problems can be effectively met.

In very general terms the solution may be said to lie in the development in individuals of the power to discriminate and make choices in a rapidly changing world. Some aspects of the new situation in politics may, for example, be mentioned by way of illustration. Throughout the world democracy is a widely shared and firmly held ideal. Attempts have been made to establish institutions through which this ideal may be achieve. Thus on the one hand technical improvements in existing media of mass communications and the invention of new forms have given statesmen access to a far wider public than ever before. On the other hand the extensive use of such media is now possible in countries where few people are in the traditional sense literate. World issues and disasters can be brought to their notice within a matter of minutes. Jet propulsion, bringing the peoples of the world within a few hours' travelling time of each other, has added yet another dimension to the problems of human relations and international politics. Quite central to the political situation, however, is the belated and somewhat reluctant recognition by political leaders that at the international level nuclear warfare can no longer be regarded as a practical extension of policy; they have been forced to rethink the processes of power politics. Too little attention has been paid, however, to the educational implications. Yet the need to develop through education, in a relatively unprejudiced atmosphere, an ability by individuals everywhere to discriminate in politics, make decisions based on evidence, and assess the consequences of choice is obvious if democratic institutions are to survive.

In the economic sphere automation is no longer an idle dream. A basic need in the process of industrialisation is electrical or nuclear power. Automation depends heavily for success on the science of electronics. The provision of an adequate supply of electrical power remains a problem in many countries. Elsewhere automation is almost a reality. One result is that consumer goods are flooding the markets of the world and are raising in acute form the need for consumer discrimination.

Another significant effect of automation will be that working hours will be shorter and the problems of leisure in vast conurbations much greater. New media have extended the range of choice. Alongside the older forms of entertainment are the new. Perhaps the theatre is now an anachronistic survival patronised by a small élite. Even the cinema and radio are losing their popular appeal in many countries. Television with all its political, social, and educational implications is taking over. One characteristic shared, however, by the newer media of entertainment is that they reach a wider public first because it is technically easier to send radio and TV programmes out to the homes of people than it is to bring them to theatre or cinema. And secondly the fundamental organs—sight and hearing—of appreciation are more easily developed than the basic reading skills. A deeper appreciation of the quality of a performance or a programme and an ability to discriminate between the values presented are, however, educational needs. Whether used in school or not, the new media are powerful educative forces and may be used to foster some attitudes and values rather than others. The power of critical aesthetic discrimination is needed by everyone exposed to cinema, radio, and TV. Equally important is the need to prepare individuals to make the moral judgements necessary to a deeper appreciation of much material presented as entertainment.

Major problems of choice have been created too by the advances made in medicine. The application of new discoveries and techniques has had profound effects on population growth and the distribution of age cohorts within a population. Today infant mortality rates are declining everywhere. Diseases like malaria and tuberculosis can now be controlled. Techniques in anaesthetics have greatly improved the possibilities of refined surgical treatment, and microbiological knowledge has made the transplantation of organs from one person to another a practical possibility. The life expectancy of those who survive a dangerous childhood in the past has now increased. The explosion of population has given rise to very serious food problems because in order to survive the teeming masses must eat. Many of them having successfully met the challenge of disease are now in danger of dying from starvation. A crude choice seems to lie between increasing the food supply of the world and improving the distribution of it and reducing the rates of population growth. Some of the solutions, of course, are technical in nature. There are many untapped sources of food, and birth control techniques have improved steadily. The technical possibilities exist of keeping the imbalance within bounds. More obdurate problems are associated with present attitudes and social institutions. Food taboos act powerfully to prevent many people from utilising available resources to the full. Economic and political considerations prevent the distribution of food to places where it is needed to prevent malnutrition or death by starvation while surpluses pile up elsewhere. Family planning often runs counter to deeply held beliefs, and many people consider abortion not only a crime but a sin. Such attitudes which have had an important part to play in the running of societies in the past cannot be dismissed as irrelevant. But a thorough study of attitudes and institutions may reveal the precise characteristics of the problem in specified areas and suggest which of the prevailing attitudes need to be changed and which institutions modified.

In general it could be argued that there has been a failure to keep pace with the rate of scientific progress both in the realm of attitudes and in the sphere of institutional change. One reason for this lag is doubtless the fact that the social sciences are much less advanced than the natural sciences. Another is educational in the narrower sense, and can be stated in a number of ways. There has been a failure, one may argue, on the part of many educators to recognise the extent to which science should necessarily form the core of a sound general education in the mid twentieth century. Certainly there is urgent need to re-examine the basic assumptions about the content of a general education in a rapidly changing world. If education is regarded as a process of providing young people with the intellectual and moral equipment to tackle problems and make decisions, then it may well be argued that no problem today, whether basically economic, political, social, or moral, can be fully understood without a knowledge of some branch of science. In other words some of the data relevant to an understanding of any problem will be drawn from science. To be sure, solutions will not necessarily emerge from a scientific analysis of the problem and a rigorous identification of relevant data. Nor are choices likely to be made solely on the basis of a careful assessment of all the possible consequences of making a choice. Insight, judgement based upon expediency or past experience, and emotions will enter into both processes. But to admit this and to recognise the limitations of science is only to emphasise the degree to which every problem today has a scientific component. Unfortunately, where there is an appreciation of this situation in the schools, ways of selecting information and methods of teaching science in a manner which would enable it to fulfil its role in general education are not yet readily available except in most general terms.

Another feature of the situation complicates matters. The manpower demands of modern industry are changing rapidly. An enormous number of highly trained specialists are now needed. The knowledge they require is grounded in the principles of pure science and should spread out into the technological applications of them. At the same time many former vocational skills are either now redundant or will soon become so. The rate of technological change will make it necessary for most industrial workers at the lower levels to be retrained several times during the course of their working lives. Experience will count for less and formal training for more in the development of these skills. Other changes of attitude will be necessary if the full benefits of automation are to be gained.

Thus the curricular problem shows two major aspects. Science should now be the basis of a sound general education and at the same time it is becoming more and more fundamental in the vocational training of future industrial workers. The question is whether or not these two demands can be reconciled within the school curriculum without imperilling those benefits which can be derived from non-science subjects and activities. Throughout Dewey's writings over more than half a century he consistently argued that not only should vocational studies constitute the core of a liberal education but that the methods of science were those appropriate to the intelligent solving of social problems and the co-operative organisation of social affairs.

It is with this kind of curriculum reform that the Soviet educators are wrestling today, and in fact their own analysis is not very dissimilar to that made by Dewey. Moreover they acknowledge that some of the ideas they accept as providing a solution to an old dilemma were anticipated in the writings of men like Thomas More, John Bellers, Comenius, Rousseau, and Pestalozzi as well as the 'great Utopian socialists' F. Fourier and R. Owen. Even Dewey and Kerschensteiner are mentioned not too unfavourably. Naturally it is the ideas of Marx as developed by Lenin and his associates which form the basis of the present attempts to reform the curricula of Soviet schools and thus break down the dichotomies which lie at the root of the problem of providing a sound general education today.

Intellectual Education and Manual Training

Before turning as a case study to the proposals for reform in the Soviet Union a brief analysis may serve to place the problems as Soviet educators see them within a European framework. It is apparent, for example, that a number of traditions dominate European thinking about the curriculum. One of them can be ascribed to the distinction Aristotle made between the liberal and the illiberal in education. He regarded any study which had a direct bearing on practical life as unworthy of the freeman. Thus a dichotomy between true education and vocational training was formulated. Moreover not every discipline or subject was worthy of attention of the citizens. The Seven Liberal Arts of the Middle Ages—Grammar, Dialectics, Rhetoric, Music, Arithmetic, Geometry, and Astronomy—were based upon Aristotle's views. His political theory held that citizenship should be restricted to warriors, rulers, and priests, and that mechanics, traders, and husbandmen—necessary servants of the State—should be excluded. Citizens should not lead the life of mechanics or tradesmen, 'for such a life is ignoble, and inimical to virtue'.

269

Thus in theory a sharp distinction was made between liberal education and vocational training. Each was appropriate to the kind of social function an individual was to perform. Moreover only certain subjects were to be regarded as truly liberal, when grouped together they may be described as language studies, music, and mathematics. Certain restrictions were also placed on the object of learning. The acquisition of knowledge for its own sake is worthy of the citizen. To acquire it for others or for paid employment is to vulgarise it. Furthermore, to attend to any subject too closely in order to 'attain perfection' in it leads to harmful results. The gifted amateur, restricting his attention to literary studies or mathematics not for their practical value, is therefore not an inaccurate picture of Europe's educated man derived from Aristotle.

In the event two characteristics can be noted. First the prestige education of Europe was acquired through a limited range of subjects whose content was quite unrelated to practical affairs. Secondly literary subjects and particularly the classical languages counted for much more than the natural sciences. In terms of approach, intellectualism was far more highly regarded than practicalism. Thus even when science began to make headway it was the pure sciences rather than the engineering subjects which were acceptable. In many countries and notably in France during the nineteenth century the difficulties of curriculum reform can be seen as due to an open conflict between the advocates of science and the supporters of the classical languages. In terms of organisation the dichotomy between mental training and manual instruction found expression in the establishment of separate institutions in continental Europe for, on the one hand, liberal studies and, on the other, vocational or professional training. The divorce could be seen both at the post-primary and tertiary stages of education. The universities remained strongholds of truly liberal education.

Certain notable exceptions should be mentioned. In England, no universities other than Oxford and Cambridge were established until the nineteenth century. Then in the civic universities technological studies either formed the foundations on which the new institutions were built or became integral parts of the curricula. Furthermore as the elementary schools for the masses developed a major decision was taken at the turn of the century to exclude vocational subjects from compulsory education. Thus in contrast to continental Europe few vocational schools were built and the curricula of elementary schools included few practical subjects and those which were included were taught with a non-vocational bias. Policies followed in the U.S.A. diverged even further from the traditional European pattern. The Land Grant Colleges established under the Morrill Act of 1862 and subsequent acts were specifically intended to provide courses in vocational subjects—agriculture and the mechanic arts—designed to further the economic growth and welfare of the nation. They quickly began to provide courses in the older liberal disciplines but were always responsive to the demands of industry and commerce in the orientation of their work. Again by the middle of the century even such older traditional colleges as Harvard and Yale were treating the subjects taught from a more practical angle. One of the most significant statements in the development of higher education in the U.S.A. was made by President Eliot of Harvard, who proclaimed that his university would teach a far wider range of subjects than had hithertofore been regarded as appropriate university disciplines.

Again the Russian tradition shows certain differences. Under the influence of Peter the Great institutions bearing the stamp of those existing in Western Europe were set up. The intention was, however, more directly utilitarian and scientific. Lomonosov, co-founder of Moscow university in 1755, exemplified this tradition. Hence the classical tradition of many Western European universities is much less in evidence in the Soviet Union. Finally it should be noted that the *grandes écoles* of France were envisaged by Napoleon as professional institutions committed to the task of training selected students for the top échelons of public service. The practical purpose for which they were devised did not prevent them from making their curricula and methods of study extremely intellectual and academic. Nevertheless they represent institutions of the highest prestige somewhat apart from the universities proper.

To the force of ideas were of course added the facts of life. Manual work was brutish for the most part. The professional classes enjoyed political power and social status. Naturally the education which prepared young men for positions of advantage in society was in greater demand than that which led to drudgery, or at best, acceptance as a craftsman into a guild.

When the demands of industry and commerce became increasingly obvious during the nineteenth century the debates about education were vigorous. As mentioned, many persons in England, continental Europe, and the United States advocated the widespread introduction of commercial and technical subjects. They were called upon to justify their claims by showing what would be the content of such courses and how these subjects could be treated in such a manner as to make them as sound a basis of a general education as the classical languages. But even practical educators who agreed with Dewey that vocational studies should and could form the core of a liberal education failed to find convincing practical proposals. Consequently the classical languages continued to dominate most of the prestige schools of Europe. In England though the classics declined the arts subjects rather than the sciences took their place in the new maintained 'secondary' schools. Yet there remain, as C. P. Snow has said, two cultures. Even in Russia, where science was more highly regarded, an academic tradition has prevailed and the literary and scientific cultures are moving further apart. In most instances, vocational studies, if they were taught at all, were relegated to the inferior schools for the masses. Even in the United States, although professional subjects grew in popularity among university students, the high school curriculum has not been liberalised by the imaginative teaching of vocational subjects.

In the U.S.S.R., from the thirties when the German threat became apparent until recently, the pressing needs of industrial development far outweighed the other aims of education in the formulation of Soviet policy. The successful creation of cadres of specialists in the scientific and technological fields before, during, and immediately after the war was not achieved without cost. In 1958, after several years of debate and experimentation in education, Mr Krushchev was able to state very succinctly what he thought was one of the most serious problems in Soviet education. In a memorandum to the Presidium of the Central Committee of the C.P.S.U. he stated that 'The chief and basic defect in our secondary and higher educational establishments is the fact that they are divorced from life'. In practice this meant that, in spite of obvious successes, 'Our ten-year schools, however, are at present not accomplishing the task of training the young people for life, and are only training them for entering college'. Successes in the preparation for higher education of well educated people with a good grounding in science were acknowledged. The reasons given for believing that reforms were necessary were that 'life was marching on' and that in the two historic tasks being fulfilled, namely 'the creation of the material and technical basis for communism and the education of a new type of man' (p. 70), the schools had two related tasks to perform. They had to contribute to the material basis by training specialists for industry and agriculture and they had to educate each individual so that through his all-round development he could contribute to the establishment of a Communist society. Prior to 1958 it was felt that the Soviet schools had performed the first task but had failed to educate 'a new type of man'. The crux of the problem was regarded as the sharp differences between intellectual and physical work which had prevented the achievement of this aim. The solution was to be found in polytechnical education, the basic principle of which has a long and honourable tradition. Some of the European and American precursors of the present emphasis in Soviet theory on the basic need to ground a satisfactory general education in productive labour have already been mentioned. Russian pioneers in this field were Chernyshevesky, Dobrolyubov, and Ushinsky. But it was Engels and Marx who provided the scientific rationale for an education which would combine instruction with productive labour. Later the theory was more fully developed by Lenin and his wife Krupskaya. The present discussions start from these ideological principles.

Basic Ideology and Expediency

At the most general level the persisting sources of Communist educational policy are not difficult to find. According to Krupskaya, 'Lenin attached particular attention to the upbringing of the growing generation. He regarded the school as an instrument for re-educating the entire growing generation in the spirit of communism.' Some indication of the methods of achieving this goal were given by Marx when referring in *Capital* to Robert Owen's factory school. He stated that all truly educative processes have their origin in productive labour. Another source of Soviet educational theory is the physiological views of Pavlov, which, it need hardly be said, gave a greater role to environmental factors than to innate abilities in the development of human beings. Finally mention should be made of Makarenko's theories of education through discipline and the collective which have, in contrast to some others, stood the test of time in the U.S.S.R. There is little doubt that within the writings of Krupskaya and Lenin, Pavlov and Makarenko can be found some of the most general and representative Communist theories of Soviet education.

Educational policy is rarely, however, determined solely by ideology. Conditions in the Soviet Union should be considered if changes in policy are to be understood. From the start of the Communist regime widespread illiteracy had to be attacked. After the confusion and destruction of the revolution and civil war, millions of homeless children remained to be cared for, and it was in this field that Makarenko won lasting fame. No doubt at first the Marxist view that true education was inevitably and closely linked with productive labour meant that intellectual work was underestimated during the nineteen-twenties. Theories not unlike those advocated by Dewey in America came into fashion under the name 'paedology'. But in the thirties and particularly after 1935 there was a reversal of policy. For some twenty years as part of the drive to catch up with and overtake the capitalist countries intellectual training was stressed. In many respects this educational policy differed little from the continental European traditions, but economic incentives made it possible to attract to science and technology large numbers of the most gifted students. Shortages of labour, the need for specialists, and the defects of the polytechnical courses which were provided all help to account for those defects of the system detected by Soviet leaders.

By 1952, in fact, the circumstances of the Soviet Union had so changed that it was possible to envisage the 'prospect of advancing rapidly from socialism to communism' (p. 49). Renewed interest was taken in polytechnical education, and the

Liberal Education and Vocational Training

1958 law strengthening the ties of the school with life represents the legislative culmination of a process of reform which has its ideological roots in the writings of many progressive educators and in particular in the works of Marx, Lenin, and Krupskaya. The difficulties it set out to solve, however, were deeply entrenched in the more detailed theory and practice of Soviet education and the debates associated with the reforms are likely to persist for some time.

The general conception of what ought to be done is neither novel nor apparently in dispute. Yet the difficulties facing those who accept the view that a sound general education should be grounded in productive labour are considerable. First, realistic regulating theories have to be devised to enable practical expression—in syllabuses, curricula, and methods of teaching—to be given to general aims. The Soviet reforms are intended to change the attitudes of young people towards productive labour, thus creating the 'new type of man' with a strengthened morality and a new awareness of the dignity of labour. At the same time school practices have to be devised which will achieve these goals—by no means an easy task in a vast country whose extensive educational system was based upon, and still resembles, certain Western European and Russian prototypes in which the Aristotelian dichotomy between liberal education and vocational training found constant and overt expression.

Sources of Inconsistencies

One aspect of the malfunctioning of the system was due to the very success of the Communist government in extending a certain type of education very widely. It raised aspirations which in time could no longer be easily satisfied. Increasing numbers of secondary school graduates—intellectuals—whose ambition was to enter an institution of higher learning were unable to do so directly. Many students leaving secondary schools, in 1957 about two in every three, entered industry, commerce, or agriculture, and were often unprepared both psychologically and technically to do so. The principal reason given by Soviet educators for this state of affairs is that pre-revolutionary Tsarist traditions have been perpetuated in the schools. Thus

275

knowledge for its own sake was prized, the content of the curriculum was abstract, and theory was often divorced from its practical applications. Moreover, in the European tradition, methods of teaching were didactic and formal. In their schools it was, and is, these characteristics which Soviet writers found unsatisfactory. It is hardly surprising, and indeed a brief visit to Soviet schools reveals the extent to which these criticisms are founded upon fact.

Against this background it is apparent that the proposals in the new law, and those being debated, represent a major attempt to reformulate basic educational theories. There is indeed about them a genuine educational aspect which, since it involves an attempt radically to change the attitudes of young people, is fundamentally moral in purpose. Because in communist theory economic activities are considered of vital significance, man's attitude towards work constitutes an important basis of morality. Since life itself centres round it, the dignity and importance of work are stressed. In a truly communist society, moreover, the most efficient use of social and economic resources is an important aim, and can be achieved through the sound organisation of labour without enforcement. The task of education then is to develop each individual to the full extent of his abilities in order that he may accept his responsibilities as a Soviet citizen and promote the growth of a communist society. Fundamental to the achievement of this aim is the inculcation in pupils of the correct attitudes towards work, of a knowledge of production methods, and of technical skills based upon theoretical principles. In practice, instruction has to be combined with productive labour or with socially useful work, and thus to bridge the gap between general education and vocational training.

Proposed Solutions—the Principles of Polytechnical Education

According to Communist theory polytechnical education provides this bridge, and should permeate the whole of education. A lengthy and detailed account of the principles and institutional proposals of this revived principle of education is given in a UNESCO monograph, *Polytechnical Education in the U.S.S.R.*, edited by S. G. Shapovalenko. It represents in fact a blueprint of Soviet education and most of the information that follows is drawn from it.

It is clear for example that polytechnical education does not simply mean vocational education. It is the basis of a sound 'liberal' education and the teaching of its 'working skills to the pupils is carried out during the process of teaching general education subjects, general technical subjects and in teaching about work and production' (p. 171). Again: 'In such subjects as physics, chemistry, mathematics, geography, natural sciences, and mechanical drawing they [children] acquire a solid foundation of the basic knowledge needed in each field of industry and agriculture; while working in the school shops and laboratories and training at the factory shops and in the collective and State farm fields, they learn to apply theory to practice.' Polytechnical education includes learning about the major branches of the economy and work in industry so as to acquire definite industrial skills. Overall in the new syllabuses for the eleven-year schools the proportions of time spent on the various groups of subjects were changed to the following: general subjects (humanities) 36 per cent; general subjects (mathematics and science) 32·5 per cent; manual and trade training, production practice, general technical subjects, 21 per cent; and artistic and physical education 10·5 per cent (p. 104).

Within this framework certain principles are to be taught as part of polytechnical education. First, there are the general socio-economic principles of socialist production, such as public ownership of the means of production, planned development and increased productivity, and the protection of workers' interests. Secondly, the technical and economic principles include the widest possible application of science to industry so as to devise new techniques, and develop automation. The third group of principles are those concerned with organisation and economic practices designed to show the implications for labour of the transformation of industrial procedures from individual work to mass production (pp. 85–6). The important areas in which these principles find expression are in power production —an index according to Lenin of society's move towards communism was the degree of electrification (p. 71)—chemical production, and agricultural production (p. 114). As is usual in the

Soviet Union, a wide range of details are available of the subject matter which is regarded as appropriate to the proper understanding of these three vital areas of production.

Yet perhaps more important than the factual content of the work are the attitudes which Soviet educators think will be required, and the degree of technical skill and know-how young people will need, in the modern industrial world. Electrification will of course provide for the all-round mechanisation and automation of production. Automation, it is recognised, will lighten the workers' tasks, increase productivity, shorten the working day, and significantly liquidate the 'existing distinction between intellectual and physical labour' (p. 74). The developments in the major areas of the chemical industry and in atomic energy will clearly involve the disappearance of certain skills and their replacement by others. In general, it is accepted that the social divisions among workers will be reduced by automation owing to a decrease in the number of trades. Fewer specialities will lead to a demand for people who have a general orientation in all branches of production, who are trained for changes in the nature of their work, and who can pass from one kind of job to another (p. 81). As for the most general values, each individual should combine 'love and respect for work; knowledge and skills necessary to work in mechanised and automated production so as to guarantee high-quality, low cost products; interest in scientific and technological developments; all-round intellectual, physical, technical, aesthetic, and manual development; high cultural and moral standards based upon an understanding of his obligations to society; a communist outlook and a devotion to his country' (p. 82).

Polytechnical education is designed therefore to perform two tasks. It will help to raise production by training workers for a new and changing industrial world. In this world they will need to possess not only the skills of a trained technician but also a wide knowledge of the principles of science and technology as well as an acquaintance with all aspects of modern production. As I. A. Kairov has put it, 'engine drivers will become genuine locomotive engineers'. On the other hand it will help to promote the all-round development of the individual so that he can participate in the establishment of a truly communist society and learn to enjoy the increasing amount of leisure time that automation will provide for him.

Institutional Reform

Acceptance of major principles has not resolved all the problems either of theory or practice. Soviet literature in translation reveals the extent to which there is uncertainty about the detailed regulating theories which are needed if institutional reforms are to succeed. There are also misgivings about some of the new practices proposed. Nevertheless major intended institutional changes were enacted in the 1958 law and subsequent statutes. In fact the new system was, and is being, introduced by steps in the Soviet Union. The principles of change were based, it is claimed, on experiments and pilot schemes (p. 52). The intention of the law was to extend compulsory education from seven to eight years and replace the ten-year school by a system in which a completed secondary education would take eleven years all told. After eight years it was intended that pupils would proceed to one of three types of school. The majority whilst in full-time productive employment will complete their schooling in evening or shift schools. Another group will attend schools providing general education and very realistic production training. A minority will go to schools providing a general polytechnical secondary education and leading, it seems, fairly directly to higher education.

In the part-time schools for workers or collective farmers, students while actively at work in factory or on farm will be granted time to complete their general education, to receive polytechnical education, and to improve their technical qualifications. In these schools, obviously, the links between work and instruction should be very close. In the second type of school students will prepare for some branch of the national economy. These schools like the technical colleges and trade schools under the previous system will co-operate very closely with local industries. Students will spend between a third and a half of their time in school, the rest will be spent in specially organised training sections and shops in local enterprises. In rural areas according to the seasons there will be alternating periods of study and participation in farm work. In principle, the work of these schools will be determined very much by local conditions. Undoubtedly they will provide local industries with highly skilled technicians and craftsmen. In the third type of school more emphasis will be given to general education, and technical or professional training.

More boarding schools were also envisaged, if parents desire them. It is felt that in the controlled environment of the boarding school the wider aims of the new law should be more easily achieved. As far as it is possible to judge, existing boarding schools enrol children from somewhat disadvantaged homes rather than from the homes of the upper middle classes.

As for the curriculum, certain changes have been made. More socially useful work has been introduced into the general curriculum at the expense of such subjects as Russian language and literature, geography, and history. Socially useful work is first taken as a subject on the timetable in the third grade, and in this and up to and including the eighth grade occupies two out of between 26 and 34 periods a week. In the last three grades of the complete eleven-year school it is intended that a third of the week (12 periods) should be given over to general technical subjects, production training (theoretical and practical), and productive work (p. 99). The precise organisation of socially useful work as part of the curriculum depends upon local conditions, but contact with factories or nearby farms will be established.

In addition extra-curricular activities, hobby circles, mass media, school visits and so on will be used to illustrate production methods, give students some knowledge of working conditions, and make it possible for them to relate theory more effectively to practice. It is also generally agreed that work in production before entering an institution of higher education would benefit all young persons. Indeed, Mr Krushchev stated that in his view 'all pupils, without exception, should be drawn into work beneficial to society at industrial establishments, collective farms, etc., after they have finished seven or eight forms at school'. Understandably the danger of underproducing young intellectuals was recognised, and the new law states that each Union Republic shall 'wherever necessary, retain a certain number of the existing secondary schools throughout the transition period', thus avoiding any interruption in the supply of young specialists.

Debates and the New Approach

Legislation can bring about certain organisational changes in the structure and curriculum of the schools. But since the problem is seen by Soviet educators as one of changing important attitudes of students and teachers, the whole approach to education is in need of modification. There is little evidence that the shackles of an earlier European tradition are going to be thrown off overnight. Some of the objections to polytechnical education are of a negative kind. Concern has been shown about the position of the humanities. Neither industrialists nor the guardians of academic standards seem, as yet, fully convinced of the value of students spending a considerable proportion of their time in factories or on farms. Certainly not all work experiences are regarded as necessarily educative. Some idea of the resistance to the movement can be gained from reports that although by 1963 out of some 12,500 schools in the R.S.F.S.R. about 10,000 had become eleven-year schools with production training, many areas in the Soviet Union had not raised the proportion of productive work to the level proposed. In 1964 policy reverted to a ten-year school.

Perhaps more important than this conservatism is the very real difficulty of formulating regulatory theories on the basis of which a vast teaching force can improve methods of teaching, syllabuses, and curricula. Prominent Soviet writers point to the lack of research and theoretical investigation in the field of polytechnical education. One comment, for example, indicates that when the law was introduced the science of didactics was not well enough developed to help put the law into effect in a scientific manner. The author goes on to point out that the isolated recommendations were not enough to solve the cardinal problem. Nor will a simple extension of vocational studies in the schools satisfy the theoreticians, because they do not wish only to devise policies which will enable the future demands for highly qualified scientists and technologists to be met. In addition they aim at inculcating skills, attitudes, values, and knowledge which will enable an individual to develop himself fully as a person and also to fulfil his other responsibilities as a citizen. Stated in another way, the fundamental problem is one of finding theories which when translated into practice will provide a form of 'liberal' education appropriate to the twentieth century.

Two methods attempted prior to the reversal of policy in the thirties have been rejected as unsuitable. The selection of subject matter solely in accordance with the needs of productive labour is no longer acceptable; nor is an approach which was subsequently advocated before the return to intellectualism occurred. In this second scheme, reminiscent of the project method, educational subject matter was centred round the numerous working activities of people. The school was to be organised like life itself. Education was to be a single indissoluble process achieved through complex programmes in which the laws of nature, labour and society were to be studied and the links between them established. The chief criticism of the 'complex' approach seems to be that the links established are artificial. The arguments against the use of labour as an organising principle are that it breaks either the logic of school subjects or the ordered sequences of labour processes. Moreover it excludes from the curriculum some subjects unrelated to labour which are nevertheless important in the general education of children.

Thus present-day discussion turns on the practical possibilities of arranging courses of study so that organic connections are made between instruction and work, so that neither the logic of the school subjects nor the regular sequences of industrial routines are broken. Some writers advocate parallel courses, others think that this is often ineffective if theory is to be related to practice, and if more than mental knowledge and manual skills are to be acquired.

There is also a debate going on in educational circles about whether or not the psychological needs and capacities of children should be the principle of constructing courses of instruction rather than either the logic of the subject matter or industrial skills. Some writers, indeed, recognise the claims of all three principles of selecting data and advocate a multilateral approach. As for methods of teaching, not only have the principles of the natural sciences to be taught but also the objective links between these and technological subjects have to be made known. The familiar principle of 'integrating' subjects by relating data from different subject fields is also discussed. In teaching any subject, in fact, an attempt should be made to reveal the direct link between scientific principles and industrial practice. In these ways attention to industrial production will permeate the teaching of every subject in the school.

Additions to the curriculum, the introduction of new items in syllabuses, work experience, and extra-curricular activities constitute substantial reform. But it should be noted that having rejected the more radical theories of curricular organisation Soviet educators have not in practice moved very far in this sphere except to introduce productive work. The present curriculum of the schools shows a heavy bias towards scientific subjects. The economic rewards for studying them, either in the form of stipends when attending institutions of higher learning or subsequent salaries, are high. After the fourth class more than half the time allocation is on the science side. The general curriculum pattern is nevertheless somewhat traditional. Even in science the teaching would appear to have been rather didactic and formal, and the content of the courses generally speaking abstract. Intellectualism in school science education has certainly helped to produce a crop of extremely competent specialists and research workers. The problem is not really to win for science a rightful place in the curriculum—tradition, Marxist theory, and economic necessity have combined to achieve these things. Rather it is a question of re-orientating the whole of formal education so that less weight will be given to intellectualism and more to what, in English terms, may be called character training or moral education. After all, whatever the social and political ends of the system, it is with the upbringing of children that Soviet educators are concerned.

Broadly speaking the situation in non-Communist Western European countries differs in that the science subjects have yet to acquire the prestige of the classical languages or humanities as an integral part of a liberal or general education. The need for scientists and technologists has been recognised. New institutions like the Colleges of Advanced Technology (to be universities) in England have been established to meet the demand. This policy reflects the one followed by many governments towards the end of the nineteenth century of setting up extensive systems of vocational schools and thus institutionalising the dichotomy between 'liberal' education and vocational training. To be sure, the English educator still gives high priority to the development of a sound moral character through the whole atmosphere of the school, extra-curricular activities, and the academic study, particularly in the sixth forms, of a rather small number of subjects. There is still a widely shared belief that specialisation in the arts subjects provides a better general education than specialisation in the sciences. Even so each subject, so the theory runs, should be taught as much for its liberalising effects as for the vocational preparation it will provide.

In France an excellent base exists on which to build technical education. Regional needs and manpower requirements at various levels can relatively easily be met by extensions to the present system. But as for a liberal education a French spokesman is inclined to emphasise the importance of clear, logical thinking best developed through mathematics, the correct use of the French language, and the study of the classics. Even the reformed curricula of the French *lycées* reflect this belief. The classics form the core of a liberal education in many countries still. The German *Allgemeinbildung* is a concept which perhaps derives from romantic and Hegelian traditions which stress the desirability of enabling individuals to penetrate the surface of appearances to the essential nature of men and things. In most cases, reform proposals have tended to emphasise the value of modern language study compared with that gained from the classics. Wherever the early European tradition has prevailed, however, esteem for the classical languages has checked the development of science and technology as school subjects.

The policy makers of today cannot safely ignore the claims of science and technology, since they are vital to economic progress. Industrial processes make it absolutely necessary that technical, production, managerial, and commercial personnel should be well grounded in these subjects. More important still, the political and moral issues of the day demand that responsible citizens in their attempts to reach decisions should be able to weigh up the relevant scientific evidence. Without this ability they can hardly be safe from either the demagogue or the technocrat. On both counts, the economic-industrial and the socio-political, science and technology and the methods appropriate to them should be essential ingredients of the core of any 'liberal' education.

John Dewey was well aware of this problem. The foundations of his educational theory were that the most important task of education was to develop the intelligence of individuals so that they could tackle the problems of a changing world co-operatively using the methods of science. For Dewey there was no end-product, just a succession of problems, but he hoped that mankind would progress and was convinced that this could come about only through the maintenance and streng-thening of democratic institutions. His philosopher's view of the situation did not lead him often to formulate specific curriculum theories or suggest specific practices. These can be found in the views of Thomas Jefferson and Herbert Spencer. Similar ones were incorporated in the Seven Cardinal Principles of Curriculum presented in 1918 by a Committee of the National Education Association of the United States. The detailed proposals need not concern us here. What is important is that they broke away from the old conception of a curriculum based upon subject matter organised in terms of the historical development of subjects like history, geography, physics, chemistry and so on. New criteria, based upon the problems young people were likely to meet, were suggested for the selection and organisation of curricular data. Thus running through American approaches to the curriculum is the belief that the subject-matter of a sound general education should be drawn from three areas—the social sciences, the natural sciences, and the language arts. Specific problems should be used in order to select relevant data for instructional purposes, and these are likely to be drawn from the three areas. There will in fact be a central core of information which is common to them. This constitutes the heart of general education; for the rest students should be free to pursue the study in greater depth of the traditional subjects provided in the timetable as electives.

It would be unwise to suggest that American theory has yet been adequately translated everywhere into effective practice. Over the years when faced with hard choices between an academic approach or intellectualism in education American educators have fairly consistently chosen to move in the direction of providing everyone with a socialising education, designed to help young people cope with their problems and in particular to help prepare them for future participation in a democracy. Many commentators feel that as a result gifted children in the United States have been neglected and that the country has failed to match the Soviet Union in the production of high-quality scientists and engineers. Strangely the Soviet dilemma reveals the degree to which educational policy geared rather intimately to rapid economic development may create difficult social, political, and indeed even economic problems. Soviet educators are approaching similar problems to the Americans from a different angle and background. To redress the balance due to specialisation they are returning to Marxist sources of polytechnical education for their general theory, which as they admit is not entirely different from that proposed by Dewey and others.

Perhaps what is needed by both groups, however, are detailed operating theories of a specific character which will enable them to change the methods of teaching and the content of the curriculum in a way which will make possible the more harmonious integration of intellectual education, productive work, and socialising experiences. But even when these theories have been more adequately worked out, teachers will have to be found who can be trained to put them effectively into practice, not with a select minority of young people but with them all. And the new curriculum and methods will have to take account of the complexity and ever-changing character of the modern world. It is a daunting problem demanding imaginative solutions, active research and experimentation, and determined implementation.

Chapter XI

INDIVIDUAL FREEDOM AND
SOCIAL RESPONSIBILITY
(JAPAN)

A PERENNIAL moral problem faces educators everywhere. It is to find an acceptable balance in education between the inculcation of, on the one hand, individualism and on the other, a sense of social conformity. Stated in another way, there is always a need to temper individual freedom with an acceptance of social responsibility. Or again the question is to what extent should individuals be expected to conform to established social norms and to what extent and in what areas should they be encouraged to question norms or indeed challenge and reject them. Popper, of course, characterises the open society as one in which freedom to challenge and reject political norms is basic. Yet one of the traditional tasks of education has been to hand down accepted norms from one generation to the next. Among these there may be two which appear contradictory. One suggests that young people should conform and obey. The other suggests that in some areas at least they ought to be prepared to challenge authority and reach their own decisions.

Philosophically the dilemma has a long history. The search for truth and the discovery of the authority for it has gone on in many societies for thousands of years. In most general terms the view that there are permanent truths external to individual men should be contrasted with the belief that man is the measure of truth, which therefore is never more than hypothetical or relative and is always liable to be modified.

Closely associated with these two contrasting views are the psychological theories about the ability of individuals to acquire knowledge. Again, the élitist position may be compared with a faith in the intrinsic reasonableness and rationality of all men.

287

Finally two views of society may be compared. One ideal postulates a static society in which change is necessarily retrogressive. At the other extreme some social theorists regard as ideal a society which is always in process of change—in the opinion of some towards a final knowable goal.

Against these contrasted concepts of knowledge, individualism, and social change can be viewed the variety of institutions through which a balance between individual freedom and social conformity is attempted. Until the twentieth century, to be sure, over large areas of the world social institutions were such as to inhibit change, restrict individual freedom of choice (at least for the masses), and promote the acceptance of authority based upon belief in absolutes. The amount of freedom varied from region to region, country to country, and between one sphere of social activity and another. Any comparative analysis of the solutions offered to the problem under consideration would therefore demand a careful study both of normative and institutional patterns.

In spite of considerable differences two generalisations may serve to direct attention to the kind of solutions offered and to one significant feature of the problem. In any society to help individuals resolve the conflict within them between self-interest and social responsibility appeals may be made to rules of conduct, to principles of judgement, or to the authority of persons. Inevitably social control involves all three elements in varying degrees. Institutional arrangements reinforce one or other of the bases of authority whenever attempts are made to promote group interests. The schools contribute to the various solutions by making known to students the rules of conduct which are expected to regulate the relations between men in society. Some of them, like good manners, are technical in nature and apply to specific relationships in rather special circumstances. The more challenging educational task, however, is to move beyond rules to the establishment within the individual of principles on the basis of which he can make judgements and subsequently act upon them in circumstances to which no specific rule applies. A particular feature of this problem is the need to ensure that the individual can operate within a variety of situations; notably the family, the school, the local community, and the nation. And today there is a growing

need to extend the context and find principles which will
enable people to find a balance between national self-interest
and international responsibility.

Concepts of individualism are well-developed, of course, in
countries whose traditions are Greco-Christian. An analysis
of different epistemological assumptions would reveal several
possible attitudes towards individual choice. For example,
Descartes' views about knowledge and how it can be acquired
('I think, therefore I am') provide support for an individualism
based upon clear logical thinking starting from personal *a
priori* premises. English empiricism suggests that consensus is
possible if based upon observations of facts and the cautious
evolution from them of hypotheses and general laws. Pragmatism in the U.S.A. lends support to the view that principles
should be tested, co-operatively, in experience and rejected or
accepted on this kind of evidence.

In all three countries acceptance of the principle that all
men should be equal before the law has not been accompanied
by any radical rejection of belief in psychological inequality.
The degree to which all men are expected to enter into decision-
taking processes varies from nation to nation, but the Periclean
contention is widely held that if only some members of society
are capable of formulating policy all should be capable of
judging it.

The social and political institutions of these three democracies also vary. Prior to de Gaulle's constitutional reforms
the French had placed great faith in the ability of members of
the legislature to formulate and execute policy. The American
Constitution was from the start founded on a theory that a
system of checks and balances was desirable, but yet gives to the
executive branch overwhelming authority in some spheres.
Government by Cabinet in the United Kingdom postulates both
individual ministerial and collective responsibility, a rationale
for which, in the absence of a written constitution, can be
found, for example, in J. S. Mill's *Representative Government*.
The organisation of local political authorities varies in a similar
way, and a comparative study of this, and family structures
and the roles accorded to various members therein, would be
necessary in order more fully to understand the way how each
of these three nations wedded to its own concepts of an open,

democratic society attempts to resolve through institutional arrangements outside the formal schools the conflict described. These and other institutions should be the subject of separate and rigorous comparative studies.

Here an attempt is made to reveal more precisely the nature of the problem in Japan and to show how, when faced with what appeared to be an authoritarian State and an obedient people, the occupying powers attempted after World War II to democratise the country through education. For a variety of reasons Japan presents a fascinating case study of a general problem. The following analysis is based upon wide reading and a stay in Japan during which lengthy discussions with Japanese colleagues helped to clarify the problem. But, it should be remembered, inability either to read the language or to enter fully into the thought processes of many colleagues and friends places limitations on the possibilities of complete comprehension which should not be ignored.

Moral Obligation and Human Feeling

Perhaps some idea of the problem in Japan can be given through a brief description of a film, *I wish I Could be a Seashell*, about a simple Japanese barber who among others was standing trial before an Allied court as a war criminal. In flashback were shown aspects of his life in his village, his conscription into the army—with much false rejoicing—and the incident of which he was accused. He had been compelled, obviously against his will, by his superior officer to bayonet before the eyes of the assembled platoon one of three captured American airmen. He was found guilty and condemned to death, without understanding how he had transgressed, but without bitterness, and with the hope that he could escape from the State Leviathan and from future responsibility by becoming a seashell. The theme of the film—the conflict in a strange context within the barber between his moral obligation or duty (*giri*) and his human feeling (*nyngo*)—was beautifully and poignantly presented.

The extent to which the context was important was also revealed. The barber faced no insurmountable questions of choice among his family and within his local community where the traditional dilemma between *giri* and *nyngo* is usually portrayed. He was modest, affectionate, benevolent, law-abiding, and a keeper of the peace. The real difficulty arose when he was projected into the wider context of national affairs as a member of the army. The film showed not only the power of the State through its appointed officers to enforce obedience, but also how, under certain circumstances, human feelings were unable to protect the individual against it. Having raised the problem so tellingly, this film—in spite of the fact that it was a powerful indictment of war—nevertheless left many questions unanswered.

There can be little doubt, however, that in pre-war Japan the educational system and other institutions enormously strengthened *duty* or *moral obligation* as the authority for behaviour. *Loyalty* and *filial piety* were basic obligations. Duty was to persons (and groups of persons) and not to abstract principles. Persons were carefully placed in a hierarchy which depended upon age, sex, social status, and position. There were many ways in which overt recognition of one's own place and that of others was expected, notably through complicated language conventions.

Perhaps this emphasis on duty strengthened the group, and weakened individual responsibility. Certainly the group was optimistic—the Japanese nation had a glorious destiny. On the contrary, the individual was inclined to pessimism and fatalism. In some situations suicide—in its nobler form a supreme expression of loyalty—became the escapist's answer. Of great importance was the tendency for the society to be paternalistic, capable of responding to wise leadership but vulnerable to take-over bids by determined cliques. Even so, other societies succumbed as easily as Japan during the nineteen-thirties and under economic and demographic difficulties no more severe. It should not be forgotten, either, that many thousands of opponents of the military régime were eliminated. Indeed many competent observers regard this decade as a grave distortion of Japan's traditions. Certainly the ultra-nationalists attempted to make education serve their purpose of imperial expansion. To some extent they succeeded.

Nevertheless the pre-war system of education in Japan and the policies of imperialism can be regarded as having developed under the impact of problems common to most countries undergoing a process of industrial development, the fact that in Japan it took place so rapidly increased the difficulties. Educational policy, for example, had to take account of the enormous increase in population—for several decades it rose at the rate of about one million every year. (Now the rate of increase has been reduced to about that of Europe.) Great demands were placed on the schools to accommodate more and more children. Industrial development created a demand for literate workers and skilled technicians. Associated changes in the social structure of the nation created problems of selection and training for political leadership. More bureaucrats were needed, and the complexities of twentieth-century life placed the extension of formal schooling for the purposes of social education high on the list of priorities.

Japan's entry into the stream of industrialisation coincided with a change in the political scene. The Emperor Meiji was restored in 1868 after a period of some three hundred years during which the Tokugawa Shogunate (the Shogun was a generalissimo who ruled on behalf of the Emperor) had maintained uneasy control of a country divided politically among many competing feudal clans. Retarded nationalism together with the feudal economy presented special problems for the new leaders. Fearful of foreign imperialism they directed all their efforts to the rapid political unification of Japan and to the development, under their own direction, of the country's economic strength. These objectives were achieved remarkably quickly and without the direct assistance of foreign powers. Several consequential changes took place. The social structure was modified through increased upward social mobility. The traditional ethics of the upper classes were disseminated first to the towns and only afterwards—and to a much lesser degree—in the countryside. The differences between urban and rural life in Japan consequently remain enormous.

Selective Cultural Borrowing

The magnitude of Japan's economic achievements is unquestioned. Equally, the nation's political system has been severely criticised. Before examining the post-war scene it would be well to consider briefly the contribution made to Japan's achievements and disasters by education and European influences.

It has often been said, of course, that the Japanese are remarkable, and by implication uncritical, imitators. This assessment does them less than justice. There is an old Japanese saying 'Japanese traditional spirit with civilised technical skills' (*Wakon-Kansai*). In the event, European technical skills were accepted and brought to a high degree of efficiency. European forms of organisation were also copied. But the traditional Japanese spirit persisted, and only in the immediate post-Meiji Restoration period was there much enthusiasm for European values and social theories. Signs of the influence of a practicalism reminiscent of Benjamin Franklin or Samuel Smiles were also evident at that time. The Constitution of 1889 was remarkably liberal in many respects, although the reaction of that decade represented a return by the leaders to some of the historical traditions and indigenous beliefs of the Japanese people. The most noticeable exception to this general trend was the introduction and academic study of German philosophy, notably Hegelianism.

The technique of selective cultural borrowing is well revealed in the educational system which was set up within three years of the Restoration. In its organisational arrangements it was, and remained up to 1945, a copy of European and American institutions. Enter a school today and the immediate impression, in sharp contrast to a private home, is of a Western institution in many ways. Its ethos, however, if not entirely different, shows many features which are distinguishable as Japanese. The pre-war organisation of education reflects the influence of European, Japanese, and Chinese traditions.

Structurally there were three divisions, elementary, secondary, and higher. Universal elementary education was quickly established after 1868. By 1900 there were four years of compulsory schooling. This period was soon increased to six years (age six to twelve). In 1941 the National Schools reform proposed an extension of compulsory schooling to eight years. There were upper or higher elementary schools. These grew in numbers and provided an extended elementary education together with handicrafts for boys and domestic science for girls. More and more schools had two years higher elementary courses, but perhaps only about half the children in the ordinary elementary courses stayed on. Perhaps not more than about 14 per cent of the students went beyond the elementary schools.

As in Europe there developed several kinds of secondary school. The middle schools set up under the Meiji leaders were for boys and the course was of five years' duration. They were principally for the middle classes, and by providing different courses in the fourth and fifth years prepared boys either for business careers or for further education. Students were admitted on the basis of competitive examinations. Exceptionally able boys could enter them after the fifth year of elementary school. Enrolments in the middle schools rose steadily. In 1935 there were over five hundred schools with more than three hundred thousand students; three times as many as thirty years before.

About the same number of girls were attending girls' high schools and special domestic high schools. The Chinese tradition introduced into Japan *circa* A.D. 400 was against co-education. According to Confucius women should be 'good wives and wise mothers'. Husbands were to be regarded as lords and worshipped as such. Writing of the objections to co-education, a Japanese educator of the thirties named the following: boys became effeminate, women masculine, and during adolescence co-education often led to immoral practices. Moreover since boys and girls have their own intellectual faculties uniform teaching consequently lowered standards. A distinction was drawn between the mode of life in Europe and the United States. Domestic science, sewing, cooking, training in the tea ceremony and in flower arrangement and ladylike etiquette were necessary if a Japanese woman was to meet the requirements of life.

Objections to higher education for women were that it deprived them of matrimonial opportunities at a suitable age, that it destroyed the domestic character of girls and many of the fine qualities which Japanese women traditionally possessed. It must be remembered that at the time women were legally very much discriminated against. They were unable to divorce their husbands, had no property rights, and could not vote. There were, one author proudly notes, no women in politics in 1935.

A third group of schools enrolled about as many students as the middle schools. These technical schools were intended to train students for industrial occupations. Local needs often determined the course. During the thirties, partly as a result of the raw silk trade, Japan was turning to the production of consumer goods. Her cheap mass-produced toys and her ability to compete in textiles became well known and feared. In the face of this shift in production emphasis was placed on the establishment of technical schools.

Still a great many adolescents received no formal training after leaving the elementary schools. Consequently an attempt was made to extend the technical continuation schools. After 1935 all youngsters between the ages of 12 and 19 were encouraged to attend, either part-time or full time, youth schools. They were not part of the compulsory system until 1939. Their aim was to fuse technical and vocational studies with social education and were intended for those pupils who did not go on to middle or technical schools. They were popular because attendance there reduced the period of compulsory military service. These schools, it is claimed, in particular became an instrument of ultra-nationalism. Against the Ministry of Education the influence of the army prevailed in them.

The higher schools were part of higher education. They were principally for boys and corresponded to the academic grammar schools of Europe. The course of study was of seven years, four of these being devoted to general education in the ordinary course, and three years being a more specific preparation for university entrance. A rather significant movement had, however, taken place. Increasingly boys entered the higher schools from the fourth year of the middle schools on the basis of competitive examinations. The courses in the higher schools were differentiated studies, one for literature, the other for science. Both courses had a common core and included two foreign languages, law and economics, mathematics and gymnastics. Neither course, however, was very specialised.

As in Europe teachers intended for different types of schools were trained in different institutions. The teachers in the higher schools were university graduates with little or no professional training. High normal schools trained teachers for the middle, girls' high, and technical schools. Recruitment for the normal schools usually came from middle schools or girls' high schools.

Entrance to university was on the basis of competitive examination. In 1935 there were 45 universities with 71,000 students. There existed in the universities a long tradition of interest in science and technology, law and medicine. The departments of literature enrolled fewer students than any of these. Since the universities remained rather free from government control they continued to exercise a somewhat progressive influence on education as a whole. The principal philosophy studied was that of Hegel. Their function was to provide bureaucrats. Even in the thirties there was very considerable unemployment among university graduates; in 1935, a period of economic crisis, more than 50 per cent of university graduates were out of work.

Within this system selection was broadly speaking on ability. Elementary schools were free, and the fees for secondary schools in 1945 were equivalent to about £5 a year and those at the universities modest. Nevertheless the composition of the various secondary schools was representative of a highly structured society. The whole structure was (and perhaps continues to be) dictated by a concept of hierarchy directly derived from the kinship of the clan. During the Tokugawa Shogunate there were four classes, the samurai or warriors, the farmers, the artisans, and the merchants. In addition there was an aristocracy of peers, and an untouchable caste, the Eta. Considerable attempts were made in the thirties to root out discrimination against the Eta. Undoubtedly the secondary schools, at first intended for the middle classes and nobility, resulted in increased social mobility. The impression prevails that selection does not present as great a problem as in England. Jean Stoetzel maintains that in spite of a philosophy of social stability the social structure of Japan is relatively flexible. Individual self-interest, however, is not dominant. 'Direct competition, which questions the validity of rank, hurts feelings, and jeopardises personal security and social stability is avoided as much as possible; thus the promoters of the recent educational reforms were being neither as original nor, by the same token, as "democratic" as they thought in taking such pains to abolish all competition in schools.'

In any case there was a pre-war movement towards a far less differentiated secondary school system than was common in many European countries. The greatest hurdle was entry into the higher schools.

One other agency of social mobility should be mentioned. The army provided for the personally ambitious an accessible route to positions of power and prestige. Poor peasants rose rapidly to positions of leadership and responsibility. Neither their informal education nor their subsequent training gave them the code of behaviour of the traditional warrior class, the samurai. It was in fact the Young Officer group which led the ultra-nationalistic movements of the late twenties and during the thirties. The mutiny that carried them to power occurred six days after the party representing liberal and business interests in Japan had won a notable electoral victory. Richard Storry in *The Double Patriots* (London, Chatto and Windus, 1947) points out that the rising class of officials—particularly in the Ministries of Home Affairs and Education—were strongly influenced by a nationalist study circle which at least for some time had been able to attract some of the Young Officers. In the *Cardinal Principles of National Entity* (*Kotutai No Hongi*) published by the Ministry of Education in 1937 Confucian filial piety was enlarged to include the supreme moral obligation of loyalty to the Imperial House.

Administration

The Ministry of Education officials were in a strong position to impose ultra-nationalism on the schools. The administrative organisation set up in 1871 was a copy of the French. A code of education followed in 1872. The country was divided into eight university districts, each to have a university and itself divided into 32 middle school districts. There were to be 210 elementary school districts in each middle school district. An elementary school was to be provided for every 600 inhabitants. Throughout the country 256 middle schools and 53,760 elementary schools were planned. By 1875 there were 24,225 elementary and 53 secondary schools. Under the Minister

297

there was an appointed vice-Minister who directed the affairs of the official bureaux. The number of these grew so that in 1935 there were seven—Higher Education, General Education, Technical Education, Social Education, Supervision, School Books, and Religious. Area inspectors concerned themselves with every aspect of school life.

As in most European countries, elementary education came more under the influence of the local administration—village headmen, town mayors, the governors of prefectures—than did secondary and higher education. Nevertheless the central Ministry exerted a considerable measure of control over most aspects of public schools. Teachers were licensed by the Ministry. Licences granted by the prefectures were not nationally recognised. Marked attempts were made to raise the prestige of teachers and in 1935 every local board had a teacher on it.

Textbooks were compiled or sanctioned by the Ministry. The greatest control was exercised over textbooks for the compulsory subjects or core subjects and for those used in elementary schools. Greater freedom was allowed in the secondary and higher schools. The main outlines of the curricula of the various types of school were determined by the Ministry, although some allowances were made for local variations in terms of special needs, particularly in the vocational field. The costs of education were shared by the national government and local authorities. In 1935 about one third of the total expenditure on education was borne by the Ministry. A far higher proportion of the money spent on higher education was provided by the Ministry, more than one quarter of which came from private sources. There were policies of equalisation and subsidy to ensure that schools were established in every part of the country.

The system certainly provided for a network of paternalistic control which accorded well with the traditional hierarchical principles based on kinship. Village headmen, town and city mayors, prefectural governors were linked to the central governments by the system of appointment rather than election. Teachers were treated as government officials and accorded the privileges and status appropriate to their position and rank. Control, it would be true to say, remained in the hands of the Establishment.

Aims of Education

The tremendous successes of this system should not be under-estimated. One purpose was social: the cultivation of national morality. After 1890 when the Imperial Rescript on education was issued there existed a blueprint to which all subsequent policy makers paid a homage amounting to reverence. Before returning to examine the special influence of the Rescript on the curriculum some of the special functions other than social-political which each type of school performed should be noted. The elementary schools stressed literacy. Since in Japan there are four scripts, and four ways of writing depending upon circumstances, the task was formidable. The picture writing is based on the Chinese ideograms, of which there are many thousands (*Kanji*). Elementary school children learned to remember a selected number. Robert King Hall's evidence suggests that school students had been exposed to some 1356 different ideograms in elementary school textbooks. An additional 450 were introduced in the seventh and eighth classes. In addition there are two native phonetic syllabary systems. Fortunately compared with the thousands of syllables into which English can be dissected there are less than 80 recognisably different syllables in Japanese words. Accents make it possible to reduce the number to about 50 (*Kana* 48).

In pre-war Japan about 40 per cent of elementary school time was taken up with the teaching of literacy and moral education. The schools were remarkably successful. About 99 per cent literacy was achieved, although some caution is necessary, since it is difficult to say precisely what standards were reached. Two things should be noted. Today the Japanese are voracious readers, yet in some public offices like those of customs and immigration, scribes still sit patiently waiting to help persons fill in difficult forms; but they seem to have very few customers.

The middle and higher schools provided a liberal education and prepared students for further education. The Chinese classics gave the essentials of a liberal education. They exercised the brain, gave emotional training, and provided a way of thinking. Otherwise the curriculum was not very different from that of a European academic secondary school. In addition to morals, Japanese language, and Chinese classics, it included history, geography, foreign languages, mathematics, science, drawing, music, practical work, and gymnastics. The kinds of differentiation which occurred at both levels have already been mentioned.

As for methods only a subjective assessment can be made. The written language itself obviously placed great demands upon memorisation. Probably this tendency was carried over into the teaching of other subjects. At least the secondary schools give the impression that very little time is devoted to experimental science. Similarly the emphasis in language teaching is on grammar and translation. But with classes even in 1959 still enormous, 56 in the higher schools, severe limitations are placed upon wholesale experimentation. Nevertheless relations between teacher and pupil seem paternal, with the teacher held in considerable respect and motivation among pupils high.

The Normative Pattern

Thus far rather few radical differences between organisation and purposes of the pre-war Japanese educational system and the European have been noted. There were some important distinguishing features. Moral education as a course of study in the curriculum was, at least as far as emphasis, uniquely Japanese. The subject-matter was selected in the light of the Imperial Rescript of 1890, and consequently represented the fundamental Japanese norms or values. The social purpose of the schools was the development of loyal citizens who would understand their duties and know what to expect of their leaders. The secondary schools were to cultivate national morality among the future leaders of the society so that they should know their responsibilities. As we have seen the object of the course of morals was to extend the rules of behaviour based upon kinship obligations from the family and clan to the nation. The textbooks compiled for the teaching of *Shūshin* (or morals) illustrate through understandable stories the rules of behaviour enshrined in the Imperial Rescript. The various sources of the Japanese ethical code are not difficult to identify in general terms. The construct proposed here is necessarily highly selective. It may nevertheless serve as a basis for further analysis.

Any Weberian construct for Japan, drawn from philosophy not empirical data, would inevitably contain aspects of Buddhism, Confucianism, and certain European theories. It was seen that few elements which cannot be reconciled with indigenous Shintoism have much chance of survival. The Imperial Rescript combined Confucianism with State Shintoism. Of European theories perhaps only those associated with Hegelianism have made much headway in Japan, although it is clear that Christian belief profoundly influenced a small minority of people, and that American pragmatism permeates much of economic life.

If the pattern is drawn up in the light of theories of society, the individual, and knowledge, its broad outlines would be of the following kind.

Social theory is derived largely from Confucian paternalism, with the principles of loyalty and filial piety blending harmoniously with the ancestor worship of Shintoism. Rules guiding the behaviour of an individual in five sets of relationships also stem from Confucianism, as does the position of women. The five relationships were those between (*a*) sovereign and subject, (*b*) father (or mother) and child, (*c*) husband and wife, (*d*) elder and younger brother or sisters, and (*e*) friends. The virtues which should guide action are clearly stated in the Imperial Rescript. Individuals should be loyal, filial, affectionate, modest, benevolent, law-abiding. A person who did not observe the rules of conduct in these relationships would be regarded as not knowing how to behave or not knowing his duty: or, stated another way, as not recognising his obligations.

As for the individual, Shinto belief was that all men were descended from the gods (*kami*), who were, however, unequal in standing and importance. Hence the acceptance of inequalities among men was justified. There is also the extremely important concept of *Jikaku*, an inner spiritual quality, acquired through introspection to give knowledge of self, possessed by some men, a minority, but not others, which derives from Zen Buddhism. One of the chief tasks of education is to develop this immensely respected ability. The paternalism of the family was extended to the nation through a revival of the ancient belief that the Emperor was divine, a direct descendant in unbroken line from the supreme deity, the sun goddess.

For a representative theory of knowledge it is perhaps necessary to turn to Zen Buddhism. About one-fifth of the population subscribes to this sect of Buddhism. In all there are thirteen major sects, each having given Japanese interpretations to an imported religion. Zen in particular has contributed to the aristocratic way of life—*Bushido*. It united aestheticism with military prowess. Indeed so strong is the aesthetic element that 'life itself has become identified with art'. The way of life of the *samurai* has been diffused among the urban population. In particular every detail of the domestic scene is so arranged as to form a unified whole—an aesthetic creation.

Learning, however, was regarded with a mild contempt. Certainly the rational logical elements were weakly represented compared with intuition. Spiritual training, however, gave assurance of discovering an ultimate reality which transcends all individual differences. Highly mystical and contemplative in approach, Zen Buddhism holds that knowledge cannot easily be verbalised. What is known is known intuitively, in experience and emotion. It is hardly surprising that of all the European epistemologies only the dialectic and mysticism of Hegel were widely accepted among Japanese scholars. Neither Cartesian rationalism nor the empiricism of a Locke or Mill is very evident.

Intuitive knowledge, together with *Jikaku*, strengthens the leader's position in the social hierarchy. His authority is very great. The freedom of the individual to exercise independent judgement is much reduced, for it is not easy to dissociate ideas from the personality of the person holding them. To attack or challenge the former is to break one's obligation to the latter.

In these terms enormous power and responsibility is vested in the leaders. The final court of appeal if the social rules of mutual obligation break down is to intuition (if we can describe so simply the complex thought processes of Zen Buddhism). This should be compared with the European appeal finally either to reason or evidence in any attempt to solve the moral problem created by the conflict between duty, social responsibility, and individual freedom. During the ultra-nationalistic phase all the agencies of State Shintoism were strengthened to enforce obedience at the expense of individual freedom.

Educational Reform in the Post-War Period

After the surrender in 1945, the occupation forces under American leadership attempted to redress the balance. Policy, however, was directed towards the achievement of two aims. The first was to prevent Japan from ever again waging an aggressive war; the second was to re-educate the Japanese. But even officials had no clearly developed idea of just what was involved. 'Government by nudge', however, achieved certain results, not all of them desired or expected. Some institutions were temporarily abolished and new ones created. Through widespread land reforms the power of the landlords was very much weakened. So too was the power of the family industrialists (*Zaibatsu*). State support of Shinto was suppressed and the Emperor denied his divinity. Positive reforms included the writing of a new constitution in which sovereignty was invested in the people, the Emperor being merely a symbol of the State. Legally women were made equal with equal rights. They were now able to divorce their husbands, could own property, and were given a vote. The main consequence of these attempts, which were resisted fairly successfully, was to give more power to organised labour and a well-organised Communist party.

Education was vulnerable. The attempted reforms were more drastic than in most other spheres. The points of attack were institutional. The power of the central Ministry of Education was reduced. It became an organisation for the collection and dissemination of information. The appointment of teachers became the responsibility of local authorities. These Boards of Education were mainly elected and not, as before, appointed. Freedom was given to the teachers to organise their own courses and select their own textbooks. Teachers were no longer State officials and were allowed in 1947 to form their own union, the Japan Teachers' Union. Decentralisation made possible take-over bids by determined leaders of this organisation.

The curriculum was heavily attacked. Morals, Japanese history, Chinese classics, geography, and the military arts

(*Kendo* and *Judo*) were removed. Social studies and civics were among the important subjects designed to replace 'morals'. The course in social studies was intended to develop courses of study through experiences in social living. One of the first tasks of the Allied forces was to censor all the textbooks in use, removing all traces of militarism. Perhaps they did so to prevent the Japanese Ministry of Education taking over textbook control again. New books had to be submitted to Occupation Head-quarters for approval. The linguistic difficulties were enormous. The results were not quite those expected. The policy showed how a determined central authority—even a minority in temporary power—could rewrite a nation's textbooks inside a year. Moreover the operation failed to make clear why and in what ways the textbooks had to be censored.

The principles of selection on the basis of academic ability were virtually abandoned. Colleges were turned into universities, so that the university population grew overnight from some 150,000 to five times that number. Compulsory education was introduced for nine years in a system of primary and lower secondary schools. Senior secondary schools completed the 6–3–3 system of America. Co-education was encouraged throughout the system and an atempt was made to latinise the script (*Romaji*) since the *Kanji* (Chinese characters) was regarded as particularly anti-democratic in its effect because so few members of the population were trained to read more than a rather limited number of them.

All these new policies were made in the interests of promoting democracy. Whether knowingly or not they were taken over with little modification from American practice. There is little purpose in asking whether or not these reforms were good in themselves. Certainly as time went on some proposals were rejected by the Japanese, simply because they were American in origin. It is also evident that not all European institutional arrangements—and the Japanese system was basically European—were regarded by the Americans as democratic. The distinguishing feature of the Japanese system was to be found in the ideological framework which surrounded it and the fundamental task of altering the Japanese philosophy of education was never seriously tackled. This assertion raises profound questions. For example, many indigenous views have not only survived the vicissitudes of Japanese history but remained to provide acceptable rules of conduct for the vast majority of the Japanese people—at least in certain contexts. However desirable an aim, the period of time and the resources available were too limited to make a change in the basic philosophy of education a practical possibility. Wished on to the Japanese were a series of institutional reforms. There were few principles on which they could call to guide them in attempting to make the new system work.

Attachment to Traditions

Conditions after the war were not propitious. Japan faced the same kind of problems as prevailed in England in 1945—only more so. Her economy was ruined, her capital assets dissipated, her export trade gone. Communications, equipment, factories, and schools had been seriously damaged or destroyed. One-quarter of the dwelling houses in Japan had been burned to the ground. In 1945 the people of Japan were short of all the necessities of life. Economic recovery began only after the United States realised what a drain the country was on her own exchequer. By 1951 Japan was on the road to recovery. This entailed a radical switch from her traditional products, raw silk, rayons, and cotton goods, to consumer products of high quality. The switch was made, and by 1955 according to G. C. Allen the economic recovery of Japan was essentially complete.

The moral condition of the people continues to create alarm among responsible persons. More divorces, more crimes of violence are instanced in support of this claim. More important perhaps is the feeling not only among young people that the basis of morality—moral obligation in its variety of forms in innumerable personal relations—has been destroyed. According to Stoetzel many people felt not only that mutual obligations were no longer being fulfilled but that in fact duties were no longer recognised or known. He also reports a profound conflict among young people. To quote one example, he writes that some women are loud in their demands for equality—but many spontaneously admit to wishing to keep to their former status. His general conclusion is that 'the attachment of youth to Japanese culture is profound and in essential ineradicable'.

Other observers note that human feeling has taken over as a guide to conduct. Self-interest and individualism are predominant. But Stoetzel's disclaimer should be noted. Certainly loyalty to the group has led to some unfortunate situations. A bitter struggle for power has for example developed between the Japan Teachers' Union and the Ministry of Education. Formed in 1947, the union enrols practically all elementary school teachers and a high proportion of lower secondary school teachers. The union leaders are fighting to retain some of the reforms introduced under the American influence; notably social studies and the greater participation of the local authorities in the appointment and promotion of teachers. The Ministry wished to introduce grading ratings for teachers in order to facilitate promotions. The Union fought this proposal vigorously. The leadership undoubtedly has Communist leanings. Teachers engage directly in political activities, and, if rumour is correct, in some instances deliberately break up meetings by violence. In some areas at least the impression is that they behave with a degree of irresponsibility which few teachers in England would condone. Many teachers may not in fact approve of Union policy, but loyalty to the group remains, and human feeling or individual judgement is suspended. Conversely the Ministry seems to have been less diplomatic in some of its actions than would seem desirable. The split between the supporters of the union and the supporters of the Ministry runs through education. Personal relations between administrators and teachers and between teacher and pupil remain in many instances extremely good in the best traditions of paternalism. Traditions of filial piety, respect for elders and people in positions of authority remain. Group loyalties to the Japan Teachers' Union or to the Ministry of Education are drawing men of good will on both sides apart rather than together. At worst group loyalties in terms of class will replace the wider loyalties and in a new context there may be a return to something like the feuds between clans of the pre-Meiji period.

New Proposals for Reform

Educators in Japan are naturally worried by these developments. Many of them are searching diligently for a new basis of moral education which will bring together in effective harmony some traditional values and some new ones. They are seeking to find some principles and develop new institutions which will enable them to reconcile (in terms used here) the conflict, or gap if you prefer, between moral obligation and human feeling, social responsibility and individual freedom, group authority and individual responsibility.

To meet the situation the Ministry of Education revised the curriculum of elementary schools in 1951, 1955 and again in 1958. A course of morals was reintroduced. In 1959 a circular dealing with primary and lower secondary school curricula was issued. In the same year the reintroduction of a revised course in moral education became effective. The course has four aims. First it is hoped that through it young people will understand and acquire daily and basic behaviour patterns. These rules of conduct will be based on the authority of family as before. The second aim is to increase moral sentiments and the power to judge between right and wrong, good and evil. Thirdly the course should assist in the development of individuality and the cultivation of creative attitudes towards life. Finally it should get pupils to form and increase those kinds of moral attitudes which are demanded of a member of a democratic nation or community and to desire to put them into practice.

The emphasis, previously lacking, on individuality and power to judge is extremely noteworthy. Even so institutions still have to be devised through which these aims can be achieved. Students' councils have existed in schools for some time, but although they provide useful outlets for student criticism they do not confer any real authority on young people. One hour a week has been allocated in the lower secondary school timetable to extra-curricular activities. Curricula generally are again coming under the control of the Ministry, and in 1961 an entirely new curriculum came into force in the elementary schools. By 1962 new courses were in operation in the lower secondary schools. These reforms represent an attempt on the part of the Ministry to establish minimum standards in the basic subjects. The lower secondary school curriculum gives more time to mathematics and science and a wider range of electives in vocational subjects is provided. The Chinese classics have been reintroduced into the upper secondary schools.

The majority of universities and about a third of the junior colleges are maintained by the national government, as are a few schools in each class. The national government appoints teachers in them. But most of the upper secondary schools are prefectural schools and the majority of elementary and lower secondary schools are run by the municipalities. The appointment of teachers to these schools is the responsibility of the prefectural Board of Education (on the advice of the principal and after an examination in some instances) and the municipal Board of Education respectively. A number of types of teachers' certificate exist granted by the prefectures. A reform of teacher training is anticipated, the intention being to standardise more rigorously university and college courses for intending teachers. Centres are being set up to advise on textbooks.

All these returns to traditional, if somewhat modified, practice should be viewed with alarm only if the pre-war tradition is regarded in all its details as vicious, and if the educational system is held to be the cause of ultra-nationalism. Moreover, education should not perhaps be regarded, as it sometimes is, as a panacea. In the evolution of a society economic policies and political struggles will no doubt play a major part. It is not for comparative educationists to judge the rights and wrongs of policies pursued in foreign countries. All that should be attempted is to predict if possible the various consequences— however minor—educational policy may bring about in other aspects of the society. In Japan will it help to direct present internal political conflicts into less violent manifestations? Can it help to furnish attitudes which will enable democratic institutions to operate more peacefully?

One change is of very considerable significance, namely the position of women in Japanese society. Many of them may find their new freedom strange, others may resent the traditional fetters which prevent them from enjoying their legal emancipation. They may wish more than anything to be 'good wives and wise mothers', but demand perhaps a greater say in the manner in which they should express these virtues. Consequently in increasing numbers young mothers through Parent-Teacher Associations are beginning to exert their influence. There can be little doubt that their influence will be for the good of education and of society generally.

Moreover in certain important respects the climate of opinion in Japan is changing. The variety of standards and the rather sudden removal of definite rules of conduct have contributed to a measure of moral confusion. Is it necessary for the Japanese, if they are to achieve their own expressed desire to strengthen democracy and live at peace, to forge new rules and principles of moral conduct? A research team from Kyushu University directed its attention to this very point and to the possibilities of borrowing again from Europe some of its educational methods of developing loyal citizens and creative individuals. How can the schools contribute to the growth of individuality tempered with social responsibility? Their task is by no means easy. They are tackling it energetically and with some success in the organisational field. As far as attitudes are concerned the consistent blend of western and Japanese norms may be more difficult to find. New techniques have been acquired but the traditions of Japan remain.

It is the very success of the process of selective cultural borrowing combined with the deeply felt sense of loyalty and obligation to the spirit of Japan that gives this universal problem such unique features in this beautiful and friendly country.

NOTES

CHAPTER I

1. Robert Owen, *A New View of Society* (Glencoe, Illinois, Free Press), pp. iv and 65, and *Letters on Education As It Is and As It Ought to Be* (May, 1851), p. 10.

2. Henry Barnard, *National Education. Systems, Institutions and Statistics of Public Instruction in Different Countries*, Part II (New York, E. Steiger, 1872), p. 515.

3. M. E. Sadler, 'The Unrest in Secondary Education in Germany and Elsewhere', in *Board of Education Special Reports on Educational Subjects*, Vol. 9, *Education in Germany* (London, H.M.S.O., 1902), p. 162.

4. William Torrey Harris in *Annual Report of the Commissioner of Education for the Year 1888–89* (Washington, 1891), I, p. xxv.

5. Matthew Arnold, *Schools and Universities in the Continent* (London, Macmillan, 1868), p. xxii.

6. Matthew Arnold, *The Popular Education of France* (London, Longman, Green, Longman & Roberts, 1861), p. xxx.

7. Henry Barnard in *Connecticut Common School Journal* (Hartford), I, No. 11, April 1, 1839, an issue devoted to 'An exposition of the Common School system of Prussia'.

8. V. Cousin, *Report on the State of Public Instruction in Prussia* (trans. Sarah Austin), 2nd ed. (London: Effingham Wilson, 1836), p. 392.

9. Horace Mann in *Seventh Annual Report of the Board of Education* (Boston, Dutton and Wentworth, 1844), p. 23. All these reports have been reproduced.

10. Cousin, op. cit., p. 292.

11. Sadler, op. cit., p. 44.

12. ibid., p. 54.

13. Harris, op. cit., p. xix.

14. Cousin, op. cit., p. 3.

15. John Eaton, Jr., in *Report of the Commissioner of Education for the Year 1879* (Washington, 1881), p. xiii.

16. Harris, op. cit., p. xix.

17. Sadler, op. cit., p. 21.

18. Arnold, op. cit., p. xi.

19. Mann, op. cit., p. 99.

20. Joseph Kay, *The Social Condition and Education of the People in England and Europe*, Vol. I (London, Longman, Brown, Green & Longmans, 1850), p. 5.

21. I. L. Kandel, *Comparative Education* (New York, Houghton Mifflin, 1933), p. xix.

Notes

22. Nicholas Hans, *Comparative Education* (London, Routledge, 1949).
23. Friedrich A. Schneider, *Triebkräfte der Pädagogik der Völker* (Salzburg, Otto Muller, 1947).
24. Mann, op. cit., p. 184.
25. Sadler, op. cit., p. 23.
26. Harris, op. cit., p. xxiii.
27. Cousin, op. cit., p. vii.
28. V. Cousin, *On the State of Education in Holland as Regards Schools for the Working Classes and for the Poor* (London, John Murray, 1838), p. lxvi.
29. *Le Musée pédagogique, son origine, son organisation, son objet*, d'après les documents officiels (15 Mai 1884), (Paris, Imprimerie Nationale, MDCCC LXXXIV, Ministre de l'Instruction Publique et des Beaux-Arts), p. 15.

CHAPTER II

1. J. S. Mill, *A System of Logic* (London, Longmans, Green and Co., 1891), Preface to 1st edition, p.v.
2. ibid., p. 606.
3. Lester F. Ward, *Outlines of Sociology* (New York, Macmillan, 1898), pp. 25–6.
4. Richard Hofstadter, *Social Darwinism in American Thought* (Boston, Beacon, 1955), p. 67.
5. Herbert Dingle, *The Special Theory of Relativity* (New York, Chemical Publishing Co., 1941), pp. 5 and 89.
6. A. J. Ayer, *Language, Truth and Logic* (London, Gollancz, 1948), p. 97.
7. Philip P. Wiener, *Evolution and the Founders of Pragmatism* (Cambridge, Mass., Harvard University Press, 1949), pp. 191, 195, 198, 200.
8. Otto Neurath, 'Foundations of the Social Sciences' in *International Encyclopedia of Unified Sciences*, 11, no. 1.
9. John Dewey, *How We Think* (New York, Heath, 1933), particularly chapter 7.

CHAPTER III

1. See B. Holmes and S. B. Robinson, *Relevant Data in Comparative Education* (Hamburg, Institute for Education, 1963).
2. See *Proceedings of the Comparative Education Society in Europe, Amsterdam, 1963* (The Hague, Nijhoff, 1964).
3. K. R. Popper, *The Open Society and its Enemies* (London, Routledge, 1946).
4. See H. H. Gerth and C. Wright Mills, *From Max Weber: Essays in Sociology* (London, Routledge & Kegan Paul, 1948), p. 324.
5. Gunnar Myrdal, *An American Dilemma* (New York, Harper, 1944).
6. J. A. Lauwerys, 'The Philosophical Approach to Comparative Education' in *Thoughts on Comparative Education* (The Hague, *International Review of Education*, 1960), p. 27. This volume, a *Festschrift* for Pedro Rossello, contains many important articles on methodology.
7. F. S. Cillié, *Centralization or Decentralization* (New York, Bureau of Publications, Teachers College, Columbia, 1940).

Notes

CHAPTER IV

1. Gunnar Myrdal, op. cit., Vol. 1, p. 111.
2. Lewis Mumford, *Technics and Civilization* (London, Routledge, 1934), p. 370, and *The Condition of Man* (London, Martin Secker & Warburg, 1944), p. 63.
3. William Ogburn, *Social Change* (London, Allen & Unwin, 1923).
4. Karl Mannheim, *Man and Society* (London, Kegan Paul, 1940), p. 39.

CHAPTER V

1. See Walter Lippmann, *The Public Philosophy* (Boston, Little, Brown, 1955); *Phantom Public* (New York, Harcourt Brace, 1925); and *Public Opinion and Foreign Policy in the United States* (London, Allen & Unwin, 1952).
2. Hans J. Morgenthau, *Dilemmas of Politics* (Chicago, University of Chicago, 1958), p. 377. See *Politics among Nations* (New York, Knopf, 1956).
3. Lippmann, *Phantom Public*, p. 88.
4. Lippmann, *The Public Philosophy*, p. 74.
5. United Nations Preparatory Educational, Scientific, and Cultural Commission, *Fundamental Education: Common Ground for All People* (New York, Macmillan, 1947).
6. Director General, Unesco, *Learn to Live* (Paris, Unesco, 1951), Foreword by James Torres Bodet, p. 7.
7. *Fundamental Education*, p. 271.
8. H. L. Elvin, 'The Philosophy of UNESCO' in *The Year Book of Education 1957: Education and Philosophy* (London, Evans, 1957).
9. Quincy Wright, *The Study of International Relations* (New York, Appleton-Century-Crofts, 1955).
10. Ministry of Education, Government of India, *Report of the Secondary Education Commission* (Oct. 1952–June, 1953, New Delhi), p. 23.
11. Philip W. Buck and Martin B. Travis, Jr. (eds.), *Control of Foreign Relations in Modern Nations* (New York, Norton, 1957).
12. National Education Association, Educational Policies Commission, *American Education and International Tensions* (Washington, 1949).
13. Frederic Lilge, in *Mid-Century: The Social Implications of Scientific Progress* (Cambridge, Mass., Massachusetts Institute of Technology, 1950), p. 318.

CHAPTER VI

1. Karl W. Deutsch, *Nationalism and Social Communication* (Cambridge, Mass., Technology Press, Massachusetts Institute of Technology, and New York, Wiley, 1953).
2. I. Schapera, *Migrant Labour and Tribal Life* (London, Oxford University Press, 1947); Sol Tax, *Penny Capitalism—A Guatemalan Indian Economy* (Washington, 1953) and U.K. Board of Trade, *The African Native Market in the Federation of Rhodesia and Nyasaland* (London, H.M.S.O., 1954).
3. Barbu Niculesco, *Colonial Planning, a Comparative Study* (London, Allen & Unwin, 1958). For a shorter account of British policy see: Brian Holmes,

'United Kingdom: Education and Development' in *Year Book of Education 1954* (London, Evans, 1954).

4. Statements of the Indian Advisory Planning Board, October 1946, in United Nations Secretariat, Department of Economic Affairs, *Economic Development in Selected Countries: Plans, Programmes and Agencies*, Vol. 1 (New York, Lake Success, Oct. 1947).

5. John Ely Burchard (ed.) *Mid-Century, The Social Implications of Scientific Progress* (Cambridge, Mass., Technology Press, M.I.T., and London, Chapman & Hall, 1950).

6. Walter Lippmann, *The Communist World and Ours* (Boston, Little, Brown, 1959).

7. Philip M. Hauser (ed.), *Population and World Politics* (Glencoe, Ill., Free Press, 1958).

8. Thorstein Veblen, *The Theory of the Leisure Class: An Economic Study of Institutions* (New York, Modern Library, 1934).

9. Pierre Mendes-France and Gabriel Ardant, *Economics and Action*, a UNESCO publication (New York, Columbia Univ. Press, 1955).

10. M. J. Bowman and G. L. Bach, *Economic Analysis and Public Policy* (New York, Prentice Hall, 1949).

11. F. A. Hayek, *Individualism and Economic Order* (Chicago, Univ. of Chicago Press and London, Routledge, 1948).

12. O. F. Raum, 'Resistance Factors in the Transformation of African Society' in *The Year Book of Education 1954* (London, Evans, 1954). This chapter owes much to the analysis and illustrations presented in this Year Book and also *The Year Book of Education 1956. Education and Economics.*

13. André Siegfried, 'The Spirit and Foundations of European Civilization' in *The Year Book of Education 1957. Education and Philosophy* (London, Evans, 1957).

14. Perry Miller, *The New England Mind in the 17th Century* (New York, Macmillan, 1939) and *The New England Mind: from Colony to Province* (Cambridge, Harvard Univ. Press, 1953); see also Max Weber, *The Protestant Ethic and the Spirit of Capitalism*, trans. Talcott Parsons, Foreword by R. H. Tawney (London, Allen & Unwin, 1930), and R. H. Tawney, *Religion and the Rise of Capitalism* (London, Murray, 1936).

15. UNESCO, *The Organization of the School Year*, Educational Studies, and Documents No. 43 (Paris, UNESCO, 1962).

CHAPTER VII

1. A. W. Halpin (ed.), *Administrative Theory in Education* (Chicago, University Mid West Administration Center, 1958). This volume provides the basis for the analysis in this chapter.

2. See H. Finer, *The Major Governments of Modern Europe* (London, Methuen, 1960) and W. G. Andrews, *European Political Institutions. A comparative government reader* (Princeton, Van Nostrand, 1962).

3. R. F. Campbell and R. T. Gregg, *Administrative Behavior in Education* (New York, Harper, 1957).

4. See R. K. Merton (ed.), *Reader in Bureaucracy* (Glencoe, Ill., Free

Notes

Press, 1952); and K. G. Heath, *Ministries of Education: Their Function and Organization*, Bulletin 1961, no. 21 (Washington, U.S. Department of Health, Education and Welfare, 1962).

5. International Bureau of Education, Geneva and UNESCO, *School Inspection*, Publication No. 174 (Geneva, 1956), A comparative study.

6. F. S. Cillié, *Centralization or Decentralization* (New York, Bureau of Publications, Teachers' College, Columbia, 1940).

CHAPTER VIII

1. See *Year Book of Education 1963: The Education and Training of Teachers* (London, Evans, 1963).

2. Henry Barnard, *German Teachers and Educators* (Hartford, Brown & Gross, 1878).

3. Myron Lieberman, *Education as a Profession* (Englewood Cliffs, N. J., Prentice Hall, 1956).

4. See A. E. Bestor, *Educational Wastelands* (Urbana, Univ. of Illinois, 1953), and *The Restoration of Learning* (New York, Alfred A. Knopf, 1955).

5. J. B. Conant, *The Education of American Teachers* (New York, McGraw Hill, 1963).

6. Robert M. Hutchins, *The Higher Learning in America* (New Haven, Yale University Press, 1936).

CHAPTER IX

1. Jean Thomas and Joseph Majault, *Education in Europe: Primary and Secondary Education* (Strasbourg, Council for Cultural Co-operation of the Council of Europe, 1963).

2. Carr Report, *Training for Skill*, Recruitment and Training of Young Workers in Industry; Report of a Sub-committee of the National Joint Advisory Council (London, H.M.S.O., Dec. 1957).

3. Barlow Report, *Scientific Manpower*, Cmnd. 6824 (London, H.M.S.O., May, 1946).

4. Zuckerman Committee, *Advisory Council on Scientific Policy, Committee on Scientific Manpower Statistics* (London, H.M.S.O., 1961).

5. *Advisory Council on Scientific Policy, Report on the Recruitment of Scientists and Engineers by the Engineering Industry* (London, H.M.S.O., 1955).

6. Percy Report, *Higher Technological Education*, Report of a Special Committee, April, 1944–July, 1945 (London, H.M.S.O., 1945).

7. *Employment Policy*, Cmnd. 6527 (London, H.M.S.O., May, 1944).

8. Joint Committee on Human Relations in Industry, *First Report* (London, H.M.S.O., March, 1953 to March, 1954).

9. R. M. Titmuss, *Problems of Social Policy* (London, Longmans, 1950), and *Essays on the Welfare State* (London, Allen & Unwin, 1958).

10. R. H. Tawney (ed.), *Secondary Education for All: A Policy for Labour* (London, Allen & Unwin, 1923).

11. Hadow Report, *Education of the Adolescent*, Board of Education Consultative Committee on Education (London, H.M.S.O., 1926).

Notes

12. Spens Report, *Secondary Education*, Board of Education, Consultative Committee on Education (London, H.M.S.O., 1938).

13. Norwood Report, *Curriculum and Examinations in Secondary Schools*, Committee of the Secondary Schools Examinations Council (London, H.M.S.O., 1943).

14. *Secondary Education for All: A New Drive*, Cmnd. 604 (London, H.M.S.O., Dec. 1958), and *Early Leaving*: A Report of the Central Advisory Council for Education, England (London, H.M.S.O., 1954).

15. Crowther Report, *15 to 18*, Report of the Central Advisory Council for Education, England (London, H.M.S.O., July, 1959).

16. Newsom Report, *Half Our Future*, A Report of the Central Advisory Council for Education (England) (H.M.S.O., 1963).

17. Robbins Report, *Higher Education*, Cmnd. 2154 (London, H.M.S.O., Oct. 1963).

18. W. R. Fraser, *Education and Society in Modern France* (London, Routledge, 1963).

CHAPTER X

The information on the Soviet educational system is based upon personal visits and, among others, the following selected publications. Page numbers given in the text refer to Shapovalenko's *Polytechnical Education in the U.S.S.R.*

The Law on Strengthening Ties between School and Life can be consulted in English in K. Galkin, *The Training of Scientists in the Soviet Union* (Moscow, Foreign Languages Publishing House, 1959) or in J. B. Conant, *The Child, the Parent and the State* (Cambridge, Mass., Harvard University Press, 1959).

N. S. Krushchev, *Memorandum on Proposals for the Reform of Education* (Soviet Booklet No. 42, October, 1958. Published by *Soviet News*).

Theses of the Central Committee of the Communist Party (Soviet Booklet No. 44, December, 1958. Published by *Soviet News*).

E. A. Asratyan, *I. P. Pavlov and His Life and Work* (Moscow, Foreign Languages Publishing House, 1953).

N. K. Krupskaya, *On Education* (Moscow, Foreign Languages Publishing House, 1957).

A. S. Makarenko, *A Book for Parents* (Moscow, Foreign Languages Publishing House, 1954) and *The Road to Life* (Moscow, Foreign Languages Publishing House, 1955).

S. G. Shapovalenko (ed.), *Polytechnical Education in the U.S.S.R.* (Paris, UNESCO, 1963).

Soviet Education (New York, International Arts and Sciences Press). A periodical containing translated articles from Soviet educational magazines.

The Year Book of Education (London, Evans) regularly includes articles on the U.S.S.R. by Soviet authors.

Center for International Studies, *Documentary and Reference Material on Education in the Soviet Union*, duplicated translated material (Cambridge, Mass., Massachusetts Institute of Technology, 1956).

M. Deineko, *Public Education in the U.S.S.R.* (Moscow, Progress Publishers, 1964).

Notes

Bereday, Brickman, Read & Schlesinger, *The Changing Soviet School* (London, Constable, 1960).

Nicholas DeWitt, *Education and Professional Employment in the U.S.S.R.* (Washington, National Science Foundation, 1961).

Leonhard Froese, *Russische und Sowjetische Pädagogik* (Heidelberg, Quelle & Meyer, 1963).

Nicholas Hans, *Educational Policy in Soviet Russia* (with S. Hessen) (London, King, 1930); *History of Russian Educational Policy* (London, King, 1931); and *The Russian Tradition in Education* (London, Routledge, 1963).

W. R. Medlin, C. B. Lindquist, and M. L. Schmitt, *Soviet Education Programs* (Washington, U.S. Government, 1960).

B. Simon (ed.), *Psychology in the Soviet Union* (London, Routledge, 1957).

L. Volpicelli, *L'Évolution de la pédagogie soviétique* (Neuchâtel Delachaux et Niestlé, 1954).

CHAPTER XI

The analysis and information presented in this chapter are based upon a personal three-month visit to Japan, frequent and long discussions with Japanese colleagues, and extensive reading in English. I am particularly indebted to Professor B. Iwahashi for reading the manuscript of this chapter and for his invaluable advice and suggestions. The following are selected references in English.

Ministry of Education:

Education in 1955–, Annual Report of the Ministry of Education, Research Section, Research Bureau, Ministry of Education. Reports are available for years 1907–38 under the Ministry of State for Education.

Education in Japan, graphic presentation, Annual 1954 (Tokyo, Research Bureau).

Japan's Growth and Education, Educational Development in Relation to Socio-economic growth. The White Paper on Education (Tokyo, Ministry of Education, 1963).

Revised Curriculum in Japan for Elementary and Lower Secondary Schools (Tokyo, Research Bureau, 1960).

Japanese National Commission for UNESCO, *Japan, its Land, People and Culture* (Tokyo, Ministry of Education, 1958).

Centenary Cultural Council Series, A Cultural History of the Meiji Era. Titles include; *Education and Morality; Society; Life and Culture Japanese; Legislation* (Tokyo, Obunsha).

Japanese Education Reform Council, *Education Reform in Japan* (Tokyo, 1950).

M. Hiratsuka, 'Some Important Moments in the History of Modern Japanese Education' in *Bulletin of the Research Institute of Comparative Education and Culture* (Fukuoka, Kyushu University, 1957).

Titsu Katayama, *Women's Movement in Japan* (Foreign Affairs Association of Japan, Kenkyusha Press, 1938).

D. Y. Kikuchi, *Japanese Education* (London, 1909).

D. T. Suzuki, *Zen and Japanese Culture* (London, Routledge, 1959).

Notes

G. C. Allen, *A Short Economic History of Modern Japan, 1867–1937* (London, Macmillan, 1946) and *Japan's Economic Recovery* (London, Royal Institute of International Affairs, 1958).

W. G. Aston, *Shinto, the Way of the Gods* (London, 1905).

Ruth Benedict, *The Chrysanthemum and the Sword* (London, Secker & Warburg, 1947).

B. H. Chamberlain, *Things Japanese* (London, Kegan Paul, 1890).

D. J. Enright, *The World of Dew* (London, Secker & Warburg, 1955).

Robert King Hall, *Education for a New Japan* (New Haven, Yale University Press, 1949); *Shushin, the Ethics of a Defeated Nation* (New York, Teachers College, Columbia, 1949 and (ed.) *Kokutai No Hongi* (Cambridge, Mass., Harvard University Press, 1949).

Donald Keene, *Japanese Literature* (London, Murray, 1953), and *Modern Japanese Literature* (London, Allen & Unwin, 1956).

Fosco Maraini, *Meeting with Japan* (London, Hutchinson, 1959).

G. B. Sansom, *Japan, a short cultural history* (London, Cresset, 1946); *A History of Japan*, Vol. 1 (London, Cresset, 1958); *The Western World and Japan* (London, Cresset, 1950).

Jean Stoetzel, *Without the Chrysanthemum and the Sword* (London, Heinemann/UNESCO, 1955).

Richard Storry, *The Double Patriots* (London, Chatto & Windus, 1957), and *A History of Modern Japan* (Harmondsworth, Pelican, 1960).

SCAP (Supreme Commander of the Allied Powers), *Post-War Developments in Japanese Education*, 2 vols. (Tokyo, 1952).

SELECTED BIBLIOGRAPHY

The following books and periodicals in English have been selected from a growing volume of literature in comparative education. They should be considered primarily as presenting different approaches to the study of comparative education. A fuller bibliography, *Teaching Comparative Education*, has been published by UNESCO (Education Abstracts, Volume XV, No. 4, 1963).

General Texts

G. Z. F. BEREDAY, *Comparative Method in Education* (Holt, Rinehart & Winston, New York, 1964): area studies.

J. F. CRAMER and G. S. BROWNE, *Contemporary Education* (New York, Harcourt Brace, 1956): descriptive.

NICHOLAS HANS, *Comparative Education, a study of educational factors and traditions* (Routledge, 1958): historical factors.

I. L. KANDEL, *The new era in Education* (London, Harrap, 1955): historical causes or determinants.

E. J. KING, *World Perspective in Education* (London, Methuen, 1962): problems.

J. A. LAUWERYS, *Morals, Democracy and Education* (Tokyo, Institute for Democratic Education, 1957): problems.

VERNON MALLINSON, *An Introduction to the Study of Comparative Education* (London, Heinemann, 1960): national character.

A. H. MOEHLMAN, *Comparative Educational Systems* (New York Library of Education, 1963): long range factors.

Major Reference Works

International Bureau of Education, Geneva, *International Yearbook of Education*, 1933–9, 1946–: also special studies which provide policy statements.

UNESCO, *World Survey of Education*, 1955 (Paris): four volumes dealing with different stages of education, over 200 descriptive studies.

UNESCO Institute for Education, Hamburg: a series of publications dealing with selected problems in education.

Year Book of Education (London, Evans Bros.; New York, Harcourt Brace): each year a theme or problem is selected and treated on a broad comparative basis.

Selected Bibliography

Periodicals

Comparative Education Review (New York, Comparative Education Society, 1957): four issues a year.
Bulletin of the International Bureau of Education (Geneva, 1927): four issues a year.
Educational Studies and Documents (Paris, UNESCO, 1953–): irregular.
International Review of Education (Hamburg, UNESCO Institute for Education, 1955): four issues a year.

Selected Problems:
Educational

FRANK BOWLES, *Access to Higher Education* (Paris, UNESCO; New York, Columbia University Press, 1963).
JAMES BRYANT CONANT, *The Child, the Parent and the State* (Cambridge, Mass., Harvard University Press, 1959).
ROBERT DOTTRENS, *The Primary School Curriculum* (Paris, UNESCO, 1962).
KATHRYN G. HEATH, *Ministries of Education: their Function and Organisation* (Washington, Government Printing Office, 1962).
TORSTEN HUSEN and STEN HENRYSSON (ed.), *Differentiation and Guidance in the Comprehensive School* (Stockholm, Almqvist & Wiksell, 1959).
O.E.C.D. *Policy for School Science* (O.E.E.C., Paris, 1962).
Supply, Recruitment and Training of Science and Mathematics Teachers (Paris, O.E.C.D., 1962).
T. L. RELLER and E. L. MORPHET (eds.), *Comparative Educational Administration* (Englewood Cliffs, N.J., Prentice Hall, 1962).

Socio-economic

ADAM CURLE, *Educational Strategy for Developing Societies* (London, Tavistock, 1963).
L. J. LEWIS, *Education and Political Independence in Africa and other essays* (Edinburgh, Nelson, 1962).
MARGARET MEAD, *Cultural Patterns and Technical Change* (Paris, UNESCO, 1953).
H. H. STERN, *Parent Education: an international survey* (Hull, University of Hull; Hamburg, Institute for Education, 1960).

Psychology

I. BENNET, *Delinquent and Neurotic Children; a comparative study* (London, Tavistock, 1960).
A. W. FOSHAY and others, *Educational Achievements of Thirteen-year-olds*

Selected Bibliography

in Twelve Countries (Hamburg, UNESCO Institute for Education, 1962).

F. HOTYAT (ed.), *Evaluation in Education* (Hamburg, UNESCO Institute for Education, 1958).

W. D. WALL, F. J. SCHONELL and W. C. OLSEN, *Failure in School* (Hamburg, UNESCO Institute for Education, 1962).

W. D. WALL, *Education and Mental Health* (London, UNESCO, and Harrap, 1955).

W. D. WALL (ed.), *Psychological Services for Schools* (Hamburg, UNESCO Institute for Education, 1956).

INDEX

Academic freedom, 196, 197

Academic schools, 224, 272, 295

Administration and control, 155, 158, 175, 181, 182, 297, 298, 303

Afghanistan, 145

Africa, 37, 38, 109, 110, 138, 152

Agrégation, 144, 217, 259

Aligarh Moslem University, India, 107

Allen, G. C., 305

America, *see* United States of America

American Journal of Education, 14

Anderson, C. A., ix, 66

Anthropomorphism, 141

Ardant, Gabriel, 130

Aristotle, 87, 269, 270

Arkansas University, U.S.A., 214

Arnold, Matthew, 7, 9, 15, 17, 187

Asia, 37, 38, 105, 151, 152

Association of Assistant Masters, U.K., 250

Athens, Greece, 195

Austin, Sarah, 22

Australia, 201

Automation, 266, 278

Ayer, A. J., 30, 32

Bach, G. L., 130

Bacon, Francis, 25, 196

Baluchistan, 89

Barlow Report, U.K., 229, 230

Barnard, Henry, 11, 14, 48, 200

Belgian Congo, 123

Bestor, A. E., 173, 204, 214

Bevin, Ernest, 112

Bill of Rights, U.S.A., 58, 77

Birth-rates, 37, 126, 191, 206, 242

Boarding schools, 280

Bode, B. H., ix, 213

Bodet, J. T., 103

Boston, U.S.A., 18

Bowman, M. J., 130

Britain, *see* United Kingdom

British Guiana, 134

Buddhism, ix, 194, 302

Buisson, M. F., 12

Bureau of Education, Washington, U.S.A., 12, 14, 16, 23

Calvin, 75

Capital, 134, 135, 242

Capital aid, 135

Carr Committee, U.K., 229

Caste, 137

Causal relations, 44, 46, 53

Centralisation, *see* Administration

Centres pédagogiques régionaux, 217

Ceylon, 107, 111

Chase, F. C., ix

Chicago University, U.S.A., 213

China, 126, 129, 133, 135

Christianity, 59, 140, 194, 195, 301

Christ's Hospital School, U.K., 9

Church and State, 7, 8, 72, 110, 155, 175, 198, 201, 204, 224, 259

Index

Index

Index

Langevin, Paul, 170, 171, 259, 260
Latin America, 125
Lauwerys, J. A., x, 65, 103
Legislation: 6, 64, 151, 222, 260, 279
    U.K., 157, 159, 169, 170, 189, 222, 225, 226, 236, 241, 246, 256, 260
    U.S.A., 172
Leicestershire Plan, U.K., 255
Lenin, 273, 275, 277
Lieberman, Myron, 203
Lilge, Frederick, 117
Lippmann, Walter, 98–100, 116, 118, 120, 124, 133, 251
Literacy, 16, 102, 106, 118, 151, 299
Local authorities, 8, 226
Locke, John, 59, 261
Lomonosov, 271
Luther, 75
Lycées, France, 7, 156, 183, 259, 261

Majault, Joseph, 222
Makarenko, A. S., 274
Manchester University, U.K., 234
Mann, Horace, 8, 11, 18, 20, 81, 201, 206
Mannheim, Karl, 83
Manpower, 87, 135, 228
Marx and Marxism, 26, 27, 75, 83, 196, 269, 273, 275, 283, 286
Mass education, *see* Universal education
Mass media, 37, 38, 79, 266
Massachusetts Board of Education, U.S.A., 18
Massachusetts Institute of Technology, U.S.A., 117
Mendes-France, P., 130, 150

Middle classes, 8
Mill, J. S., 27, 36, 91, 289
Miller, Percy, 140
Ministry of Education, 8, 168, 174
Mirabeau, 7
Moral education, 276, 300, 307
Moral problems, 89, 118, 305
Morgenthau, H. J., 100, 104
Mudiliar, Sir Ramaswami, 124
Mumford, Lewis, 78, 83
Myrdal, Gunnar, 57, 75, 78, 184

Napoleon, 7, 140, 156, 271
National Education Association, U.S.A., 82, 115, 212, 285
National Health Service, U.K., 234
National Union of Teachers, U.K., 201
Nationalisation, 233
Nationalism, 5, 10, 61, 109, 291
Nepal, 146
Neurath, Otto, 31
Newsom Committee, U.K., 248
Newton, Sir Isaac, 29
Nigeria, 109, 134
Nineteenth century, 7, 8, 10, 12, 16, 22, 26, 38, 50, 60, 61, 70, 77, 157, 201
Nomenclature, 15
Norwood Report, U.K., 171, 226, 240

Objectives, 45
Ogburn, William, 83
Ogden, C. K., 103
Ohio, U.S.A., 208, 210, 213
Organisation of schools, 22, 143, 147
Owen, Robert, 5, 26, 75, 140, 274

324

Index

325

The International Library of

Sociology

and Social Reconstruction

Edited by W. J. H. SPROTT
Founded by KARL MANNHEIM

ROUTLEDGE & KEGAN PAUL
BROADWAY HOUSE, CARTER LANE, LONDON, E.C.4

CONTENTS

PRINTED IN GREAT BRITAIN BY HEADLEY BROTHERS LTD
109 KINGSWAY LONDON WC2 AND ASHFORD KENT

GENERAL SOCIOLOGY

Brown, Robert. Explanation in Social Science. *208 pp. 1963. (2nd Impression 1964.) 25s.*

Gibson, Quentin. The Logic of Social Enquiry. *240 pp. 1960. (3rd Impression 1968.) 24s.*

Homans, George C. Sentiments and Activities: Essays in Social Science. *336 pp. 1962. 32s.*

Isajiw, Wsevelod W. Causation and Functionalism in Sociology. *165 pp. 1968. 25s.*

Johnson, Harry M. Sociology: a Systematic Introduction. *Foreword by Robert K. Merton. 710 pp. 1961. (5th Impression 1968.) 42s.*

Mannheim, Karl. Essays on Sociology and Social Psychology. *Edited by Paul Keckskemeti. With Editorial Note by Adolph Lowe. 344 pp. 1953. (2nd Impression 1966.) 32s.*

Systematic Sociology: An Introduction to the Study of Society. *Edited by J. S. Erös and Professor W. A. C. Stewart. 220 pp. 1957. (3rd Impression 1967.) 24s.*

Martindale, Don. The Nature and Types of Sociological Theory. *292 pp. 1961. (3rd Impression 1967.) 35s.*

Maus, Heinz. A Short History of Sociology. *234 pp. 1962. (2nd Impression 1965.) 28s.*

Myrdal, Gunnar. Value in Social Theory: A Collection of Essays on Methodology. *Edited by Paul Streeten. 332 pp. 1958. (3rd Impression 1968.) 35s.*

Ogburn, William F., and **Nimkoff, Meyer F.** A Handbook of Sociology. *Preface by Karl Mannheim. 656 pp. 46 figures. 35 tables. 5th edition (revised) 1964. 45s.*

Parsons, Talcott, and **Smelser, Neil J.** Economy and Society: A Study in the Integration of Economic and Social Theory. *362 pp. 1956. (4th Impression 1967.) 35s.*

Rex, John. Key Problems of Sociological Theory. *220 pp. 1961. (4th Impression 1968.) 25s.*

Stark, Werner. The Fundamental Forms of Social Thought. *280 pp. 1962. 32s.*

FOREIGN CLASSICS OF SOCIOLOGY

Durkheim, Emile. Suicide. A Study in Sociology. *Edited and with an Introduction by George Simpson. 404 pp. 1952. (4th Impression 1968.) 35s.*

Professional Ethics and Civic Morals. *Translated by Cornelia Brookfield. 288 pp. 1957. 30s.*

Gerth, H. H., and **Mills, C. Wright.** From Max Weber: Essays in Sociology. *502 pp. 1948. (6th Impression 1967.) 35s.*

Tönnies, Ferdinand. Community and Association. *(Gemeinschaft und Gesell-schaft.) Translated and Supplemented by Charles P. Loomis. Foreword by Pitirim A. Sorokin. 334 pp. 1955. 28s.*

SOCIAL STRUCTURE

Andreski, Stanislav. Military Organization and Society. *Foreword by Professor A. R. Radcliffe-Brown. 226 pp. 1 folder. 1954. Revised Edition 1968. 35s.*

Cole, G. D. H. Studies in Class Structure. *220 pp. 1955. (3rd Impression 1964.) 21s. Paper 10s. 6d.*

Coontz, Sydney H. Population Theories and the Economic Interpretation. *202 pp. 1957. (3rd Impression 1968.) 28s.*

Coser, Lewis. The Functions of Social Conflict. *204 pp. 1956. (3rd Impression 1968.) 25s.*

Dickie-Clark, H. F. Marginal Situation: A Sociological Study of a Coloured Group. *240 pp. 11 tables. 1966. 40s.*

Glass, D. V. (Ed.). Social Mobility in Britain. *Contributions by J. Berent, T. Bottomore, R. C. Chambers, J. Floud, D. V. Glass, J. R. Hall, H. T. Himmelweit, R. K. Kelsall, F. M. Martin, C. A. Moser, R. Mukherjee, and W. Ziegel. 420 pp. 1954. (4th Impression 1967.) 45s.*

Jones, Garth N. Planned Organizational Change: An Exploratory Study Using an Empirical Approach. *About 268 pp. 1969. 40s.*

Kelsall, R. K. Higher Civil Servants in Britain: From 1870 to the Present Day. *268 pp. 31 tables. 1955. (2nd Impression 1966.) 25s.*

König, René. The Community. *232 pp. Illustrated. 1968. 35s.*

Lawton, Denis. Social Class, Language and Education. *192 pp. 1968. (2nd Impression 1968.) 25s.*

McLeish, John. The Theory of Social Change: Four Views Considered. *About 128 pp. 1969. 21s.*

Marsh, David C. The Changing Social Structure in England and Wales, 1871-1961. *1958. 272 pp. 2nd edition (revised) 1966. (2nd Impression 1967.) 35s.*

Mouzelis, Nicos. Organization and Bureaucracy. An Analysis of Modern Theories. *240 pp. 1967. (2nd Impression 1968.) 28s.*

Ossowski, Stanislaw. Class Structure in the Social Consciousness. *210 pp. 1963. (2nd Impression 1967.) 25s.*

SOCIOLOGY AND POLITICS

Barbu, Zevedei. Democracy and Dictatorship: Their Psychology and Patterns of Life. *300 pp. 1956. 28s.*

Crick, Bernard. The American Science of Politics: Its Origins and Conditions. *284 pp. 1959. 32s.*

Hertz, Frederick. Nationality in History and Politics: A Psychology and Sociology of National Sentiment and Nationalism. *432 pp. 1944. (5th Impression 1966.) 42s.*

Kornhauser, William. The Politics of Mass Society. *272 pp. 20 tables. 1960. (3rd Impression 1968.) 28s.*

4

Laidler, Harry W. History of Socialism. Social-Economic Movements: An Historical and Comparative Survey of Socialism, Communism, Co-operation, Utopianism; and other Systems of Reform and Reconstruction. *New edition. 992 pp. 1968. 90s.*

Lasswell, Harold D. Analysis of Political Behaviour. An Empirical Approach. *324 pp. 1947. (4th Impression 1966.) 35s.*

Mannheim, Karl. Freedom, Power and Democratic Planning. *Edited by Hans Gerth and Ernest K. Bramstedt. 424 pp. 1951. (3rd Impression 1968.) 42s.*

Mansur, Fatma. Process of Independence. *Foreword by A. H. Hanson. 208 pp. 1962. 25s.*

Martin, David A. Pacificism: an Historical and Sociological Study. *262 pp. 1965. 30s.*

Myrdal, Gunnar. The Political Element in the Development of Economic Theory. *Translated from the German by Paul Streeten. 282 pp. 1953. (4th Impression 1965.) 25s.*

Polanyi, Michael. F.R.S. The Logic of Liberty: Reflections and Rejoinders. *228 pp. 1951. 18s.*

Verney, Douglas V. The Analysis of Political Systems. *264 pp. 1959. (3rd Impression 1966.) 28s.*

Wootton, Graham. The Politics of Influence: British Ex-Servicemen, Cabinet Decisions and Cultural Changes, 1917 to 1957. *316 pp. 1963. 30s.*
Workers, Unions and the State. *188 pp. 1966. (2nd Impression 1967.) 25s.*

FOREIGN AFFAIRS: THEIR SOCIAL, POLITICAL AND ECONOMIC FOUNDATIONS

Baer, Gabriel. Population and Society in the Arab East. *Translated by Hanna Szöke. 288 pp. 10 maps. 1964. 40s.*

Bonné, Alfred. State and Economics in the Middle East: A Society in Transition. *482 pp. 2nd (revised) edition 1955. (2nd Impression 1960.) 40s.*
Studies in Economic Development: with special reference to Conditions in the Under-developed Areas of Western Asia and India. *322 pp. 84 tables. 2nd edition 1960. 32s.*

Mayer, J. P. Political Thought in France from the Revolution to the Fifth Republic. *164 pp. 3rd edition (revised) 1961. 16s.*

CRIMINOLOGY

Ancel, Marc. Social Defence: A Modern Approach to Criminal Problems. *Foreword by Leon Radzinowicz. 240 pp. 1965. 32s.*

Cloward, Richard A., and **Ohlin, Lloyd E.** Delinquency and Opportunity: A Theory of Delinquent Gangs. *248 pp. 1961. 25s.*

5

Downes, David M. The Delinquent Solution. A Study in Subcultural Theory. *296 pp. 1966. 42s.*

Dunlop, A. B., and **McCabe, S.** Young Men in Detention Centres. *192 pp. 1965. 28s.*

Friedländer, Kate. The Psycho-Analytical Approach to Juvenile Delinquency: Theory, Case Studies, Treatment. *320 pp. 1947. (6th Impression 1967). 40s.*

Glueck, Sheldon and **Eleanor.** Family Environment and Delinquency. *With the statistical assistance of Rose W. Kneznek. 340 pp. 1962. (2nd Impression 1966.) 40s.*

Mannheim, Hermann. Comparative Criminology: a Text Book. *Two volumes. 442 pp. and 380 pp. 1965. (2nd Impression with corrections 1966.) 42s. a volume.*

Morris, Terence. The Criminal Area: A Study in Social Ecology. *Foreword by Hermann Mannheim. 232 pp. 25 tables. 4 maps. 1957. (2nd Impression 1966.) 28s.*

Morris, Terence and **Pauline,** assisted by **Barbara Barer.** Pentonville: A Sociological Study of an English Prison. *416 pp. 16 plates. 1963. 50s.*

Spencer, John C. Crime and the Services. *Foreword by Hermann Mannheim. 336 pp. 1954. 28s.*

Trasler, Gordon. The Explanation of Criminality. *144 pp. 1962. (2nd Impression 1967.) 20s.*

SOCIAL PSYCHOLOGY

Barbu, Zevedei. Problems of Historical Psychology. *248 pp. 1960. 25s.*

Blackburn, Julian. Psychology and the Social Pattern. *184 pp. 1945. (7th Impression 1964.) 16s.*

Fleming, C. M. Adolescence: Its Social Psychology: With an Introduction to recent findings from the fields of Anthropology, Physiology, Medicine, Psychometrics and Sociometry. *288 pp. 2nd edition (revised) 1963. (3rd Impression 1967.) 25s. Paper 12s. 6d.*

The Social Psychology of Education: An Introduction and Guide to Its Study. *136 pp. 2nd edition (revised) 1959. (4th Impression 1967.) 14s. Paper 7s. 6d.*

Homans, George C. The Human Group. *Foreword by Bernard DeVoto. Introduction by Robert K. Merton. 526 pp. 1951. (7th Impression 1968.) 35s.*

Social Behaviour: its Elementary Forms. *416 pp. 1961. (3rd Impression 1968.) 35s.*

Klein, Josephine. The Study of Groups. *226 pp. 31 figures. 5 tables. 1956. (5th Impression 1967.) 21s. Paper 9s. 6d.*

Linton, Ralph. The Cultural Background of Personality. *132 pp. 1947. (7th Impression 1968.) 18s.*

Mayo, Elton. The Social Problems of an Industrial Civilization. With an appendix on the Political Problem. *180 pp. 1949. (5th Impression 1966.) 25s.*

Ottaway, A. K. C. Learning Through Group Experience. *176 pp. 1966. (2nd Impression 1968.) 25s.*

Ridder, J. C. de. The Personality of the Urban African in South Africa. A Thematic Apperception Test Study. *196 pp. 12 plates. 1961. 25s.*

Rose, Arnold M. (Ed.). Human Behaviour and Social Processes: an Inter-actionist Approach. *Contributions by Arnold M. Rose, Ralph H. Turner, Anselm Strauss, Everett C. Hughes, E. Franklin Frazier, Howard S. Becker, et al. 696 pp. 1962. (2nd Impression 1968.) 70s.*

Smelser, Neil J. Theory of Collective Behaviour. *448 pp. 1962. (2nd Impression 1967.) 45s.*

Stephenson, Geoffrey M. The Development of Conscience. *128 pp. 1966. 25s.*

Young, Kimball. Handbook of Social Psychology. *658 pp. 16 figures. 10 tables. 2nd edition (revised) 1957. (3rd Impression 1963.) 40s.*

SOCIOLOGY OF THE FAMILY

Banks, J. A. Prosperity and Parenthood: A study of Family Planning among The Victorian Middle Classes. *262 pp. 1954. (3rd Impression 1968.) 28s.*

Bell, Colin R. Middle Class Families: Social and Geographical Mobility. *224 pp. 1969. 35s.*

Burton, Lindy. Vulnerable Children. *272 pp. 1968. 35s.*

Gavron, Hannah. The Captive Wife: Conflicts of Housebound Mothers. *190 pp. 1966. (2nd Impression 1966.) 25s.*

Klein, Josephine. Samples from English Cultures. *1965. (2nd Impression 1967.)*
1. Three Preliminary Studies and Aspects of Adult Life in England. *447 pp. 50s.*
2. Child-Rearing Practices and Index. *247 pp. 35s.*

Klein, Viola. Britain's Married Women Workers. *180 pp. 1965. (2nd Impression 1968.) 28s.*

McWhinnie, Alexina M. Adopted Children. How They Grow Up. *304 pp. 1967. (2nd Impression 1968.) 42s.*

Myrdal, Alva and Klein, Viola. Women's Two Roles: Home and Work. *238 pp. 27 tables. 1956. Revised Edition 1967. 30s. Paper 15s.*

Parsons, Talcott and Bales, Robert F. Family: Socialization and Interaction Process. *In collaboration with James Olds, Morris Zelditch and Philip E. Slater. 456 pp. 50 figures and tables. 1956. (3rd Impression 1968.) 45s.*

Schücking, L. L. The Puritan Family. *Translated from the German by Brian Battershaw. 212 pp. 1969. About 42s.*

7

THE SOCIAL SERVICES

Forder, R. A. (Ed.). Penelope Hall's Social Services of Modern England. *288 pp. 1969. 35s.*

George, Victor. Social Security: Beveridge and After. *258 pp. 1968. 35s.*

Goetschius, George W. Working with Community Groups. *256 pp. 1969. 35s.*

Goetschius, George W. and **Tash, Joan.** Working with Unattached Youth. *416 pp. 1967. (2nd Impression 1968.) 40s.*

Hall, M. P., and **Howes, I. V.** The Church in Social Work. A Study of Moral Welfare Work undertaken by the Church of England. *320 pp. 1965. 35s.*

Heywood, Jean S. Children in Care: the Development of the Service for the Deprived Child. *264 pp. 2nd edition (revised) 1965. (2nd Impression 1966.) 32s.*

An Introduction to Teaching Casework Skills. *190 pp. 1964. 28s.*

Jones, Kathleen. Lunacy, Law and Conscience, 1744-1845: the Social History of the Care of the Insane. *268 pp. 1955. 25s.*

Mental Health and Social Policy, 1845-1959. *264 pp. 1960. (2nd Impression 1967.) 32s.*

Jones, Kathleen and **Sidebotham, Roy.** Mental Hospitals at Work. *220 pp. 1962. 30s.*

Kastell, Jean. Casework in Child Care. *Foreword by M. Brooke Willis. 320 pp. 1962. 35s.*

Morris, Pauline. Put Away: A Sociological Study of Institutions for the Mentally Retarded. *Approx. 288 pp. 1969. About 50s.*

Nokes, P. L. The Professional Task in Welfare Practice. *152 pp. 1967. 28s.*

Rooff, Madeline. Voluntary Societies and Social Policy. *350 pp. 15 tables. 1957. 35s.*

Timms, Noel. Psychiatric Social Work in Great Britain (1939-1962). *280 pp. 1964. 32s.*

Social Casework: Principles and Practice. *256 pp. 1964. (2nd Impression 1966.) 25s. Paper 15s.*

Trasler, Gordon. In Place of Parents: A Study in Foster Care. *272 pp. 1960. (2nd Impression 1966.) 30s.*

Young, A. F., and **Ashton, E. T.** British Social Work in the Nineteenth Century. *288 pp. 1956. (2nd Impression 1963.) 28s.*

Young, A. F. Social Services in British Industry. *272 pp. 1968. 40s.*

SOCIOLOGY OF EDUCATION

Banks, Olive. Parity and Prestige in English Secondary Education: a Study in Educational Sociology. *272 pp. 1955. (2nd Impression 1963.) 32s.*

Bentwich, Joseph. Education in Israel. *224 pp. 8 pp. plates. 1965. 24s.*

Blyth, W. A. L. English Primary Education. A Sociological Description. *1965. Revised edition 1967.*

1. Schools. *232 pp. 30s. Paper 12s. 6d.*
2. Background. *168 pp. 25s. Paper 10s. 6d.*

Collier, K. G. The Social Purposes of Education: Personal and Social Values in Education. *268 pp. 1959. (3rd Impression 1965.) 21s.*

Dale, R. R., and Griffith, S. Down Stream: Failure in the Grammar School. *108 pp. 1965. 20s.*

Dore, R. P. Education in Tokugawa Japan. *356 pp. 9 pp. plates. 1965. 35s.*

Edmonds, E. L. The School Inspector. *Foreword by Sir William Alexander. 214 pp. 1962. 28s.*

Evans, K. M. Sociometry and Education. *158 pp. 1962. (2nd Impression 1966.) 18s.*

Foster, P. J. Education and Social Change in Ghana. *336 pp. 3 maps. 1965. (2nd Impression 1967.) 36s.*

Fraser, W. R. Education and Society in Modern France. *150 pp. 1963. (2nd Impression 1968.) 25s.*

Hans, Nicholas. New Trends in Education in the Eighteenth Century. *278 pp. 19 tables. 1951. (2nd Impression 1966.) 30s.*
  Comparative Education: A Study of Educational Factors and Traditions. *360 pp. 3rd (revised) edition 1958. (4th Impression 1967.) 25s. Paper 12s. 6d.*

Hargreaves, David. Social Relations in a Secondary School. *240 pp. 1967. (2nd Impression 1968.) 32s.*

Holmes, Brian. Problems in Education. A Comparative Approach. *336 pp. 1965. (2nd Impression 1967.) 32s.*

Mannheim, Karl and Stewart, W. A. C. An Introduction to the Sociology of Education. *206 pp. 1962. (2nd Impression 1965.) 21s.*

Morris, Raymond N. The Sixth Form and College Entrance. *231 pp. 1969. 40s.*

Musgrove, F. Youth and the Social Order. *176 pp. 1964. (2nd Impression 1968.) 25s. Paper 12s.*

Ortega y Gasset, José. Mission of the University. *Translated with an Introduction by Howard Lee Nostrand. 86 pp. 1946. (3rd Impression 1963.) 15s.*

Ottaway, A. K. C. Education and Society: An Introduction to the Sociology of Education. *With an Introduction by W. O. Lester Smith. 212 pp. Second edition (revised). 1962. (5th Impression 1968.) 18s. Paper 10s. 6d.*

Peers, Robert. Adult Education: A Comparative Study. *398 pp. 2nd edition 1959. (2nd Impression 1966.) 42s.*

Pritchard, D. G. Education and the Handicapped: 1760 to 1960. *258 pp. 1963. (2nd Impression 1966.) 35s.*

Richardson, Helen. Adolescent Girls in Approved Schools. *Approx. 360 pp. 1969. About 42s.*

Simon, Brian and Joan (Eds.). Educational Psychology in the U.S.S.R. *Introduction by Brian and Joan Simon. Translation by Joan Simon. Papers by D. N. Bogoiavlenski and N. A. Menchinskaia, D. B. Elkonin, E. A. Fleshner, Z. I. Kalmykova, G. S. Kostiuk, V. A. Krutetski, A. N. Leontiev, A. R. Luria, E. A. Milerian, R. G. Natadze, B. M. Teplov, L. S. Vygotski, L. V. Zankov. 296 pp. 1963. 40s.*

SOCIOLOGY OF CULTURE

Eppel, E. M., and **M.** Adolescents and Morality: A Study of some Moral Values and Dilemmas of Working Adolescents in the Context of a changing Climate of Opinion. *Foreword by W. J. H. Sprott. 268 pp. 39 tables. 1966. 30s.*

Fromm, Erich. The Fear of Freedom. *286 pp. 1942. (8th Impression 1960.) 25s. Paper 10s.*

The Sane Society. *400 pp. 1956. (4th Impression 1968.) 28s. Paper 14s.*

Mannheim, Karl. Diagnosis of Our Time: Wartime Essays of a Sociologist. *208 pp. 1943. (8th Impression 1966.) 21s.*

Essays on the Sociology of Culture. *Edited by Ernst Mannheim in co-operation with Paul Kecskemeti. Editorial Note by Adolph Lowe. 280 pp. 1956. (3rd Impression 1967.) 28s.*

Weber, Alfred. Farewell to European History: or The Conquest of Nihilism. *Translated from the German by R. F. C. Hull. 224 pp. 1947. 18s.*

SOCIOLOGY OF RELIGION

Argyle, Michael. Religious Behaviour. *224 pp. 8 figures. 41 tables. 1958. (4th Impression 1968.) 25s.*

Nelson, G. K. Spiritualism and Society. *313 pp. 1969. 42s.*

Stark, Werner. The Sociology of Religion. A Study of Christendom.
Volume I. Established Religion. *248 pp. 1966. 35s.*
Volume II. Sectarian Religion. *368 pp. 1967. 40s.*
Volume III. The Universal Church. *464 pp. 1967. 45s.*

Watt, W. Montgomery. Islam and the Integration of Society. *320 pp. 1961. (3rd Impression 1966.) 35s.*

SOCIOLOGY OF ART AND LITERATURE

Beljame, Alexandre. Men of Letters and the English Public in the Eighteenth Century: 1660-1744, Dryden, Addison. Pope. *Edited with an Introduction and Notes by Bonamy Dobrée. Translated by E. O. Lorimer. 532 pp. 1948. 32s.*

Misch, Georg. A History of Autobiography in Antiquity. *Translated by E. W. Dickes. 2 Volumes. Vol. 1, 364 pp., Vol. 2, 372 pp. 1950. 45s. the set.*

Schücking, L. L. The Sociology of Literary Taste. *112 pp. 2nd (revised) edition 1966. 18s.*

Silbermann, Alphons. The Sociology of Music. *Translated from the German by Corbet Stewart. 222 pp. 1963. 32s.*

SOCIOLOGY OF KNOWLEDGE

Mannheim, Karl. Essays on the Sociology of Knowledge. *Edited by Paul Kecskemeti. Editorial note by Adolph Lowe. 352 pp. 1952. (4th Impression 1967.) 35s.*

Stark, W. America: Ideal and Reality. The United States of 1776 in Contemporary Philosophy. *136 pp. 1947. 12s.*

The Sociology of Knowledge: An Essay in Aid of a Deeper Understanding of the History of Ideas. *384 pp. 1958. (3rd Impression 1967.) 36s.*

Montesquieu: Pioneer of the Sociology of Knowledge. *244 pp. 1960. 25s.*

URBAN SOCIOLOGY

Anderson, Nels. The Urban Community: A World Perspective. *532 pp. 1960. 35s.*

Ashworth, William. The Genesis of Modern British Town Planning: A Study in Economic and Social History of the Nineteenth and Twentieth Centuries. *288 pp. 1954. (3rd Impression 1968.) 32s.*

Bracey, Howard. Neighbours: On New Estates and Subdivisions in England and U.S.A. *220 pp. 1964. 28s.*

Cullingworth, J. B. Housing Needs and Planning Policy: A Restatement of the Problems of Housing Need and "Overspill" in England and Wales. *232 pp. 44 tables. 8 maps. 1960. (2nd Impression 1966.) 28s.*

Dickinson, Robert E. City and Region: A Geographical Interpretation. *608 pp. 125 figures. 1964. (5th Impression 1967.) 60s.*

The West European City: A Geographical Interpretation. *600 pp. 129 maps. 29 plates. 2nd edition 1962. (3rd Impression 1968.) 55s.*

The City Region in Western Europe. *320 pp. Maps. 1967. 30s. Paper 14s.*

Jackson, Brian. Working Class Community: Some General Notions raised by a Series of Studies in Northern England. *192 pp. 1968. (2nd Impression 1968.) 25s.*

Jennings, Hilda. Societies in the Making: a Study of Development and Redevelopment within a County Borough. *Foreword by D. A. Clark. 286 pp. 1962. (2nd Impression 1967.) 32s.*

Kerr, Madeline. The People of Ship Street. *240 pp. 1958. 28s.*

Mann, P. H. An Approach to Urban Sociology. *240 pp. 1965. (2nd Impression 1968.) 30s.*

Morris, R. N., and Mogey, J. The Sociology of Housing. Studies at Berinsfield. *232 pp. 4 pp. plates. 1965. 42s.*

Rosser, C., and Harris, C. The Family and Social Change. A Study of Family and Kinship in a South Wales Town. *352 pp. 8 maps. 1965. (2nd Impression 1968.) 45s.*

RURAL SOCIOLOGY

Chambers, R. J. H. Settlement Schemes in Africa: A Selective Study. *Approx. 268 pp. 1969. About 50s.*

Haswell, M. R. The Economics of Development in Village India. *120 pp. 1967. 21s.*

11

Littlejohn, James. Westrigg: the Sociology of a Cheviot Parish. *172 pp. 5 figures. 1963. 25s.*

Williams, W. M. The Country Craftsman: A Study of Some Rural Crafts and the Rural Industries Organization in England. *248 pp. 9 figures. 1958. 25s. (Dartington Hall Studies in Rural Sociology.)*
    The Sociology of an English Village: Gosforth. *272 pp. 12 figures. 13 tables. 1956. (3rd Impression 1964.) 25s.*

SOCIOLOGY OF MIGRATION

Humphreys, Alexander J. New Dubliners: Urbanization and the Irish Family. *Foreword by George C. Homans. 304 pp. 1966. 40s.*

SOCIOLOGY OF INDUSTRY AND DISTRIBUTION

Anderson, Nels. Work and Leisure. *280 pp. 1961. 28s.*

Blau, Peter M., and Scott, W. Richard. Formal Organizations: a Comparative approach. *Introduction and Additional Bibliography by J. H. Smith. 326 pp. 1963. (4th Impression 1969.) 35s. Paper 15s.*

Eldridge, J. E. T. Industrial Disputes. Essays in the Sociology of Industrial Relations. *288 pp. 1968. 40s.*

Hollowell, Peter G. The Lorry Driver. *272 pp. 1968. 42s.*

Jefferys, Margot, with the assistance of Winifred Moss. Mobility in the Labour Market: Employment Changes in Battersea and Dagenham. *Preface by Barbara Wootton. 186 pp. 51 tables. 1954. 15s.*

Levy, A. B. Private Corporations and Their Control. *Two Volumes. Vol. 1, 464 pp., Vol. 2, 432 pp. 1950. 80s. the set.*

Liepmann, Kate. Apprenticeship: An Enquiry into its Adequacy under Modern Conditions. *Foreword by H. D. Dickinson. 232 pp. 6 tables. 1960. (2nd Impression 1960.) 23s.*

Millerson, Geoffrey. The Qualifying Associations: a Study in Professionalization. *320 pp. 1964. 42s.*

Smelser, Neil J. Social Change in the Industrial Revolution: An Application of Theory to the Lancashire Cotton Industry, 1770-1840. *468 pp. 12 figures. 14 tables. 1959. (2nd Impression 1960.) 50s.*

Williams, Gertrude. Recruitment to Skilled Trades. *240 pp. 1957. 23s.*

Young, A. F. Industrial Injuries Insurance: an Examination of British Policy. *192 pp. 1964. 30s.*

ANTHROPOLOGY

Ammar, Hamed. Growing up in an Egyptian Village: Silwa, Province of Aswan. *336 pp. 1954. (2nd Impression 1966.) 35s.*

Crook, David and Isabel. Revolution in a Chinese Village: Ten Mile Inn. *230 pp. 8 plates. 1 map. 1959. (2nd Impression 1968.) 21s.*
    The First Years of Yangyi Commune. *302 pp. 12 plates. 1966. 42s.*

Dickie-Clark, H. F. The Marginal Situation. A Sociological Study of a Coloured Group. *236 pp. 1966. 40s.*

Dube, S. C. Indian Village. *Foreword by Morris Edward Opler. 276 pp. 4 plates. 1955. (5th Impression 1965.) 25s.*
India's Changing Villages: Human Factors in Community Development. *260 pp. 8 plates. 1 map. 1958. (3rd Impression 1963.) 25s.*

Firth, Raymond. Malay Fishermen. Their Peasant Economy. *420 pp. 17 pp. plates. 2nd edition revised and enlarged 1966. (2nd Impression 1968.) 55s.*

Gulliver, P. H. The Family Herds. A Study of two Pastoral Tribes in East Africa, The Jie and Turkana. *304 pp. 4 plates. 19 figures. 1955. (2nd Impression with new preface and bibliography 1966.) 35s.*
Social Control in an African Society: a Study of the Arusha, Agricultural Masai of Northern Tanganyika. *320 pp. 8 plates. 10 figures. 1963. (2nd Impression 1968.) 42s.*

Ishwaran, K. Shivapur. A South Indian Village. *216 pp. 1968. 35s.*
Tradition and Economy in Village India: An Interactionist Approach. *Foreword by Conrad Arensburg. 176 pp. 1966. (2nd Impression 1968.) 25s.*

Jarvie, Ian C. The Revolution in Anthropology. *268 pp. 1964. (2nd Impression 1967.) 40s.*

Jarvie, Ian C. and Agassi, Joseph. Hong Kong. A Society in Transition. *396 pp. Illustrated with plates and maps. 1968. 56s.*

Little, Kenneth L. Mende of Sierra Leone. *308 pp. and folder. 1951. Revised edition 1967. 63s.*

Lowie, Professor Robert H. Social Organization. *494 pp. 1950. (4th Impression 1966.) 50s.*

Mayer, Adrian C. Caste and Kinship in Central India: A Village and its Region. *328 pp. 16 plates. 15 figures. 16 tables. 1960. (2nd Impression 1965.) 35s.*
Peasants in the Pacific: A Study of Fiji Indian Rural Society. *232 pp. 16 plates. 10 figures. 14 tables. 1961. 35s.*

Smith, Raymond T. The Negro Family in British Guiana: Family Structure and Social Status in the Villages. *With a Foreword by Meyer Fortes. 314 pp. 8 plates. 1 figure. 4 maps. 1956. (2nd Impression 1965.) 35s.*

DOCUMENTARY

Meek, Dorothea L. (Ed.). Soviet Youth: Some Achievements and Problems. *Excerpts from the Soviet Press, translated by the editor. 280 pp. 1957. 28s.*

Schlesinger, Rudolf (Ed.). Changing Attitudes in Soviet Russia.
2. The Nationalities Problem and Soviet Administration. Selected Readings on the Development of Soviet Nationalities Policies. *Introduced by the editor. Translated by W. W. Gottlieb. 324 pp. 1956. 30s.*

Reports of the Institute of Community Studies

(*Demy 8vo.*)

Cartwright, Ann. Human Relations and Hospital Care. *272 pp. 1964. 30s.*

Patients and their Doctors. A Study of General Practice. *304 pp. 1967. 40s.*

Jackson, Brian. Streaming: an Education System in Miniature. *168 pp. 1964. (2nd Impression 1966.) 21s. Paper 10s.*

Jackson, Brian and **Marsden, Dennis.** Education and the Working Class: Some General Themes raised by a Study of 88 Working-class Children in a Northern Industrial City. *268 pp. 2 folders. 1962. (4th Impression 1968.) 32s.*

Marris, Peter. Widows and their Families. *Foreword by Dr. John Bowlby. 184 pp. 18 tables. Statistical Summary. 1958. 18s.*
Family and Social Change in an African City. A Study of Rehousing in Lagos. *196 pp. 1 map. 4 plates. 53 tables. 1961. (2nd Impression 1966.) 30s.*
The Experience of Higher Education. *232 pp. 27 tables. 1964. 25s.*

Marris, Peter and **Rein, Martin.** Dilemmas of Social Reform. Poverty and Community Action in the United States. *256 pp. 1967. 35s.*

Mills, Enid. Living with Mental Illness: a Study in East London. *Foreword by Morris Carstairs. 196 pp. 1962. 28s.*

Runciman, W. G. Relative Deprivation and Social Justice. A Study of Attitudes to Social Inequality in Twentieth Century England. *352 pp. 1966. (2nd Impression 1967.) 40s.*

Townsend, Peter. The Family Life of Old People: An Inquiry in East London. *Foreword by J. H. Sheldon. 300 pp. 3 figures. 63 tables. 1957. (3rd Impression 1967.) 30s.*

Willmott, Peter. Adolescent Boys in East London. *230 pp. 1966. 30s.*
The Evolution of a Community: a study of Dagenham after forty years. *168 pp. 2 maps. 1963. 21s.*

Willmott, Peter and **Young, Michael.** Family and Class in a London Suburb. *202 pp. 47 tables. 1960. (4th Impression 1968.) 25s.*

Young, Michael. Innovation and Research in Education. *192 pp. 1965. 25s. Paper 12s. 6d.*

Young, Michael and **McGeeney, Patrick.** Learning Begins at Home. A Study of a Junior School and its Parents. *About 128 pp. 1968. 21s. Paper 14s.*

Young, Michael and **Willmott, Peter.** Family and Kinship in East London. *Foreword by Richard M. Titmuss. 252 pp. 39 tables. 1957. (3rd Impression 1965.) 28s.*

The British Journal of Sociology. *Edited by Terence P. Morris. Vol. 1, No. 1, March 1950 and Quarterly. Roy. 8vo., £3 annually, 15s. a number, post free. (Vols. 1-18, £8 each. Individual parts £2 10s.*

All prices are net and subject to alteration without notice

1268 H.B.